Douglas McGill, a native of Rochester, Minnesota, is a former staff reporter for *The New York Times* and bureau chief for *Bloomberg News* in Tokyo, London, and Hong Kong. Dubbed "Glocal Man" by National Public Radio, he now lives in Rochester, which he writes about as a journalist from a global perspective. In 2003, he broke the news of an African genocide of the Anuak tribe by interviewing refugees in Minnesota. His articles illuminate the international connections linking local Minnesota communities, to the rest of the world. The Executive Director of the World Press Institute at Macalester College since January, 2007, Doug also teaches a citizen journalism workshop, Largemouth, where citizens learn the skills of professional journalism, and visiting journalists learn from citizens. His reports and essays are published on The McGill Report at www.mcgillreport.org. and the Local Man blog at www.localman.org.

here

here

A Global Citizen's Journey

DOUGLAS McGILL

artpacks

Text copyright © 2007 by Douglas McGill

Published by artpacks
    535 22nd Street NE
    Rochester, MN   55906
    507.273.2529

Grateful acknowledgment is made to *The Rochester Post-Bulletin*
for permission to reprint the articles that appear in this volume in the chapter
entitled "The Up Escalator." The chapter entitled "The Refugees of Pochalla"
appeared first in *The New Republic*.

Book and cover design
by Virginia Woodruff, Anastasia Woodruff, Karen Snyder
Book and cover design © artpacks
Author Photo © Douglas McGill
Designed, printed, and bound in the United States of America

Library of Congress Cataloging-in-Publication Data
McGill, Douglas
    Here : A global citizen's journey/Douglas McGill.
       p. cm.
    ISBN 13: 978-0-9790247-0-2 (hardcover)
    ISBN 10: 0-9790247-0-6 (hardcover)
    ISBN 13: 978-0-9790247-1-9 (pbk.)
    ISBN 10: 0-9790247-1-4 (pbk.)
    1. Globalization
    2. Cosmopolitanism—Case studies.
    3. Rochester (Minnesota)—Social conditions.
    4. Global Citizenship.

HN80.R6M34 2006
303.48'27760090511—dc22
                              2006100268

To Caren with deepest love

ACKNOWLEDGMENTS

The people whose stories I tell in this book were true collaborators in the creative process. So my deepest thanks goes to them for helping me understand their lives.

Bill Boyne, the enlightened publisher and editor of my local newspaper, the *Rochester Post-Bulletin*, for many years, published many of the stories collected here in a weekly column called "Global Rochester." Jay Furst, the paper's managing editor, supported my early coverage of the Anuak genocide, as did the John S. and James L. Knight Foundation, which provided a grant allowing me to travel to Ethiopia and Sudan.

Special thanks goes to John McMeel, the chairman of Andrews McMeel Publishing, who administered the Knight grant and from the very beginning was a guardian angel watching over my "local-global" journalism. My deepest gratitude goes also to Stella Ye for her unfailing support, and whose adventurous, joyful and realistic spirit lies behind every word in this book.

Other people who generously shared their brilliance are Rick Plunkett, Carol Christenson, Chris Gomez, Jackie Bernard, Louis Smith, Luisa Kreisberg, Mark Kramer, Jay Rosen, Andrew Cline, JSG Boggs, Bill Buzenberg, Michael Skoler, Andrew Haeg, Steve Perry, Yogish Kudva, Raman Narayanan, Bill Mitchell, Margo Melnicove, Jina Moore, Jeremy Iggers, Jacquelin Cheung, Rebecca Hoffman, Sandy Close, Doug Glass, David Pyle, Greg Aamot, Mark Neuzil, Wendy Wyatt, Kris Bunton, Lynda McDonnell, Mary Turck, Bob Craig, Joel Bleifuss, Eleanor Gasparik, Samantha Powers, Dick Longworth, Dru Sweetser, Jonathan Landreth, Alexa Olesen, and Joachim Stroh.

It took me a long time to write this, my first book. I was able to do it because at long last, thanks to my Mom and Dad, I was able to find my true home.

CONTENTS

Introduction: A Journey in Global Citizenship

I Did a 9/11 Hijacker Live in Rochester?................1

II Who Are We Today?

The Most Beautiful Place on Earth.................................19
The Global Citizen's Dual Address...............................22
Thai Curry and Awakened Heart................................. 25
Shooting Ourselves in the Future.................................28
The World Music of Quetico.......................................31
The Mississippi, the Yangtze, and Me..........................34
The Ya Ba Crisis...37
The Shame of Olmsted County...................................40
America's Most Globlized Town..................................43
Who Runs Minnesota Agriculture?..............................47
Husbanding Hogs and Democracy..............................50
Who Are We Today?...53
The World in an Ear of Corn......................................56
A Global Killer Comes to Minnesota............................59
Avoiding Food and Sex Like the Plague.......................62
Schmoozing for National Security...............................65
The Global Citizen's Vote..67
Presidential Innocence Abroad.................................. 70
The Saudi Royals, By George.....................................73
Let's Not Get Jay-Walked..76
The Round Goby and World Peace..............................79
The Siberian Tigers of Minnesota............................... 83
The Hmong Wisconsin Death Trip...............................87
A Very Sudanese Christmas...................................... 90
Globalization at Fourth and Broadway.........................93
L'Affaire de Janet's Breast...96
A Seasonal Song of Spam..99
Sex on a Human Scale...102

III United Dreams Of America

Becoming Americans

Just Plain Smart...107

A Rabbi Who Loves God and the Vikings.................................110

A Kazakh Artist's American Vision..113

From Russia With 800 SATs..117

Minnesota's Uighur-American...120

"No Cow's Here"...123

Wishing You a Prosperous 1383!...126

The Up Escalator

"What's it Going to Be in My Life?"...129

Sugar Stirred into Minnesota Milk..136

Lakes + Snow + Cold = Home..143

Education is the Sun and Moon...149

The Best of Two Cultures...156

Better Life for the Kids...163

Learning from Strangers

The Heroism of Hospitality..169

"Teacher Bill, Do You Like Beer?"...172

Teaching Beyond Arrogance..175

Little Johnny on the Top of the World......................................178

The Flag Lady of Rochester..181

Learning from Strangers...184

A Red Stain of Bewitching Beauty...186

Minnesota's Mensch...189

Whole Child, Whole World...192

Foreigners Are Us

Rainbows from Tibet..195

No Jobs. No Money. No Life...198

Heirlooms for Africa...201

From Kathmandu to Clarks Grove..204

Foreigners Are Us...209

Outsource Yourself...212

A Patriot of Venezuela and Minnesota.....................................215

A Love Letter (Unrequited, Alas)...218

Fix Immigration Now..226
Assimilate, then Celebrate...229
Somalis for Dean..232
Importing Dharma..235
The Great State of Minnisootaa.......................................238
"I Thought Things Couldn't Get Worse".........................241

IV The Minnesota Anuak

Minnesota Interviews

A Lost African Tribe of Minnesota..................................247
Minnesota Anuak Fear 400 Dead in Ethiopian Massacre............254
How News of an African Genocide Broke on a Minnesota Blog...257

A Trip to Africa

Stranded in Nairobi..260
A Gunfire Evasion Seminar..263
"Sir, Are You Conducting an Ethnic Cleansing?".........266
Ethiopia's Minister of Genocide......................................269
Genocide of the Anuak Broadenes to Women,.............272
    Children, and Villages
The Refugees of Pochalla..278

Back to Minnesota

Another Darfur Victim: The Anuak of Ethiopia.............284
"We Were in Over Our Head, But We Loved Them"........289
Diapers and Death..291
An Easter Message to the Minnesota Press....................297

V A Global Citizen Thinks About War

A Global Citizen Thinks About War..................................303
At a War Rally, Echoes of Earlier Wars...........................316
Baghdad in the BWCA...318
Alden Pyle at Abu Ghraib..321

VI Nine Paths of Global Citizenship...........325

Postscript: A New Story for a New World...........341

here

INTRODUCTION

A Journey in Global Citizenship

On the afternoon of Sunday, December 14, 2003, I received an alarming telephone call from a man named Obang Kono Cham, whom I'd interviewed earlier for an article in The McGill Report, my international news blog written from my home in southeast Minnesota.

Obang was an immigrant from Ethiopia to Minnesota and a member of an African tribe called the Anuak, a dark-skinned people who live in the remote western Ethiopian state of Gambella. Obang himself had originally moved to Minnesota after surviving a massacre of Anuak by Ethiopian soldiers in the village of Dimma in 1992, in which 26 Anuak were slaughtered. Now, Obang was telling me about a far bloodier massacre of Anuak men and boys that was underway in Gambella *at that very moment.*

He had spent most of the previous day, Obang said, talking on his cell phone to friends and family members who still lived in Gambella. They told Obang that several troop trucks filled with uniformed Ethiopian soldiers had arrived in their town, called Gambella the same as the state, in the early afternoon of Saturday, September 13. The soldiers were carrying AK-47 assault rifles and they spread through town, going door to door calling out Anuak men and boys. Some of the soldiers, the eyewitnesses said, were carrying lists of names and addresses. When the Anuak men came to their doors the soldiers grabbed them roughly, dragged them into the street, and told them to run. When they ran they were shot in their backs, and sometimes were hacked to death with machetes by lighter-skinned Ethiopians whom the soldiers were encouraging to kill Anuak. According to later confirmed reports, more than 425 Anuak died in the slaughter that Saturday, December 13, and on Sunday, December 14.

Over the next two days, I took call after call from Anuak immigrants living in Minnesota who were in a total panic, feeling helpless as their loved ones were being gunned down half a world away. Worst of all, the Minnesota Anuak were listening to all the sounds of the massacre through their cell phone connections which they kept open for hour upon hour. Through their phones the Minnesota Anuak listened to their friends and loved ones frantically describe their situation, sometimes even as the soldiers approached their homes. "They are coming to get me! They are coming to get me!" one Anuak in Ethiopia, Omot Bowar, whispered to a friend in Minnesota, a man named Obang Jobi. "I told Omot 'Keep talking to me! Keep talking to me!'" Jobi later recalled. "But then the soldiers came and you could hear the door crash open, and they took the phone from Omot and threw it down, and the line went dead. My wife and I were silent for almost 30 minutes in our house. We thought that Omot had been killed."

As a journalist, I found my situation perplexing. Within a week of the first phone call from Obang Kono Cham, I'd called a spokesman for the Ethiopian government at its embassy in Washington, who denied that any massacre had taken place. I'd read international newspapers and news sources including The New York Times, BBC, and Reuters, and scanned the Internet for any accounts to corroborate the large-scale, targeted killing of the Anuak that I was hearing about in Minnesota. I scrutinized the web sites of the U.S. Embassy in Addis Ababa, the United Nations, Human Rights Watch, and Amnesty International. From all these sources, nothing remotely corroborated an event of the scale that the Minnesota Anuak were claiming.

On the other side, what kind of information had I collected in Minnesota? Basically, I'd heard dozens of stories from people who had spent hours on cell phone conversations, talking to eyewitnesses to the massacre and listening also to the sounds of the killing as it happened. The people in Gambella were the actual eyewitnesses, always the most important and credible source in any news story. So what kind of sources were the Anuak of Minnesota? One might perhaps call them "earwitnesses," based on the sounds of the massacre they'd heard over their cell phones. But who on earth had ever heard of "earwitnesses" before? Anyway, could I really trust the interpretation the Anuak were giving to their telephone calls? Those conversations with eyewitnesses to the killings were certainly chilling, but they were also second-hand after all, which gives a journalist pause.

It boiled down to a gut decision, and after nine days I decided I'd gathered enough facts, and heard enough stories, to publish. Yet it was terribly difficult because what I'd concluded was not only that more than 425 people had been killed in Gambella (I'd called survivors of the massacre and asked them to count corpses in the streets and mass graves), but also that the massacre of December 13 was part of a larger, ongoing genocide of the Anuak. My story accused a sovereign government of consciously attempting to murder an entire minority group among its population. I was literally trembling when I published the story on The McGill Report, nine days after the phone call I'd received from Obang Kono Cham.

It took more than five months before a mainstream news source wrote about the massacre (The New York Times sent a reporter to Gambella in June, 2004), and more than a year before a major human rights organization, Human Rights Watch, sent a team to Ethiopia and corroborated virtually every detail of my original account. But almost within minutes of publication on the Internet, my story found an eager audience of readers among the thousands of Anuak refugees living in the U.S. and around the world, who were eager to get news of the massacre. Within about a week, I'd received some 75 emails from Anuak refugees living in Canada, Europe, Australia, South Africa, Kenya, and the U.S., thanking me for providing a detailed account of the December 13 massacre in their home village. Several of these emails indicated that my account was the only one published anywhere in the world. Further, several Anuak told me that their tribe had suffered massacres of a similar scale over a period of some 15 years, but that my story was the first time any of these atrocities had been globally publicized.

Two other groups were quick to respond to my first Anuak story, followed by several follow-up pieces I wrote for The McGill Report. The first were human rights groups dedicated to preventing genocide, especially one called Genocide Watch based in The Hague. "You were the first to report on this and we're very grateful," Gregory Stanton, the group's president, emailed me in late December. Within a month, Genocide Watch had sent a researcher to Ethiopia who conducted extensive interviews with survivors of the Gambella massacre. His report reached the same conclusion as I had, that the Ethiopian government was using violent ethnic cleansing—massacres—to eliminate the entire Anuak tribe.

The second group to quickly respond to my Anuak stories were churches throughout Minnesota, and in Washington state, which had Anuak refugees in their congregations who were devastated by the December 13 massacre. Pastors from a half dozen Minnesota churches, and from one in Washington, quickly invited me to speak at Sunday gatherings and to ask for advice on how best to respond. Several of these churches subsequently raised funds for relief aid sent to refugee camps, and one began a website giving background on the Anuak tribe, the Ethiopian genocide campaign against them, and regular news updates.

But the most startling impact of my stories I learned only after travelling to Sudan in April, 2004 to a refugee camp where Anuak had fled following the massacre of four months earlier. Interviewing one young Anuak man in the refugee camp in the middle of the south Sudan desert, I introduced myself as Doug McGill from Minnesota.

"Do you mean, Doug McGill of The McGill Report?"

My eyes widened.

"How do you know that?" Not only was there no computer in the south Sudan desert, there was no electricity, nor a single telephone or electric light.

It was simple, the young man explained. I had become known in Gambella, and among the Anuak generally, as the most reliable source of news and information about what was happening to their tribe. My articles were printed out in Internet cafes and passed around, often in secret.

"You are famous among the Anuak," he said.

I was similarly taken aback when, a few days later in Addis Ababa, I arrived at a government office building to interview Barnabas Gebre-Ab, the Minister for Federal Affairs for the Gambella region. He had been the civilian chief of the Ethiopian Army that was posted in Gambella, and was the superior officer to the field commander, Tsegeye Beyene, who had been in charge in Gambella on December 13 and the months following. My reporting indicated that it was probably Gebre-Ab who had personally ordered Tsegeye to kill as many Anuak men, especially the educated and the political leaders of the tribe, as possible on December 13.

"You are causing me a lot of trouble," Gebre-Ab said when I entered his office. He gestured to a pile of my McGill Report articles, downloaded from the Internet, which lay on his desk. "I just got a telephone call this afternoon from Sweden's foreign aid minister. He said, 'What's all this I see on the Internet, about a genocide in Ethiopia?' He told me that unless all this bad publicity stops, Sweden will cut off its foreign aid to Ethiopia. You are really causing me a lot of trouble!"

When Ethiopia held national elections in May, 2005, the impact of my Minnesota-based coverage of the Anuak became even more clear. During those elections, the Anuak genocide, for the first time in Ethiopian politics, became a prominent issue widely raised by parties opposing the repressive regime of Prime Minister Meles Zenawi. Articles published in The McGill Report were often cited and passed around, and while reading articles published on Ethiopian political web sites I often found facts and snippets of my articles lifted word-for-word. Other times, links to my many articles about the Anuak were given. For the first time, by using the Internet to bypass the government-controlled Ethiopian press, the Anuak genocide had become widely known and in great detail, openly talked about and publicly aired. Most important, it had become an irrefutable historical fact.

❧

For me, a major lesson of the Anuak story is that global citizenship rests on the development of a fundamental human skill which, notwithstanding it is a skill we must either quickly learn or quickly die, is rarely discussed. This skill is the ability first to decipher, then to assess, and finally decide to act or not to act upon the image of the world that the media puts into our heads. This may seem quite an abstract leap to make after the vivid, all-too-concrete account just given of the Anuak genocide and its aftermath. But I want to argue that it's vitally important to make that leap, and to learn the skill. Indeed, the fate of humanity rests upon our doing so.

Consider: what can we truly ever know, to any degree of certainty, about the world beyond the borders of our own skin, perceptions, feelings, and thoughts? Make an inventory of the original sources of your knowledge about China, Iraq, India or Peru. Or even about a nearby town or city that you've never personally visited. Where does your information about this place and its people come from? The further a place or person is from your own direct experience, the more your mental images are built from symbols created and distributed by electronic mass media. That is, the pictures of the world that we carry in our heads are built mainly from words and images, symbols that have no inherent weight or meaning but pack a visceral emotional punch.

The great 20th-century newspaper columnist and philosopher of the press, Walter Lippmann, described this in his landmark 1922 essay, "The World Outside and the Pictures in Our Heads." The essential dilemma, Lippmann argued, is that the world outside can never be exactly replicated inside our heads. Instead, the awesome complexity of the world is inevitably distilled into clusters of symbols—words and images—that come nowhere close to giving an accurate picture of reality.

Lippmann therefore depressingly concludes that "men respond as powerfully to fictions as they do to realities, and that in many cases they help to create the very fictions to which they respond." The mass media, he said, creates vast mental "pseudo-environments," which are the fictions that we generally respond to, instead of the real world itself. This leads inevitably to the "worldwide spectacle of men acting upon their environment, moved by stimuli from their pseudo-environments."

Lippmann was pessimistic that the public could ever escape their entrapment in these scary pseudo-worlds. They simply didn't have the intellectual candlepower to penetrate beyond the symbolic pseudo-worlds of the mass media. Only experts deeply knowledgeable in the ways of symbols could do that. Lippmann's prescription for society was therefore based on the formation of expert classes of symbolic encoders and decoders. These ivory-tower experts would define the real world for the masses by using symbols hopefully ethically, but perforce also in a manner that was obviously elitist, manipulative, and propagandistic.

The story of the Anuak genocide, and the other stories in this book, I believe suggest that another way is possible. This book is filled with the stories of people who, through the power of their own moral imaginations, have lived far beyond the borders of their own local worlds. They haven't needed the help of priests or experts in mass media symbols to know the world accurately, and to act in the world morally and ethically. By doing this, they have created and still are creating a more peaceful world. The Minnesota church leaders who read about the suffering of the Anuak in Ethiopia, and in turn succored the Anuak in their local congregations, did exactly this. So did a Rochester woman who married an Iranian man, and joyfully celebrates both Iranian and Western New Year's for the sake of their children. So did another Rochester woman who in August of 2001 comforted a disheveled, terrified, utterly despondent young Saudi man in her arms, only to find out later that he was Mohand Alshehri, one of the hijackers of 9/11.

That technology can be a powerful aid to moral imagination is clearly true and is a motif of these stories. When a cellular telephone brings to you the voice of a loved one who is facing imminent violent death, virtually all levels of symbolic encodement are removed, and new possibilities open for wise moral action. The similar role played by cellular telephones in the dramas of the Anuak of December 13, and between the passengers on the airplanes of 9/11 and their loved ones at home, comes to mind. A sense of helplessness was a part of all those conversations, but so too was the fact of tender human contact, comforting love, and possibilities for redemption.

My own personal story lies behind the stories in this book. I was irresistibly drawn to meet, to befriend, to learn and finally to tell the stories of the people in this book. To me the people in these pages are true heroes, pioneers of global citizenship, masters of a survival skill we must all learn.

I returned to live in rural Minnesota after a decade working as a foreign correspondent based in Tokyo, London, and Hong Kong. A few things struck me immediately. First, I noticed that in certain ways, rural Minnesota didn't look much different from all the exotic places I'd just lived.

One in ten people in Rochester hadn't been born in the United States. In the 1980s, three thousand Hmong and Cambodian refugees had resettled in the area. In the 1990s, more than 2,000 Somalis had arrived, along with about the same number of Sudanese and Ethiopians, and several hundred Bosnian Muslims. Virtually every restaurant kitchen in southern

Minnesota was staffed by Mexican cooks and dishwashers, and most hired farmhands in the area were now Mexican, too. In some Rochester classrooms, one in two children didn't speak English as their native language.

But the immigrant influence only began to tell the story of the intimate integration of my region—financially, socially, culturally, environmentally—with the rest of the world. One day, I decided to investigate the material world of southern Minnesota including the food we ate, the clothes we wore, our fishing rods and backyard grills, the furniture in our homes, and all the appurtenances of our comfortable lives. To provide a statistic basis for what began as a hunch, I went to the local Penny's department store and examined the label in the first 25 pieces of clothing I picked up. The items were from Disney, Dockers, Oshkosh, Stafford, and Van Heusen, solid American brand names one and all. But their places of manufacture told a completely different tale. They were made in China (5 items), Vietnam (4), the Dominican Republic (3), India (2), Thailand (2), Cambodia, Sri Lanka, Guatemala, Colombia, Nicaragua, Indonesia, Pakistan, Bulgaria, Mexico, and Korea. Only one in 25 of the items I randomly picked was made in Ameica— Gold Toe brand socks. The Minnesota Vikings t-shirts? Made in Korea. The "I Visited Rochester" coffee mugs? Made in China.

Next, I explored the underlying values that Americans cherish and use to guide our key decisions. I quickly realized that our most cherished marker of American uniqueness—our very American identity—is nothing but a patchwork of international practices and beliefs.

Our main religion, Christianity, was born in the Middle East, and its holy book was written there. Our legal system is based on Common Law from England. The very notion of liberty, at the heart of the American dream, was invented by European intellectuals such as John Locke of England, Baron de Montesquieu of France, and Hugo Grotius of Holland.

Our nation's founding fathers were under no illusions about this. They in no way saw themselves as "pure" Americans. Quite the opposite. They saw themselves as planting the seed of liberty, an idea born in Europe, in fertile American soil. If you could turn back its collar, the American Dream itself would have a tag inside that says "Made in Europe."

It finally dawned on me that both our physical bodies and our spiritual lives are composed not of unique American building blocks but rather of an amalgam of global constituent particles of ideas, people, money, history, currents of cultures and values and material things. And if this was true in colonial times, how much more so is it true today in the era of global travel, the Internet, and the globalized economy.

And yet, freshly returned to the U.S. from my world travels, how little my fellow Americans seemed to know about the rest of the world, or to care. "Where have you been?" I'd be asked. "Tokyo, London, and Hong Kong," I'd answer. Then a long silence would typically follow which was not unlike the awkward gap that starts a bad date, during which time you realize that you have some long hours ahead to spend together, with very little to say.

Journalism, as a branch of literature, I thought could act as one possible antidote to American ignorance of the rest of the world, and to my own. I realized that in today's profusely and intimately interconnected world, I didn't need to live in New York or Washington or London to practice this form of journalism. Indeed it would be better to stay right where I was. In Rochester, Minesota. Right here. If my hypothesis was correct, the entire world could be seen through its interconnections with my local home.

It was an experiment, and this book is the hopeful result.

৵৵

| **DID A 9/11 HIJACKER LIVE IN ROCHESTER?**

Late one evening in August of 2001, Nancy Hanlon finished her shift as the cardiac ward secretary at St. Mary's Hospital in Rochester and headed to C.J.'s, a downtown bar where she sometimes stopped for a drink after work.

In a town whose civic identity is dominated by a paragon of straitlaced professionalism, the Mayo Clinic, C.J.'s has always stood out. A cavelike, beer-and-peanuts honky-tonk located two blocks from Mayo's front door, the club's walls are lined with bright-red Bud signs, dart-team trophies, and VFW plaques.

Its patrons have long included an eclectic crowd of local office workers and farmers, clinic patients, and members of the dwindling tribe of Mayo doctors and support staff who steal away for a smoke.

During the 1990s, C.J.'s also played host to a more rarefied clientele: extremely wealthy visitors from Saudi Arabia, the United Arab Emirates, and other Middle Eastern countries. It was this crowd of English-speaking, cognac-sipping, cosmopolitan Arab men that attracted Hanlon on those summer nights in 2001.

The men were neither especially charming nor very warm, in her view, but they were nonetheless a source of intrigue in Rochester, where social life can oscillate between dead slow and perfectly moribund. They were smart, worldly, and ready for verbal sparring, especially on matters of sex and politics. The latter was the most uncomfortable subject of all. None of them liked America much, as it turned out.

Peering into their world was a welcome counterpoint to the workaday routine of her own life. As the single, 46-year-old mother of two young daughters, Hanlon kept very busy. Besides her job as a ward secretary at the hospital, she was studying for her nursing degree at a local community college. It was nice to be able to leave it all behind for an hour or two.

On the August night in question, Hanlon was actually hoping to run into one particular Middle Eastern man she had encountered the night before, an elegant and mysterious fellow named Khalid.

3

But Khalid wasn't there, so she took a seat at the bar next to a Saudi man of an entirely different sort. Young, disheveled—and utterly despondent.

"He was slumped over a glass of beer," Hanlon recalls. "He was wearing jeans and a khaki-colored plaid shirt right out of the Ward's catalog. I looked at him and said, 'Hi,' and he looked up at me. It was overwhelming—the despair that a person can give out! Out of every part of him. His face.

"I said, 'You look like you're carrying the whole world on your shoulders.' And he looked at me and said, 'I am. I am.'"

His name was Mohand, he said. He would not go into the details of his troubles, but they sounded bad. "Several times he told me to quit talking to him, because he was a dead man," Hanlon says. "'You are talking to a dead man,' he said. 'I don't exist. I'm a ghost. I'm not even here, I'm dead.' I thought he was going to kill himself, maybe even that night."

They talked for three hours. There was no piercing his fatalism, but the brooding man did brighten a few times when he talked to Hanlon about "this great big wonderful thing," in her words, that he claimed was forthcoming. "We are really going to show your country something," she says he told her. "Something big. It's going to be really big." She had no idea what he meant; he was clearly distraught, and she wasn't sure any of it meant anything. But each time, the spells of euphoria passed as quickly as they came and he would be morose.

Hanlon never saw him again, and after a few days she had little time or reason to think of him any further. The events of September 11 shocked her, but for whatever reason they never caused her to think of the young man Mohand—until a year later, when every television network was running nonstop documentaries and news reports dedicated to the 9/11 anniversary.

Even then, it was nothing she saw that prompted her to think of him. Rather, it was what she heard. The recycled words of the terrorists and radical clerics she heard sounded uncannily like the sentiments that Mohand and the other men at the bar had been expressing the summer before. Hanlon contacted the FBI. Soon she found herself sitting in the bureau's Rochester office looking at mug shots. Finally, there he was.

"I know him," Hanlon says she told Agent David Price. "I really know this guy. Where is he? What ever happened to him?"

"And Price said, 'Nancy, he was on the plane. The only good thing about him is that he is dead. He's one of the terrorists—one of the monsters.'"

The young man's name was Mohand Alshehri. He was 22 years old and part of the team of hijackers aboard United Flight 175 out of Boston, the second jet to crash into the World Trade Center.

Nancy Hanlon's story conjures a lot of questions, first among them the matter of its own credibility. The most glaring objection is the obvious one: Rochester? How plausible is it that a member of the 19-man terrorist cadre that carried out the 9/11 atrocities would be living in or visiting Rochester, Minnesota, only weeks before the attack?

Quite plausible, actually, though the reasons why are largely invisible to anyone unfamiliar with the exceptional history and character of the city. That exceptional nature begins with the fact that Rochester is a company town. The company is the Mayo Clinic. Renowned worldwide for the quality and breadth of its medical services, Mayo has always drawn a vastly disproportionate share of the world's wealthiest and most powerful people to southern Minnesota.

They have included some of the most important figures from various Middle Eastern countries. Jordan's King Hussein, battling advanced-stage kidney cancer, ran his entire government from a suite at St. Mary's hospital for the last year of his life. During that time, his personal jetliner, emblazoned with the bright green seal of the Hashemite Kingdom of Jordan, remained parked in the cornfields at Rochester International Airport. His wife, Queen Noor, became a familiar figure to the owners of local shops where she popped in occasionally to buy flowers and gifts.

5

The notion that Rochester might have been on the international terrorism map occurred some time ago to many local residents and to the FBI, which for years has had two permanent agents stationed in Rochester. Since 9/11, they have worked closely with the local police and sheriff's office as part of the FBI's Joint Terrorism Task Force.

A thriving Middle Eastern subculture sprang up in Rochester in the 1990s, thanks to a steady flow of patients from the region who flocked to Mayo, often with large families and royal retinues in tow. Citizens of the United Arab Emirates were the most populous group of Middle Easterners living in Rochester in those days, but Saudi Arabian visitors made the biggest splash in economic and cultural terms.

For decades, Mayo Clinic doctors have seen patients from the Saudi royal family—including King Fahd, for whom it sometimes even dispatched physicians to Riyadh on an emergency basis. In the 1990s, young Saudi princes who were only distantly related to the royal family (but nonetheless traveled on handsome monthly stipends from the House of Saud) became frequent long-term visitors to Rochester. It was not unusual to see these princes wandering the downtown shopping district, dressed in tailored Western suits or ankle-length white robes, blowing thousands of dollars on expensive shoes, liquor, gold watches, and cars purchased with cash. Local residents were sometimes surprised to look out their windows and see Saudi women—obviously unaware that lawns are usually private property in the U.S.—sitting on their front yards chatting intimately, their veils billowing in the breeze.

The impact of wealthy Middle Easterners on the city's day-to-day life went beyond mere tourism. An infrastructure of local businesses grew up to serve them, including several restaurants, a grocery, a downtown storefront prayer room, a travel agency, a real estate firm, and an   express package service specializing in deliveries to Saudi Arabia.

There was something else, as well. Rochester, for reasons

that had nothing to do with the Mayo Clinic, was also a heated symbol to radical Islamists, and al Qaeda adherents in particular. One of fundamentalist Islam's most exalted spiritual leaders, Sheikh Omar Abdel Rahman—widely known as "the blind Sheikh"—resided in Rochester from 1998 to 2002, at the Federal Medical Center prison.

Abdel Rahman, a diabetic with heart problems, was sentenced to life in prison in 1996 for conspiring to blow up the United Nations, New York's FBI office, and all the bridges and tunnels going into New York City. An outspoken advocate of violent action against America's infidel, pro-Israel regime, Abdel Rahman had previously attracted hundreds of young acolytes to live near his homes in other cities. They came to seek his teachings, or sometimes in pilgrimage.

Could this have happened in Rochester, too?

The possibility was surely entertained by the U.S. government, which after 9/11 turned the city's Federal Medical Center prison into a fortress surrounded by razor-wire fences and roaming guards with machine guns. Alarm over the Sheikh's presence in Rochester rose even higher when, after 9/11, Osama bin Laden announced that he planned to free the cleric, by violence if necessary. There was talk of kidnapping U.S. officials and holding them for ransom. Gil Gutknecht, Minnesota's Republican congressional representative for the First District, complained so vehemently about the security threat posed by the blind Sheikh's presence in Rochester that Abdel Rahman was ultimately transferred to another federal prison in April 2002.

However unmistakable its presence may have been, though, Rochester's Middle Eastern subculture existed almost entirely outside the prevailing Midwestern folkways of the place. Mostly the visitors made their way around town without incident. Culture clashes did erupt from time to time.

One letter to the editor of the Rochester Post-Bulletin complained of how Saudi men acted at a local grocery store, especially how they forced their wives to walk several steps behind them. On another occasion, a messy lawsuit was brought against a local hotel's management for allegedly failing to stop sexual harassment of its maids by Middle Eastern guests.

But for the most part, the Middle Eastern contingent made its accommodations with the local culture—each tacitly acknowledging the ways it needed the other but remaining wary and distant all the same.

Somehow, Rochester never got mentioned in national discussions about terrorism and domestic security. Even after a major al Qaeda suspect—Zacarias Moussaoui, the so-called 20th hijacker who briefly attended Pan Am International Flight Academy in Eagan—got busted in the Twin Cities, even after it was publicly reported that members of the Saudi royal family had supported al Qaeda financially, there was never any public acknowledgment of the potential significance of the quiet little city 80 miles south of the metro where powerful Saudis, among others, had come and gone for years without suspicion.

As the bartenders at C.J.'s recall it, their Middle Eastern customers in the days shortly before 9/11 came in two varieties—old ones and young ones. The older customers seemed friendly, worldly, easygoing. They were receptive to casual conversation. The younger ones, by contrast, kept to themselves more, talking intensely in quiet voices and casting a chilly eye on strangers. But sometimes the younger Saudi men would welcome a local woman to their table and engage her in a conversational dance that was part flirtation, part mutually curious observation of an alien species, part political debate.

"They were from a different culture, and I gave a certain amount of respect to that, but some of their views were racist and ignorant," Hanlon says. "I'd say 'Where is your wife, why don't you bring her here?' And they would say, 'I would never bring her, it would never happen.'

"They also made it clear they were no friends of Americans. They had no love for us as a people or country. Every Saudi guy in the place would say, 'You Americans need to get out of our country, take your troops and planes and get out, and you need to back off in Israel. You are totally aligned with Israel, so you are our enemy.' I'd ask them, 'If you can't stand us, what are you doing here? Why are you here in Rochester?'"

One night Hanlon met a Saudi named Khalid who was "immaculately dressed, in a perfectly snow-white shirt with a high collar—almost clerical. Black dress pants with a kind of sheen to them. And a gold money clip right on the bar."

She bantered with Khalid in the usual way, asking about his home and family and jibing him about his absent wife. When she mentioned that her own home was located near the Rochester airport—an incidental detail in her mind—he perked up. "He just lit up like a Christmas tree," she says. "Just the word 'airport' seemed to have some significance for him. I was like, 'What? What's that all about?'"

The next night Hanlon returned to the bar after work, thinking she might see Khalid again and rekindle their conversation. He was nowhere to be found. She took a seat at the bar, next to the man she would later identify as Mohand Alshehri.

Hanlon remembers their three-hour encounter in striking detail. It was the way he looked as much as his words. "He just seemed like a frightened boy," she says. "A little man, slight and frail. Not dangerous. He was suffering and I extended myself to him.

"I said, 'Tell me what's wrong.' At first he was like, 'I can't tell you, I don't want to talk about it.' He fought against it. Then he kind of sighed and said, 'I've got myself into something there is no way out. There is no way out.'"

He wouldn't explain what he was talking about. Hanlon tried other approaches. She asked what he did for a living.

He claimed he was a pilot. "I looked at this guy and just couldn't see it," she says. "This disheveled wreck of a man, cheaply dressed with matted hair—I thought he was talking about crop dusting back in Saudi Arabia." The man saw her

9

skepticism and pulled some kind of pilot's identification card from his wallet. It looked real; his picture was on it.

Gradually he began sharing a few personal details. He had a wife and a daughter in his country, he told Hanlon.

"I put my arm around him, and he let me," she says. "He just crumpled. It was like he wanted to start crying. But he couldn't, because he was a man. I said, 'You need to think of your wife and children. You are so young, whatever you've done, maybe if you go to the authorities, even if you have to go to prison, it would still be worth it. You still could see your wife and your child again. You really need to think about that.' He said, 'I am thinking about that, but this is really the end of the road.'

"One odd thing he said is, 'It has been decided. He has decided it. It is done. It is finished, Nancy.' Which was very religious-sounding to me. Always when I felt I was getting to him, that there was a way out, it was as if he'd start to argue with himself. He'd say, 'No, it is decided, he has decided, he has spoken.' He.

"And I said 'Who is He? Do you mean Allah? Has Allah spoken?' I assumed he was talking about Allah, because it sounded so prophetic. But today I think it was probably bin Laden."

The hour grew late. Nothing she said seemed to help. When it was time to go, says Hanlon, "He turned and took hold of my arm. The last thing he said to me was, 'Nancy, promise me you won't forget me. And remember the things I told you.'" He kept insisting on the last point, she claims: "You remember what I told you."

The Rochester FBI office has declined to comment on her story, reiterating its conventional line that the agency never discusses interviews it conducts with tipsters. Paul McCabe, the bureau's regional spokesperson in Minneapolis, also declined to comment on Hanlon's story, offering only that "members of the Joint Terrorism Task Force continue to work numerous counter-terrorism matters and cases." (After I summarized

Hanlon's claims and previewed her story in my weekly Rochester Post-Bulletin column, the Star Tribune wrote a follow-up in which McCabe went further: "The FBI could not substantiate the tipster's claims. We have no reason to believe that Mohand Alshehri has ever been in Rochester, Minnesota.")

Besides the seeming incongruity of terrorists in semi-rural Minnesota, the other inescapable question concerning Hanlon's credibility is why it took her a year to reexamine her experience and contact the FBI.

It was only by an accident of circumstance that Nancy Hanlon wound up telling her story to me. I grew up in Rochester, and Hanlon was in my grade at school. I lost touch with her, along with most of my classmates, when I left town for college and a career in journalism. Twenty-eight years later I moved back to Rochester. After I signed up for a high school class reunion, Hanlon found my e-mail address and wrote to me. She had been reading my columns in the Post-Bulletin, the note said, and there was a story she wanted to tell me about a guy she'd met at a local bar.

In the dozen or so meetings I had with her in reporting this story, Hanlon could never say with any assurance why it took her so long to see any connection between her encounters at C.J.'s and 9/11. She admits she can't entirely explain it herself. Certainly her own small-town outlook played a part. Never an avid reader of political news, she was one of the people who could see no reason to think there might be terrorists in the city she sometimes refers to, without any sense of irony, as "little old Rochester."

Still, a year? Shouldn't bells have gone off when she heard of the arrest of Moussaoui? Maybe. But it didn't happen. The thought didn't dawn on her until September 2002, when the media launched their 9/11 one-year anniversary coverage.

When the possible tie did occur to Hanlon, she says, it scared her. The aspect that haunted her most was the uncanny resemblance between the words ascribed to al Qaeda leaders in the media's anniversary retrospectives and the ones she had heard from some of the Saudi men in C.J.'s the summer before. She realized it didn't prove anything, but she remembers being struck by a wave of dread that only grew the longer she thought about it.

"I was at a football game with my kids when it really hit me. The floodgates kind of opened. I was in the middle of a big crowd and I just said, 'We have to go home, I feel sick.' I remembered all the conversations I'd had with these guys. They hated America, they said the same things the terrorists were saying—it was all just too close. I couldn't watch the news and I quit reading newspapers and magazines. Finally one day I picked up the phone and called the FBI and said, 'I think I know these guys, I'm sorry it took so long.'"

At the FBI office in Rochester, Hanlon says that Agent David Price showed her photographs of dozens of suspected terrorists, but was particularly interested in one of them—Khalid Sheikh Mohammed, the top al Qaeda operative who is believed to have masterminded 9/11 and would later be apprehended in March 2003. But no, Hanlon said, that was certainly not the Khalid she met in the bar prior to meeting Mohand. The Khalid at C.J.'s was a slender man. He didn't look anything like the terrorist Khalid.

"No, no, no, no, no," she said as Price showed her photo after photo. She couldn't positively identify any of the men shown in the pictures—until, on her third and final visit to his office, Price pulled out another file. The men in these photographs were of less urgent concern to the FBI, because their present whereabouts and activities were no mystery. They had all died in the planes they hijacked on September 11. The man she knew as Khalid wasn't there. But Mohand was.

Having her apprehensions confirmed only made Hanlon more upset. After leaving Price's office, "I got in my car and I just wept. Then I wished I had never ever walked into that bar. I wished it hadn't happened to me.

"I crawled into bed for three days. My kids were scared."

Dr. Brandi Witt, Hanlon's family physician at the Mayo Clinic, corroborates that Hanlon came to her in the late fall of 2002 with symptoms of depression. "She remembered she'd spent some time with a man who she later found out was one of the 9/11 hijackers," Witt recalls. "She was having some feelings of guilt. She was wondering if she should have known, or if there was something she could have done."

Witt and Hanlon's mother, Barbara Hanlon, both confirmed to me that Nancy Hanlon told them exactly the same story in fall 2002 that she was telling me now. Barbara Hanlon adds that her daughter was "upset and overwhelmed" at the time, but says "she kind of shut up about it" after her first attempts to share the experience were rebuffed by friends.

"They looked at me like I was nuts," Nancy Hanlon remembers. "People just didn't want to hear about it. They didn't want to imagine that this might have happened right here in Rochester, Minnesota. One of my girlfriends said, 'I wish you hadn't told me that.' Like I'd befriended a mass murderer. But he wasn't a mass murderer when I met him—not that I know of."

Others simply didn't believe her. There is no material evidence to support her story, after all. She didn't take a photograph of Alshehri, and she received no gifts or notes from him. Their conversation was not noticed by anyone who would recall it later. At C.J.'s, the bartenders confirm that Saudi men frequented their establishment until 9/11, when they disappeared over-night. But they don't recognize a picture of Alshehri.

But if there is no proving that Hanlon's encounter with Alshehri ever occurred, there is some additional circumstantial corroboration of her story's plausibility. The CIA's timeline of his whereabouts prior to 9/11, for example, has him arriving in the U.S. in Miami on May 28, 2001. Other timelines show him traveling from Fort Lauderdale to Newark on September 7, 2001, and the Boston Globe reported that on September 10, he and three other hijackers stayed at the Milner Hotel in Boston, where they called several escort services but ultimately made no deal. The available record of his movements features a large gap that includes the month of August 2001.

The portrait that Hanlon paints of Mohand Alshehri as a despondent waif is also consistent with the little that's been revealed about him elsewhere. In testimony given by former CIA director George Tenet to the U.S. Congress, Tenet said the 9/11 hijackers fell into three main groups—the Hamburg Cell (including the alleged ringleader, Mohammed Atta), al Qaeda veterans, and young Saudis. Mohand Alshehri was in the third group. Some of the young Saudis "had struggled with depression or alcohol abuse, or simply seemed to be drifting in search of purpose," Tenet told Congress.

After 9/11—quite literally the day after, in many cases—the Middle East Arab subculture that had flourished in Rochester seemed to disappear altogether. No more billowing white Saudi robes were seen downtown. The city's shop owners bemoaned the end of the lavish shopping sprees they had learned to expect. Mayo Clinic disclosed that its international patient traffic, especially from the Middle East, had dried up. The downtown prayer room closed. So did the Arab travel and real estate agencies.

The sudden change felt suspicious to some locals, though it really wasn't. The same thing occurred all over the United States as Arabs of all nationalities felt the sting of the new public paranoia, and also of new federal policies that singled out Middle Easterners for scrutiny. Citizens of Saudi Arabia, especially those connected to the royal family, beat a path back home in the days immediately after September 11, some of them on planes authorized for takeoff while the rest of the American commercial and private aviation system remained grounded.

Perhaps the fact that the milieu she's talking about has vanished so completely from Rochester makes Hanlon's story even harder for some to believe today. She knows she can't do anything about that. "I kept quiet for a long time because I was asked to," Hanlon says. "The FBI said they would appreciate if I kept the story to myself. I always thought it would come out some other way, that they were here. I expected it would come out through the FBI. Then the years passed and no one said anything. It's hard to believe that it has to be me.

"This really happened," she sighs finally. "It's real." ●

II WHO ARE WE TODAY

The Most Beautiful Place on Earth

I'm lucky to have lived in some very interesting places around the world. For most of my adult life I've worked as a journalist in New York City and in Tokyo, London, and Hong Kong. I've also traveled extensively through China, Europe, Southeast Asia, Africa, and the Middle East.

Since I moved back to Rochester, Minnesota, where I grew up, two years ago, the most common question I got (and still get) is: "Why do you want to live in this tiny Midwestern town?"

Let me answer that question, once and for all.

Rochester is as beautiful as any place on earth. Please visit Silver Lake Park on a summer afternoon. Plunk down at a picnic table and watch the Zumbro River float by like liquid chocolate fringed with weeping willows, pines, maples, aspen, elm, and oaks as green as emeralds. Check out those same trees glazed with ice during the winter, encased in diamond sheaths to the last twiglet, shooting off sunbeams like cut-crystal chandeliers.

Drive through the dun-colored Minnesota prairie in late autumn. Take a look at the popcorn clouds, the corn-row clouds, the spun sugar clouds, and the Zeus'-anvil clouds that populate our Midwestern sky. Take in the mighty Mississippi River.

Minnesota is as interesting as any place on earth.

England is where our language and lots of our science, politics, and culture were born, and it's got the Royal Family, too. Japan has a fascinating social system; and Switzerland makes wonderful watches; and 5,000-year-old China now has the world's largest population, the fastest-growing economy, and is exporting sports stars (like Yao Ming), scientists (David Ho), Nobel novelists (Gao Xingjian), and virtuoso musicians (Lang Lang) as if by assembly-line. So what else is new? There will always be more in the big wide world than there is right here, or in any other specific locale.

Meanwhile, Minnesota is a specific marvel. We've got great men (George Bonga, Father Hennepin, O.E. Rolvaag, Floyd B. Olson, Will and Charlie Mayo) and great women (Harriet Bishop, Martha Ripley, Nellie Stone Johnson, Meridel LeSueur) in our history. Our tradition of civic service is the envy of 49 other states. We are a sane and sober bunch yet, endearingly, we go absolutely nuts from time to time (in 1998 we elected Governor Petulant Loudmouth with a pink feather boa).

I don't miss living abroad, because foreigners are us. I love the variety and challenge of living abroad, yet I find plenty of both commodities right here. I volunteer teach at the Adult Literacy Center here, where my students are Somalis, Sudanese, Russians, Chinese, Bosnians, Mexicans, Colombians, and many other nationalities. That's more ethnic variety than I ever saw while living in Tokyo.

Most ethnic groups in Rochester have churches, restaurants, and festivals that are open to all. I take Chinese language lessons from a Shanghai native who lives in town, and along with words and sentences I try to soak up Chinese history and attitudes and points of view.

One in 10 citizens of Rochester wasn't even born in America, and every immigrant I've met here has a vital perspective and fascinating stories they're eager to share.

At some point in my world travels, I concluded there are really only two basic puzzles a person needs to solve in life. Puzzle #1 is to decide what "home" really means, and then to find and make your own true home. Puzzle #2 is how to live in a way that's consistent with the fact that in a wider sense, the whole world is our home and all people are our neighbors.

To be honest, I'm still stumped on Puzzle #2.

But I do know this: You can't solve #2 until you've solved #1. And in Rochester, Minnesota I've found the perfect place to do that—because it's beautiful, because it's interesting, and because it's my home. ●

The Global Citizen's Dual Address

The Polish philosopher Leszek Kolakowski once wrote: "When I am asked where I would like to live, my standard answer is: deep in the virgin mountain forest on a lake shore at the corner of Madison Avenue in Manhattan and the Champs-Elysees, in a small tidy town."

I like this answer very much, but part of me distrusts it, too. If this is a picture of global citizenship, I'm skeptical. Cosmopolitanism without a home place is unserious, lonely, somehow barren. It can take without giving. It speaks of being lost and confused, as in a bad dream.

In a world like ours, already strange and surreal, I want to know exactly where I stand and live, where I come from. I want the nourishment of roots, and I want to get my mail. I want the security of a simple address in a single town, a specific avenue crossing a specific street.

"Global citizenship?" What is that? Don't we need to know what it truly means to be a "citizen" before we move to "global citizen?" Do we really know what it means to be a citizen in the United States today?

I read recently about a Korean grocer in Los Angeles, one Charles Kim, who definitely knows what it means. He apprehended a black teenager robbing his store and called the cops. When the cops came, the kid talked about his life, and Kim, instead of pressing charges, had him work off the penalty in his store. Then he hired him. Then he organized other Korean grocers to hire young black teenagers from the neighborhood.

When a reporter asked what payback he got from all this,

Kim said "the priceless taste of love." What a global citizen!

When was the last time we as a society thought about citizenship, as Charles Kim does, as a spiritual path? Not just as a dutiful annual slog to the polling booth, but as a means of personal growth—a way to heal the self by healing society? Or as a form of expression available to every person that's every bit as potent as writing a book or singing an opera, and just as necessary?

The "Self-Improvement" section at B&N is piled high with tomes on diets, meditation, massage, astrology, career counseling, divorce guides, sex guides, and so on. Many of these books are valuable and useful, I'm sure. Yet in the aggregate they form a tower to the lonely Self.

Then there is the "Current Events" section, a tower to Society you might say, with its own prescribed solutions in foreign affairs, education policy, crime, and the horribly biased news media.

I'd like to see a new section called "Society and Self" with books on how to heal the individual self, by healing society. How to cure your headache by volunteering at a shelter. This third section of books would take some imagination, which, returns us to Leszek Kolakowski.

Because if there's one thing we need these days, it's imagination. Not only to imagine how the U.S. is connected to China and Somalia and Mexico and Iraq; but also how the Chinese and Somali and Mexican communities in southeast Minnesota are connected to each other and how they are, in fact, us. Hopefully, we are all becoming one.

In the meantime, we are still many. The pasts and the passions of these foreign lands are all now well planted in our soil. It's a good idea to go to these lands and to visit with the people who live there before they come, possibly in conflict, to visit us. We need to befriend the other.

And to do that kind of travel takes imagination—to peer behind the strange languages, customs, and costumes, to see the human beings beneath.

We all need two addresses. A specific address to keep us rooted, to assure us who we are and where we are from, and to point us home. And an address in the imagination to connect us to the far reaches of humanity, to the other.

Shuttling between these two addresses, reflecting deeply about the one while visiting the other, is how to travel globally in our small tidy towns.

Thai Curry and Awakened Heart

Rochester has restaurants from 16 countries; three Asian, two Mexican, and two Middle Eastern groceries; and retail shops selling every exotic goody from Danish porcelains and Norwegian sweaters to tooled-leather Mexican boots, Swiss watches, Thai curries, Russian vodka, and Somali scarves.

Now there's a place in Rochester to get some *boddhicitta*, if you are running low. It's not a typical consumer item but it's very useful nonetheless—something you'd love your spouse and kids to have.

Bodhicitta is the essential quality of the Buddha. It literally means "awakened heart" and it contains the qualities of compassion, altruism, loving-kindness, and tenderness for life.

It's said to be made of two equal parts: wisdom and love. These two parts work together like the wings of a bird, the Buddha said, allowing men and women to rise above suffering and to be an inspiration to others.

"If it looks like wisdom but is unkind rather than loving, it's not wisdom," Buddha said. "If it feels like love but it's not wise, it's not love."

You can directly experience boddhicitta for yourself at the new temple of the Buddhist Support Society, out on 29th Street SE in Marion township, a half mile east of Marion Road. Just park under the American flag that's flying in front, knock on the door, and in a moment you will be greeted by one of the three young Cambodian monks who run the temple.

No matter how cold it is outside, they will be dressed in a simple orange robe that covers only one shoulder. Their feet will be bare. They will greet you pleasantly, let you in and listen with an utterly open attitude to whatever is on your heart.

You may feel an oddness, a strange kind of neutral feeling, because the monks sort of float by, listening very carefully when you talk and taking every care to make sure you are comfortable, but not saying much either. They will answer if you speak, of course, and what they say will likely be simple and wise, maybe even childlike. But mainly, they just listen.

This gives the flavor of boddhicitta, the very quality that no less an authority than the Dalai Lama has said "lies at the heart of all spiritual endeavor" and can even help a person understand "the true goal, the true meaning of life."

The monks don't give you boddhicitta directly, of course. Rather they embody it with their very being. It's what they are trained to do. It's in their job description to welcome all people with absolute openness and to impart by their being this feeling of simplicity, purity, and calm.

The three Cambodian monks at the temple – Sokhom Roth, Synat It, and Sopheab Loeung—have all spent more than a decade following 227 strict moral rules designed by Buddha to cultivate boddhicitta in human beings.

"Not just the Buddha but everyone can have it," explains Sokhom Roth. "You fill your heart with kindness and compassion and don't allow thoughts of greed, hate, or delusion." Of course, it takes some practice, which is what the daily rituals and meditations of Buddhist practice are all about.

"People may be from America or Cambodia or any nation on earth, but if they have developed boddhicitta they are like one," Sokhom said. "They become like water in the ocean. Each person comes from a different river but the ocean is one water, and you can't tell which river they come from."

Sokhom and Synat told me the essence of boddhicitta is to "try to live for the benefit of all living things in the universe." The Dalai Lama goes even further. He says the first step to developing boddhicitta is to imagine that "every sentient being in the universe is our dear old mother"!

How's that for an exercise in developing gratitude?

Here then is a suggested list for your next ethnic shopping trip in Rochester:

> *Swiss Chocolates: $2*
> *French Wine: $12*
> *Mexican Boots: $150*
> *Bodhicitta: Priceless.* ●

Shooting Ourselves in the Future

A single room in southeast Minnesota looks more like a United Nations lobby than any other: the crowded waiting room of Michael York, the area's only full-time private practice immigration attorney.

His Rochester office is bustling like never before as worried immigrants line up seeking help dealing with an increasingly tough and unforgiving U.S. immigration policy.

Somali women in rainbow chiffons. Russian computer programmers in white button shirts. Mexican laborers in coveralls. Chinese doctors in suits and ties.

Two years after 9/11, enforcement of immigration law throughout the U.S. has tightened dramatically as new federal and state laws, combined with heightened local police vigilance, has cast a widening net for illegal aliens.

At the national level, the detention of more than 5,000 foreign nationals in various anti-terrorism programs has grabbed headlines. The "special registration" fingerprinting of 85,000 men from Arab and Muslim countries raised protests so loud the government last month announced it would end the program. But detentions, deportations, and overall immigration enforcement continues to tighten as the U.S. makes it harder than ever for foreign visitors to get into the country or to extend their visits here.

York's office reflects those trends with some local twists.

"People are trying desperate things," York said. "They are anxious about their visa status and wanting a way to fix it."

It's not unusual, he said, for illegal immigrants—as are many migrant workers and students or tourists on expired visas----to close bank accounts, to not report household and neighborhood crimes, and otherwise take steps to ensure they never cross paths with police. They're going underground.

The police, for their part, are checking immigration status much more carefully and routinely, such as during stops for traffic violations, York said.

Before 9/11, detentions on suspected immigration violations tended to occur only after the Immigration and Naturalization Service (now the Citizenship and Immigration Service) made a request or complaint. Now, it's not uncommon for people to spend some time in a local Minnesota jail pending a full immigration hearing, even before the CIS is involved.

Educated professional people from foreign countries that have been America's allies are as nervous as everyone else, York said.

"You'd be amazed how many come in from Western Europe," he said. "I've had clients from Greece, the U.K., Canada, Australia, France, Germany, Sweden. They are all antsy about their visa status."

Local computer and medical employees originally recruited on so-called "J1" or "work visas" are doing everything they can to ensure they can stay here legally, such as by getting permanent residence status (a "green card"), and by avoiding any potential negative attention from the CIS.

Two common pieces of advice York is giving to immigrant clients these days is to be sure to report one's current address to the CIS, because reporting discrepancies raise a red flag; and also to apply for all categories of visa for which one might possibly be eligible.

The byzantine U.S. immigration bureaucracy created since 9/11 is also stifling efforts by foreign nationals to enter and stay in United States. There is far more paperwork and longer waits at all stages. A common procedure, upgrading to permanent resident "green card" status, once took six months and now takes about 18 months on average, York said.

Around the world, the visa departments at U.S. embassies have also made it virtually impossible to get previously routine non-immigrant visas.

"It was never easy but it's ten times more difficult now," York said. "In some cases it's infinitely more difficult. There is almost a presumption of fraud. The interviewers will argue with you over everything. They'll demand several forms of proof for even basic facts."

The overall picture is deeply troubling on two counts.

First, the tighter-than-ever immigration enforcement is a threat to the local economy. IBM, Mayo Clinic, and satellite companies to the area's two largest employers must hire the best talent both from the U.S. and abroad to stay competitive in a global marketplace.

What's going to happen now that this vital labor supply line is cut? The question applies not only to Rochester but to all America, of course.

Second, think of those tens of thousands of foreign-born dreamers, geniuses, entrepreneurs, and freedom lovers who once idolized the U.S. and saw themselves making their lives and futures here. Now they're sitting at home, stinging from a futile and humiliating interview at the U.S. embassy.

For them, America the beautiful is now America the bully. We are making enemies of the people whose friendship we need most to secure our future. ●

The World Music of Quetico

This past week I spent my days not tapping out clusters of symbols on a computer screen but rather chopping wood, making fires, and stamping my feet in the damp cold.

It was glorious.

Each August I spend a week canoeing through Quetico-Superior, the two million-acre wilderness that straddles the U.S.-Canada border in northern Minnesota. I do it to clear my mind, to remind myself of life's basics, and to open my soul.

What a precious global resource we have under our stewardship in Quetico-Superior, this labyrinth of glacial lakes that offers a clear window into humankind's prehistoric past.

This year I traveled with my best friend from Rochester and his 14-year-old son. At our last camp site, in the sprawling Lake Saganagon, we pitched our tent among seven towering cedars that soared a hundred feet high and surrounded us like gods.

Thanks to American and Canadian wilderness protection laws, Quetico-Superior today looks much the way it probably did in 8,000 B.C., when the glaciers of the last Ice Age receded. I carried one book with me this year, but even more I carried, as I do every year, a mind filled with a year's worth of the daily grind.

It takes a day or two of canoeing and portaging before that noise subsides. After that I start to hear the morning bird calls, the forest insects' hum, and the piercing cries of the loons.

My book was a selection of essays by Sigurd Olson—another precious Minnesota resource—called The Meaning of Wilderness. A canoe guide in Quetico-Superior before he became a popular nature writer, Olson believed that wilderness was an essential counterbalance to fast-paced modern life.

If that was true in his day, how much more true in ours. I wondered if Olson had advice about how the experience of wilderness might encourage not only individual spiritual strength but also communal civic strength. Was this even possible?

The first three days of our trip this year, it rained. The three of us dripped and shivered and huddled happily. We gulped down our days in the wet woods like refreshing tonic against the soul-parching weeks we'd spent in the office.

Then the fourth day broke blue and sunny and we duffed lazily all day long at our cedar-scented Lake Saganagon site, stretching our bare legs in the 100% mosquito-free air.

Olson's great passion was to prove why natural wilderness was critical to humankind. The reasons he offered changed over the years. As a young man in his 20's and 30's, Olson stressed the simple pleasures of enjoying pristine nature, of getting hard outdoor exercise, of breathing clean air, and of making lifelong friendships on the trail and around the campfire.

In his middle years, he broadened his pro-wilderness stance to include economic (wilderness as recreational resource), educational (wilderness as a natural history classroom), scientific (wilderness as a biology laboratory), and ecological and environmental arguments for wilderness preservation.

In his 60's and 70's, Olson at last began to plumb the subject that all along had seemed to lurk just beneath the surface of all his writings—the spiritual value of wilderness. Humankind was born and for 100,000 years or more had lived in the wilderness, he argued. Wilderness and its challenges had shaped the core of human character.

Thus, when modern technological man goes into the wilderness he feels in his bones that he is returning home.

"While some of his spiritual roots have been severed, he still has his gods," Olson wrote of modern man. "He needs to know that the spiritual values that once sustained him are still there in the timelessness and majestic rhythms of those parts of the world he has not ravished."

It is the same song inside all of us. If we can only hear it, nature itself is a unifying force that transcends all the superficial boundaries that divide mankind.

The bald eagles swoop. The fish jump. The loons cry, giving us goose-bumps. The full moon falls pianissimo, and the sun rises like cymbals crashing.

Inside and outside, we connect. ●

The Mississippi, the Yangtze, and Me

We are water-crazed here in Minnesota.

The Water-Ski Days in Lake City, with its parade of floats depicting rural America, was held the other day, and the Minneapolis Aquatennial is being held all this week. Waterama in Glenwood, the Hoyt Lakes Water Carnival, and Catfish Derby Days in Franklin are coming up this weekend.

If you're still up for a watery fest, the Riverboat Days Festival in Wabasha will be held next weekend, with its famous Fireman's Water Fight.

We even celebrate the official state liquid in frozen form, holding pagan coronation and dethroning rituals for winter gods in the state's capital every year. Not to mention our passion for the ancient rite of ice fishing, a freeze-framed genuflection to the bounties of the deep.

These celebrations of our state's life-sustaining ponds, streams, lakes, and rivers are at the heart of what makes us Minnesotans.

The waters of Minnesota also connect us with the world. Growing up here, I thought of Minnesota's waters—for me the Zumbro River, Lake Superior, and the Mississippi River—primarily as signifiers of the state itself. They defined my place, my home, and my own identity to a large degree.

Today, I see these great waters not just as landmarks that define Minnesota but also as living connectors—like blood vessels or super-sensitive membranes—between our state and the rest of the world.

Partly I've developed this perspective because of traveling

I've done; partly it's due to the vision of the world that science and ecology gives us; and partly, I think, it's just a matter of getting older and thinking more about civic responsibility.

For a couple of years in the 1990s, I worked in mainland China, and I frequently stayed in Shanghai. There I would stand on the banks of the Huangpo River, on the boulevard called the Bund, and I would see this mighty artery of commerce bearing coal barges and container ships and tiny tattered junks hauling pigs to market and every kind of ship imaginable.

When I returned to live in Minnesota in 2000, I visited Lake City and stood on the shores of Lake Pepin. I played hockey on Lake Pepin in the winter as a kid, and I sailed and motor-boated there in the summer, and somehow the Mississippi River never seemed terribly grand to me then. When I returned home, though, having seen the Huangpo River, somehow the Mississippi had grown in stature in my eyes, and in my soul, too.

That's because I can now see the Mississippi not only as a great American river—greater than I ever knew it was—but also as just a part of the world's great web of ponds, lakes, rivers and oceans.

The ecological view also fosters apprehension of Minnesota's global connectedness. The health of our state's waters is increasingly seen not just as a mirror of our own health, but of the world's environmental health.

Gone are the days when pollution in one of Minnesota's lakes could be traced to a local source. Today, any of dozens of toxins in local fish could have originated in Russia, China, or Japan. Invasive species arrive in our lakes and rivers via Great Lake barges, our shoe bottoms, and Internet mail orders.

So what is our global responsibility as stewards of one of the world's most complex water- land ecosystems? To me, above and beyond the practical matter of keeping our waters clean, a spiritual responsibility is implied.

Hamline University's Center for Global Environmental Education uses a quote by the Japanese conservationist, Tanaka

Shozo, as a motto: "The care of rivers is not a question of rivers, but of the human heart."

That means that here in Minnesota—with our 11,842 lakes and 6,564 streams and rivers—we've been granted unusual access to someplace precious, little-known, and deep. The world needs to learn some things about this place, and quick. With each lake and river a potential portal to the human heart, we've got a powerful natural resource here indeed.

Maybe we could each go to our favorite place by the water this summer, get quiet, and learn a little something about that place and about ourselves.

Now that would be worth a festival. ●

The Ya Ba Crisis of Minnesota

I wonder if St. Paul Mayor Randy Kelly, on his recent trip to Thailand to meet a new group of Hmong refugees heading to America, noticed a rampaging social problem that Thailand shares with Minnesota: an epidemic of methamphetamine abuse.

Thailand's Prime Minister Thaksin Shinawatra has called methamphetamine—in Thai it's called "ya ba" for "crazy medicine"—the nation's #1 national security problem. That's because of the vast tax sums Thailand has had to spend on education, interdiction, seeking out and destroying meth labs, prison overcrowding, and rehabilitation of addicts.

Sound familiar, Minnesota?

The sickness is more advanced in Thailand than here—so far.

Up to one in five Thais have used methamphetamine, which is also called "the diligent drug" in Thailand because it's used by truck drivers, cabbies, factory workers and others who need to work long hours to make enough money to survive. Meth in Thailand is usually taken in pill form, while the inhalable powder form is more popular in Minnesota.

In mid-1997, Thailand's economy crashed, shrinking by 12% in one year and putting two million Thais out of work. Many of the jobless took "ya ba" for relief. Quickly sucked into addiction, they started selling the pills themselves to make money to buy more, creating a direct-sales network that accelerated and amplified the epidemic many times. By 2002, 90% of all drug cases involved methamphetamines.

Worst of all was the "Ruthless Campaign" launched by the

Thai government last year to snuff out the crisis. Started on February 1, 2003, the campaign began with a mass media anti-drug blitz but quickly turned darker.

Prime Minister Thaksin, known as the toughest Southeast Asian leader since Lee Kwan Yew of Singapore, announced that "it may be necessary to have casualties. If there are deaths among dealers, it's normal."

Over the next two months—until an international outcry brought attention to the executions—as many as 3,000 Thais, mostly drug dealers but also many innocents, were caught in the crossfire. Night after night, Thai TV showed images of methamphetamine dealers lying in pools of blood. After liberal Thai newspapers began to protest, the government backed off the "Ruthless Campaign" and the killings stopped.

That last bit doesn't sound like Minnesota, thank God.

But make no mistake, the meth crisis in this state is part of the same global contagion that Thailand is suffering from. We have many of the same contributing factors to the epidemic that contributed to the Thai crisis, just mixed in a less lethal form. A main similarity is an economic downturn feeding the problem, which begins in rural areas and moves to the cities.

We can learn many lessons, positive and negative, from studying Thailand's handling of the epidemic. The brutal approach, for instance, was a non-starter of a solution. After retreating from the Ruthless Campaign the government launched a new tack to fight meth, employing some of the same educational techniques it used in its anti-HIV/Aids campaign. The centerpiece of that campaign was intensive social education about the risks of HIV and the steps to prevent it, carried out in schools, markets, brothels, and in the media.

Those steps won international praise for Thailand, which was thought to be in danger of HIV infection rates so high the country might collapse. It didn't happen.

Just to see the meth problem as one of state security, as

Thailand properly saw the HIV/Aids threat, is a major positive step. In Thailand, this is easier because most of the "ya ba" in Thailand is manufactured by rebel states in neighboring northern Burma (Myanmar), which uses drug trafficking to finance their war for independence.

It may be harder for us in Minnesota to see our connection to Burma than it is for the Thais, but the same connections are there. Drugs, just like the flu, start in one place in the world and find their way to another. Wars of revolution in one part of the world morph into drug crises in another.

We saw it happen with cocaine. Now with meth. Sometimes the route of infection is direct, such as in California, where Thai drug smugglers use the state's large Thai immigrant population as cover to import millions of Burmese "ya ba" pills into the state, fueling a meth crisis there.

Other times a variant strain arises, such as in Minnesota where the home-cooked, powdered form of meth is favored.

In any case, we've caught the bug. And we can learn from Thailand's mistakes and successes to help us get over it. ●

The Shame of Olmsted County

Quick! From what foreign country do most of Olmsted County's immigrants come? Is it Somalia? Cambodia? Laos? How about China?

Good guesses, as immigrants from all of these countries have had a major and very visible impact on life here over the past decade.

But they are all wrong. The correct answer is: Mexico.

According to the 2000 U.S. Census, some 1,783 immigrants from Mexico live in Olmsted County, far outstripping the 1,242 immigrants from Somalia, and the 583 immigrants from Vietnam, 466 from Cambodia, 425 from Laos, and 362 from China.

If you add to the 1,783 Mexican immigrants living in Olmsted, immigrants from Colombia, Chile, Guatemala, Peru and other Central and South American countries, the number of Latino immigrants here rises to 2,959.

Would you ever have guessed it? Probably not, because the Latino immigrant explosion—in Olmsted County just as in the United States—has happened stealthily, often invisibly.

I asked a few friends last week where they thought most of the foreign-born population in Olmsted County comes from. Somalia and Cambodia were the top two answers. But those were the correct answers for the 1990s and the 1980s, respectively. Three years into the 2000s, the man on the street remains unaware of the massive Latinization of our community.

Why is that? Our Mexican neighbors blend in visually more than do our Somali or Asian neighbors, of course. But there is a more important reason that is rarely discussed, because it's a hard thing to bring up.

That is, many of our Mexican neighbors are living here illegally. They live and work here, often for many years, yet have neither a valid visa nor a permanent residency document, usually called a "green card."

Lacking legal status, these immigrants try to stay invisible. They go straight home from their jobs in restaurant kitchens, on assembly lines, on landscaping and construction crews, on the corn pack line, or on the farm. They don't hang out.

They either don't drive, or they drive in abject fear because to get picked up without a license might mean a one-way ticket back to hopelessness in Mexico.

Nona Yancy, a caseworker at the Intercultural Mutual Assistance Association in Rochester, says the number of Latino immigrant cases at the aid group is on pace to more than double in three years, from 460 cases in 2000, to 935 cases so far in 2003.

About 80 percent of those IMAA cases are living here illegally, she says.

Since by definition the IMAA sees immigrants with documentation problems, 40% of local Latino immigrants here illegally is probably closer to the mark. No definite statistics are kept on the number.

Nationwide, depending whether you use pro- or anti-immigration interpretations of the raw U.S. census figures, between 20 and 40 percent of the country's 7.9 million Mexican immigrants are here illegally.

The shame doesn't lie with the immigrants. If you lived in poverty and had a chance to make a living, what would you do? The shame lies with the United States, which maintains strict immigration standards but fails to enforce them.

And why do we not enforce them? Because our corporations love cheap labor and lobby hard for lax enforcement of immigration law.

And, because we love to eat affordable food, wear affordable clothes, and to have someone to nanny the kids.

These attitudes lock millions of our Mexican neighbors—including as many as 700 men, women, and children in Olmsted County—into a desperate twilight existence. They can't apply for health insurance; they can't drive; they can't apply for food stamps or any public assistance.

If a child gets a cough or cold—not to mention something more serious—the parents face an excruciating and humiliating choice: Go to the doctor and face possible exposure and deportation? Or avoid the doctor and risk the child's life?

"Anyone here not with a legal status is a lifelong sitting duck," says Michael York, a Rochester immigration attorney.

Shouldn't we decide what we want as a society?

Do we want to allow in lots of Latin immigrants to take the low-wage jobs that lowers consumer prices and raises standard of life? Or do we want to limit immigration for reasons of physical, social, and cultural security?

As things stand, we've chosen the former. And yet, in return for the improvement in living standards these immigrants bring us, we refuse to pay the price. Instead, we make *them* pay the price in the form of lives spent in debilitating fear.

What would it take to bring this invisible problem to light nationally? Could we do it here in Olmsted County? ●

America's Most Globalized Town

The town that faces more globalization issues than any other town its size in America is plunked down here in the cornfields of southeastern Minnesota.

It's our town, Rochester, Minnesota. Home to the world-famous Mayo Clinic and also, less well known, to one of IBM's largest manufacturing plants. For decades the two institutions have recruited the world's best doctors, scientific and medical researchers, software programmers and engineers.

They've thus created a knowledge-based, globally competitive economy that could be a model for thousands of small towns and cities trying to achieve the same trick.

That's according to John Recker, an economist at the University of Ohio and the author of a report on Rochester's economic contribution to the State of Minnesota.

The report pictures Olmsted County, where Rochester is located, to be "an economic jewel rising from the prairie lands of southeastern Minnesota."

Olmsted ranks No. 1 in the nation for its concentration of high-tech production, and third in the nation for the number of patents filed in the U.S. per capita during the 1990s, according to the report and to other studies cited in the report.

With a population of 89,000, Rochester constantly deals with globalization issues that normally only America's largest cities have to face, Recker said.

"Most cities the size of Rochester are still trying to build a knowledge-based economy to compete in a global world," he said. "They are still trying to retain their college graduates.

43

Rochester has already done that. It has a strong knowledge-based economy and is now dealing with the ramifications of that, such as a big immigrant influx and the fact that an international war can directly affect its local economy."

As a result, Rochester will now be judged on how well it rises to the challenge its truly global economy has brought to the community, Recker said.

"Rochester can never ignore what's going on in the outside world, because its economy is so tied to the outside world," he said. "It's a great position to be in, but at the same time, if for example there is a global downturn in the economy, Rochester is going to feel that ahead of some other places."

IBM, which employed 4,600 workers in Rochester at the end of 2002, made more sales that year outside than inside the U.S.—$41.4 billion and $36.4 billion, respectively. Any slowdown in foreign high-tech sales therefore directly contributes to local layoffs—as 200 workers at IBM and 550 workers at Rochester's high-tech Celestica plant, which was shuttered two months ago, know all too well.

Last month, the real estate company that is marketing the Celestica building said it would look for new buyers or renters around the world because "there aren't that many companies in Minnesota" who can afford it. The real estate company has 252 offices in 52 countries globally.

The Mayo Clinic is likewise sensitive to a myriad of international trends. One concern is international patient flow. During the 1990s, hundreds of Saudi and other Middle Eastern patients flooded the town, sometimes staying for months at a time with their families in local hotels. King Hussein of Jordan stayed in Rochester for more than a year with his wife and royal retinue while he was being treated for cancer.

Both Mayo Clinic and IBM officials say their greatest concern is the post-9/11 tightening of visa restrictions for doctors, researchers, and computer workers from overseas who want to train or establish careers in the U.S.

Hiring the best and the brightest workers, no matter where they live in the world, is a competitive necessity and among the top priorities at both the Mayo Clinic and IBM.

"We source talent wherever we can find it in the world," said Tim Dallman, IBM's local spokesperson.

Yet recruiting foreigners to live and work in Rochester is a matter of great public sensitivity, especially when times are hard in the U.S. So both Mayo and IBM have to balance the need to attract foreign talent, with hiring local workers and being seen as strong corporate citizens of Rochester and Olmsted County.

Even the DM&E railroad proposal, in which a private company is trying to run a coal train through downtown Rochester, is at its core a classic new economy/old economy confrontation.

"An industrial sector railroad doesn't fit with Rochester's knowledge-based economy," Recker said.

The most important globalization issue of all facing Rochester, Recker said, is whether it is perceived as welcoming of foreigners—both the highly-educated doctors and computer workers, and those who come to work in support jobs in the community.

One of the greatest dangers to the city's growth is that one of the racist incidents that occasionally crop up here—such as the recent appearance of racist anti-immigrant fliers in a local park—could attract national attention.

Just as a single national magazine article—the 1993 Money magazine listing of Rochester as the nation's most livable city —drew hundreds of people to come live here, a highly-publicized racist incident could scare away thousands of future tourists, patients, doctors, programmers, cooks, bellhops, and waitresses.

"To be welcoming to outsiders makes good economic sense," Recker said.

Addressing Rochester citizens in a recent newspaper article, he added: "Why not make a strategic plan to develop your cultural assets? Showcase the many cultures you have in Olmsted Country—the cuisines, languages, art, music, dance. That's the beauty of globalization, to get a sense of what's out there in the world, beyond Minnesota." ●

Who Runs Minnesota Ag?

I did a major double-take when I heard Governor Pawlenty, in a press conference last week at the Gar-Lin farm in Eyota, criticize the dangerous levels of political power that Minnesota townships have amassed and are using to throw the future of Minnesota agriculture into mortal peril.

Decision-making has gone seriously amok at the state's 1,802 rural townships, in which roughly a quarter of Minnesota's population resides, the governor suggested. In his 15-minute remarks, Pawlenty stressed how local governments in Minnesota—counties too!—are failing to exercise their civic responsibility to the state when they forbid new agribusinesses and factory farms from opening in rural jurisdictions.

The press conference was called to announce the findings of a task force the governor appointed last year, to determine how Minnesota's livestock industries can become more globally competitive. It was a fine summer day, a little chilly, with the governor flanked by a dozen gorgeous fat dairy cows obliviously chewing their breakfast of enriched corn fodder.

"Be productive," the governor joked as he passed the cows.

The task force's main finding, the governor told the crowd, is that Minnesota agriculture is healthy except for four major obstacles that endanger its ability to exploit the rapidly changing demands of the global agricultural marketplace. Three of those obstacles are 1) a confusing environmental permit and review process; 2) limited access to capital; and 3) insufficient funds spent on new products, systems, and technologies.

But the biggest obstacle is local Minnesota government.

"Barriers are making it difficult for livestock producers to grow, change, and modernize," Mr. Pawlenty said. "These barriers are being put up at the township and local level, sometimes it seems based on politics rather than good science or good facts."

Tensions between rural and state government, especially between independent farmers and bureaucrats in St. Paul, are as old as the state itself. But those stresses are starting to rise again, possibly on their way to new levels, as a result of the genuinely new trend sometimes called globalization, or more accurately, global economic integration.

It is absolutely true, as the governor said at the Gar-Lin farm, that the demands of a global agricultural marketplace are putting new pressures on local farmers and on the state itself to respond flexibly, or face failure.

Yet it's really important to be clear about the exact nature of the phenomenon—that is the whole system that puts food on our tables. And especially important to be clear about whom it is that runs that system, who benefits and who loses, and what parties if any are being played the fool.

For that, a much better report than the livestock task force report to consult is one by Dr. William Heffernan, a rural sociologist at the University of Missouri, called (pardon the ungainly title) "Multi-National Concentrated Food Processing and Marketing Systems and the Farm Crisis."

Basically, Heffernan's work demonstrates the exact opposite of the trend that the Pawlenty task force describes. He shows that over the past 20 years, power has flowed away from local farmers and local governments and into the hands of an increasingly small group of giant agricultural companies.

Only two companies, Cargill and Archer Daniels Midland, today control about 75 percent of the grain and corn that's traded in the world, Heffernan says. The three largest beef processors sell about three-fourths of the beef in the U.S.; the four largest pork processors handle 60 percent of country's pork; and four companies process half the nation's broiler chickens. And so on through virtually every agricultural sector.

In such a situation, the very definition of farming must change. Today's farm crisis is as much about identity as economics. Nearly all farmers are torn between their commitment to the agrarian life, which entails a proud tradition and history, and deep personal ambivalence about working on a contract basis to a single buyer, and to following strict rules for farming "production" set by entities beyond their control.

The real power hasn't flowed from state to local government or the reverse, but rather from local farms and governments to mega-corporations. In particular, to the handful of global agribusinesses that control the lion's share of all markets.

By rights, then, a representative for global agribusiness should have stepped forward at the Gar-Lin press conference to explain its activities and influence on the Minnesota economy and rural life across the state.

Come to think of it, considering the philosophy behind the governor's task force report as well as its recommendations, perhaps one did. ●

Husbanding Hogs and Democracy

Paul Sobocinski, showing me the straw manure-catching system he uses at his hog farm in Wabasso, MN, reminds me of farmers I've met in Japan.

I was living in Tokyo and researching environmental problems around Japan. Every week I'd interview Japanese farmers, environmentalists, and ordinary citizens about a different issue such as the fertilizer pollution of a scenic Japanese lake, or acid rain in Tokyo caused by coal-fired power plants, or coral reef loss caused by construction waste runoffs.

When I asked Japanese farmers and citizens what they believed was the best solution to each local problem, they seldom gave a technical, scientific, or environmental answer.

Instead they nearly always answered: "We need more democracy." Time after time they traced the root of their local problems to the Japanese political system that centralized power in government ministries that doled out patronage to powerful corporate and political interests.

Which is exactly what Paul Sobocinski says. An outspoken activist and organizer for the Land Stewardship Project, a Minnesota-based group that promotes sustainable agriculture, Sobocinski spends almost as much time husbanding state legislation to promote democracy in Minnesota's rural communities, as he does tending his 240-acre farm.

"A few packers now control the whole pork industry," he said, sounding his main theme. "That's bad for producers and for communities, because they find themselves bargaining with a major entity that holds all the cards."

The recent Minnesota legislative session produced a bumper crop of issues that kept Sobocinski and his LSP colleagues busy writing e-mails and staging rallies. A major victory was defeating six pieces of "big ag" legislation that would have restricted local townships' ability to block agribusiness companies from building farms and processing plants locally.

That victory capped a hard-fought battle in which state agriculture officials had blamed local governments around the state for recent declines in Minnesota's livestock industry. Harold Stanislawski, a livestock business advisor for the Minnesota Department of Agriculture, told a meeting of farmers last November that local residents shouldn't have the final say on whether new livestock facilities go into their communities, because agriculture is now a global industry.

At the meeting, Stanislawski also praised a Ripley Town Board member from Dodge County for saying, "We can't just look at what the residents want. We have to look at the big picture. If this upsets you, I'm sorry."

Not that Sobocinski and others at the Land Stewardship Project disagree that agriculture is a global industry. They agree wholeheartedly. Their objection is that the consolidation of nearly every U.S. agricultural sector into a small handful of mega-companies is driving a ferocious bottom-line approach that harms the environment and the social cohesion of local communities.

And the health of the world community, too. Factory farming methods that depress costs, and government subsidies that artificially drive costs down further, means that many U.S. agricultural products are now sold so cheaply in foreign markets that they undercut goods produced locally, even by farmers in the developing world like China, Mexico, and South America.

"We're in a race to the bottom around the world, playing one country's people off against another's, just for the benefit of a few large corporations," Sobocinski says.

At his farm, Sobocinski has resisted the temptation to sign

51

multi-year contracts to produce pork for the biggest pork packaging companies, Smithfield Foods Inc. and IBP, Inc. Instead he uses environmentally sound methods to raise his hogs, using no antibiotics in the feed, and collecting manure in straw beds that are later used for fertilizer, instead of in giant manure lagoons that seep toxins and smell something dreadful.

His buyer, Niman Ranch of California, pays a premium for the pork and passes the premium along to consumers at restaurants and grocery stores who seek healthy and environmentally-friendly and pork products.

Thomas Jefferson saw a mystical bond between farmers and democracy. "Cultivators of the earth are the most valuable citizens," Jefferson wrote. "They are tied to their country and wedded to its liberty and interest by the most lasting bonds." I ran the idea past Sobocinski, who agreed to a point.

"The difference between now and Jefferson's time," he said, "was that our government was fresh and new then. They had thrown out the huge money people from England who had stifled them. They didn't have the PAC money and the big farms from St. Paul and Washington that we have today.

"They did have them in England. That's why they left." ●

Who Are We Today?

Growing up in Rochester in the late 1950s and 1960s, two architectural landmarks symbolized the city's dual identity: the Plummer Building and the Libby's (now Seneca) corncob water tower.

The Gothic-style Plummer Building, covered with stone carvings representing human progress in science and the arts, and chiming the hours of our days from its carillon, was Rochester's secular cathedral. It assured us that the light of human reason will safely illuminate our path to the future.

The corncob-shaped water tower at the Libby's food processing plant was no less powerful a symbol of our community's roots in agriculture and the land. Even today it unmistakably reminds us that our community's life began on the farm with its dawn-to-dusk rhythms, its animal sounds, and its earthy smells.

Today we may need a new symbol for a town that's grown into a new phase of life, one that's profoundly multicultural.

It's often said that at the turn of the century, Rochester, like the entire United States, was more multicultural than it is today. In 1910, more than half of Olmsted County's population of 22,500 were either born, or their parents were born, outside of the United States. Today, only about one in ten people living in Rochester was born outside of the U.S.

Similarly, there are fewer immigrants today on a percentage basis in the United States, than there were a century ago. In 1900, about 14 percent of the U.S. population was foreign-born, compared to about 11 percent today.

Yet in three important ways, multiculturalism is far more pronounced today than ever before. First, mass immigration that began in the 1960's opened the door to some 30 million immigrants now living in the U.S., a far larger number than at any time in American history.

Second, America's first wave of immigrants came mostly from Europe and thus, despite language differences, they were a relatively homogenous group in terms of religion and shared history. Our recent immigrants by contrast represent many dozens of cultures and languages from all over the globe.

Third, the enormous numbers of recent immigrants has allowed numerous cultural subgroups to form within American society. These strong identity groupings allow, to a much greater extent than previously, the retention of native languages, cultures, and customs.

All three of these themes play out in Rochester every day.

The Indian Rice & Spice grocery, at the corner of 4th Street and Broadway, is like a Bombay market with the women wearing saris and henna tattoos, engaging in long friendly chats, with the smell of sandalwood incense and the sounds of the Hindi and Gujarati languages filling the air.

Just across the street, at Tejano Western Wear, another conclave of recent immigrants to Rochester meets to socialize—but the smell is leather from the boots and vests on sale in the shop, and the language spoken is Spanish.

A new immigration trend in Rochester is probably the most important of all. Our city is filled with a new breed of immigrant that sociologists called "transnationals."

These immigrants move not for the old reasons of political persecution or to escape abject poverty, or war, but simply because they found a better job here than they did in their country. For them, a wage comparison trumps all.

Last Spring I led a weekly English conversation class with a half-dozen Chinese immigrants from mainland China, who work at the Mayo Clinic as laboratory researchers and doctors.

Had they stayed in China, all of them would have had good jobs and enjoyed high standing in Chinese society. They had chosen Rochester over a Chinese city as other Mayo employees chose Rochester over, say, Atlanta or San Francisco or Detroit.

Cities with many transnationals in their workforce are "fragile ones, whose survival and successes are centered on an economy of high productivity and advanced technologies," warns immigration scholar Saskia Sassen.

In other words, the minute another city offers a better job, there go our employees. Er, I mean our citizens. There's nothing else to keep them here but salaries.

A community's sense of identity, despite obvious pitfalls if taken to extremes, is also a great potential source of strength and cohesion. When things get tough it may be all a community has to rely on to hold together.

Once upon a time, Rochester had a corncob water tower and a Gothic carillon tower to tell us who we are.

Who are we today? ●

The World in an Ear of Corn

It's summer. Before too long, locally grown green-and-gold sweet corn straight off the stalks will be selling from the backs of pickup trucks around town.

I can't wait. I love sweet corn and I'll be one of the first customers. But when I take that first bite, I'll remember that by doing so I'm taking part in a global agricultural market to which Minnesota is a major contributor—and not always a fair and square contributor, either.

Put simply, the Minnesota corn market, like most of the largest crop markets in the United States, is rigged so that the largest growers and sellers benefit while farmers in the developing world are being driven from business.

"There is a direct link between government agricultural policies in the U.S. and rural misery in Mexico," says a 2003 report from Oxfam International entitled: "Dumping Without Borders: How U.S. Agricultural Polices are Destroying the Livelihoods of Mexican Corn Farmers."

The U.S. government currently spends $15 billion a year in subsidies paid directly to farmers, theoretically to protect them against fluctuating market prices. In fact, they allow giant agricultural firms here in the world's richest country to sell crops globally at prices that actually undercut those of farmers in developing nations like Mexico, China, and the Philippines.

This practice has directly contributed to the crisis presently afflicting corn farmers in Mexico, where corn prices have fallen more than 70 percent since 1994. More than 15 million

Mexican corn farmers have been affected, often plunging them and their families into destitution.

Minnesota was the fourth-largest state recipient of corn subsidies between 1995 and 2002, taking in $3.31 billion during the period. Including all crops, Minnesota ranked fifth-highest with $6.7 billion in subsidy payments. However, the top 20% of farms here received 78% of the subsidies, with individual payouts in that bracket averaging $219,000, according the Environmental Working Group, in Washington, D.C.

The news last week that five Minnesota farmers were charged by a federal grand jury with defrauding the U.S. government of more than $5.3 million in agricultural subsidies, is another example of how the federal subsidy program has grown out of control. Similar frauds are occurring in many states, the U.S. General Accounting Office has found.

One word runs like a thread through all of these stories of giant agricultural companies undercutting Third World farmers and fraudulently reaping illegal windfalls.

The word is greed.

Pure capitalists believe that greed is a fine motive that delivers the greatest good to the greatest number.

The problem is, food is not any old consumer product. It's a pillar of life and national security. It's both dependent upon, and contributes to, a healthy natural environment, and it's deeply entwined with every nation's sense of pride and identity. All these matters reach far beyond price.

"Everything today is geared to producing at the cheapest possible level," said Ben Lilliston, a spokesman for the Institute for Agriculture and Trade Policy, based in Minneapolis. "That's in Minnesota or Brazil or wherever." Agricultural producers "aren't placing values on livelihoods, or on whether we think it's a good idea to have many farmers in the community as opposed to one or two giant farms" serving many communities, Lewiston said.

An agricultural system where prices reflect solid values on

human health, community, and the environment is where we as a society should try to head.

"Just thinking about the food at your local grocery store is a good place to start," Lilliston added. For example, paying a little more for locally-grown fruits and vegetables helps the local economy and also potentially helps crop farmers in Mexico, the Philippines, China, and other third world countries.

That's because each small local transaction says to the global agricultural giants: "Neither of us, consumer nor farmer, will play your game." Today, many farmers feel pressured to over-produce commodity crops, because that's the way to qualify for subsidies and to sell to the giant agricultural firms. That's what allows those same agri-giants to sell so cheaply to developing nations, putting farmers there out of work.

When we buy our sweet corn out of the back of pickup trucks this summer, let's ask if was grown subsidy-free. If it was, we'll have done just a little bit for our farmer neighbors south of the border.

And the corn will taste all the sweeter. ●

A Global Killer Comes to Minnesota

Handguns are a deadly global virus.

Around the world, about a half billion handguns and small arms cause about 10,000 deaths a week, or 500,000 deaths a year.

The World Health Organization classifies the spread of small arms and the subsequent violence it causes as a global health threat on the level of AIDS and infectious diseases like hepatitis, yellow fever and plague.

The passage of a new Minnesota handgun law makes the state more vulnerable than ever to this global contagion. The state estimates that the number of Minnesotans carrying handguns in public will rise in the next three years from 11,000 to 90,000.

We've never looked at the handgun issue in a global context, as the World Health Organization does. We should.

In at least two important ways, gun violence burdens the state's health care system just as severely as global bug-caused illnesses do. For one thing, the psychological trauma caused by gun violence stresses health care givers, social services, and society at large.

And for another, a person sickened by a speeding bullet racks up health care costs just as fast as any patient—or, as in the case of head injuries or multiple wounds, much faster and over a longer time. The World Health Organization calculates that in the late 1990s, the cost of health care provided to gunshot victims in the United States totaled more than $126 billion.

Let's divide that number by 50 for a rough estimate of annual Minnesota health care expense on treating gun-related injuries: $2.5 billion.

Governor Pawlenty, have you considered imposing stricter gun control laws in Minnesota as a way to trim the state's enormous budget deficits?

The global health model as applied to gun violence suggests that extremely strong gun control measures are the best way to stop the problem.

A virus like SARS is killed by trapping and eradicating it.

As with the corona virus, why not with the Colt?

As with HIV/AIDS, why not with handguns?

Japan has already done it. Private handgun ownership in Japan is banned. Less than 1 percent of Japanese households own a gun, while up to 48 percent of American households do.

As a result, Japan has the world's lowest "intentional gun death rate" in the world (less than one tenth of one percent per hundred thousand people), while the United States has by far the highest (13.5 per hundred thousand).

I lived in Japan for four years, from 1989 to 1993, in Tokyo, and I cannot tell you how safe I felt there. It's a very definite sensation that all Americans who live in Japan—especially American women—notice immediately. In Japan you feel utterly safe on the streets, for the first time in your life. A woman can walk through the toughest neighborhood of Tokyo at 3 a.m., or stand alone at any subway station at any time, and have not the slightest worry for her safety.

I wonder if we would feel the same standing at the corner of Broadway and Second Street in Rochester, or at Hennepin and Fifth in Minneapolis, at any hour of the night?

One more lesson from abroad. From Sudan to Colombia, from Afghanistan to Germany, where the smuggled handgun trade is a growing public health threat, experts who study the global handgun virus point to a self-perpetuating cycle by which the virus divides, replicates and spreads.

"Fear leads to arming, which breeds violence, which leads to insecurity, which leads to further arming," writes Wendy Cukier, coordinator of the Small Arms/Firearms Education and Research Network.

When we passed the "conceal-carry" law in Minnesota, we caught the global bug. ●

Avoiding Food and Sex Like the Plague

Next month I am traveling to Ethiopia, so I stopped by Mayo Clinic last week to get my vaccinations. The nurse came in with a fistful of green syringes, each with a tag identifying the dreadful diseases the shots were meant to ward off—yellow fever, typhoid, meningitis, hepatitis A, and polio.

After my upper arms were swathed in Band-Aids, the nurse showed me a diagram explaining how to self-treat for diarrhea. A brochure checklist warned me not to have sex with anyone on the trip; not to drink the local water; not to drink anything containing ice cubes made from local water; and not to eat leafy vegetables. A portable water purifier; bug repellant; and a mosquito net for sleeping were all recommended purchases.

Was this Ethiopia I was going to visit, or a lower circle of Hell?

What really shook me up was when the nurse looked up for emphasis and warned me severely: "*Never eat anything from a street vendor.*"

No food from street vendors?! After ten years of traveling as a journalist, one of my sweetest memories—often literally sweet—is of the fantastic smells, sights, and flavors imbibed at outdoor food stalls. The savor of our miraculous world is available precisely on the street where most people in this world live, under the blue sky and amid the hubbub of the bazaar.

In Laos, a penny at a food stall buys you a leafy bouquet of fresh "mak heol," which you carry through the afternoon picking out the pea-sized nuts to eat as snacks. In Thailand the glistening white "rambutan," moist pearls of fruit encased in a soft spiky skin, is a delicious snack of choice.

If you skip the street food "hawkers" of Singapore and Malaysia, you'll miss one of the greatest eating experiences on this earth. Fancy hotel restaurants in both countries compete to hire the best hawker cooks.

Of course, I want to stay healthy. Of course, I am grateful for vaccinations that can protect my life, and I'll take the shots every time. But something in me rebels against the image of the world that's implied as we erect around ourselves a wall of fears, vaccinations, sprays, and nettings.

Tourism is the world's biggest industry, affecting 240 million jobs and with a half trillion dollars in sales in 2000, according to the World Tourism Organization. Yet the American tourism industry, the trend-setter globally, sells travel as a form of entertainment. It strives to make international trips more like visits to Disneyland than to anyplace real.

Taking all possible steps to prevent meningitis and other killer diseases is one thing. But succumbing to the view that the world beyond America is rife with danger and disease, which then steels you to visit those places protected by an armament of vaccines and Disneyesque illusions, is another.

Being human, which means being open and vulnerable within limits, is essential to good travel. This means that as you travel you are susceptible to some embarrassment and even heartbreak. Because make no mistake, the real world will show you to yourself—and that can be embarrassing.

One day while walking to the Tokyo subway, I saw a Japanese housewife making silly noises while playing with a kitten in her yard. "Wow!" I thought to myself. "Japanese people love kittens just like Americans do!"

I was so ashamed when I realized what I'd thought. How little I knew, how unconsciously ignorant and callous I was. How much I had much to learn.

The real world will break your heart too. I held a beautiful baby girl once in Jakarta who was red-cheeked and smiling with spontaneous joy, as little girls and boys do. But she lived in a diphtheria-ridden slum on a vast and stinking garbage heap, and I knew she would likely never grow old.

I still feel the anger of that moment and I cherish it, because it motivates me to remember that little girl and to try to do good journalism in her memory.

So bring on the shots for typhoid, yellow fever, and all the rest. But let's not try to vaccinate ourselves against the complex pains of being human, an illuminating gift of honest travel. ●

Schmoozing for National Security

I asked a Mexican friend who is an expatriate executive living in Minneapolis, how Mexicans view the United States.

"We have two very distinct views of Americans," he said. "On the one hand we think Americans are a very kind, warm, and generous people, who maybe also are a little bit naive," he said.

"In Cuernavaca, where I'm from, we get this image from the many Americans who come to study Spanish. On the other hand, we also see America as a very aggressive, unfair, and even warlike country. This comes from American companies and the U.S. government. Your companies use many unfair commercial practices for their advantage, and we often see the U.S. government interfere in trade practices and militarily in Central and South America."

In sum, Mexicans base their opinions about America on three main sources: individual Americans, U.S. corporations, and the U.S. government. Of these three, only individual Americans provide foreigners with a positive image of our country.

This has been my experience as well. In Japan, England, Hong Kong, and China, where I have lived and worked, my personal relationships have always contained elements of warmth, devotion, appreciation, and trust that have been lacking in my attitude toward the other person's government or their national corporations.

My Japanese friends would say the same thing about how they viewed individual Americans, as opposed to the U.S. government or U.S. multinationals.

Let's leave aside the philosophical question of how groups of good people can behave wickedly. Practically speaking, doesn't it make sense to think about increasing the amount of face-to-face contact between America and foreign countries as a part of our overall national security policy?

As a part of our war on terrorism? A certain level of trust, or at least mutual respect, must precede even the simplest political negotiations. On the face of it, our government and companies aren't engendering that respect, while individual people are.

If individual Americans don't step up to do this important work for peace right now, who will? ●

The Global Citizen's Vote

John Kerry said at an election rally in Rochester today that the first priority of his Presidency would be to heal damaged relations between our country and other countries around the world.

"Our troops are safer, and taxpayers pay less money, when there is a president who understands the importance of having real alliances" with other nations around the world, Kerry said in his speech at the Mayo Civic Center before a standing-room-only crowd of about 4,000 people.

This was the first point that Kerry made in his speech—it came before his points on the U.S. economy, health care policy, homeland security, and the war on Iraq. And it drew deafening applause, cheers, and whistles.

When was the last time we heard a presidential candidate use an appeal to global citizenship as an applause line, much less make it the cornerstone of his candidacy, as Kerry did today?

The folks at the Gallup and the Pew Research Center polling organizations wouldn't be surprised. Their recent polls have showed that most Americans now believe, for the first time since the Vietnam War, that foreign policy and national security issues are even more important than the economy.

A recent Pew survey found 41 percent of Americans believed that "war/foreign policy/terrorism" is the most important problem facing the nation, with 26 percent choosing the economy. The last time a survey found foreign policy issues topped the economy among Americans was in the election of 1972; from

1976 to 2000 the reverse was been true, with economy first.

Even more noteworthy, the poll shows that a majority of Americans have in the last four years shifted from being basically isolationists (seeing a lone-wolf America in the world as good thing), to being internationalists (believing America should belong to a global partnership of nations).

Three fourths of Americans, the Pew poll showed, say the U.S. should share leadership in the world, as opposed to 11 percent who say that the U.S. should be the single world leader. And 66 percent say that the U.S. is less respected in the world than it was in the past, and this is a serious national security issue.

Now that we know that the American populace is internationalist in outlook, there's no time to waste. We need to press the presidential candidates to flesh out the details of their international visions. For example:

1. *The biggest threat facing America today, Bush and Kerry agreed in their first debate, is that a terrorist group will get a nuclear weapon and set it off in an American city. Yet six days from the election there has yet to appear any serious follow-up on this deadly-serious point of agreement between the candidates. Citizens—let's not call ourselves media consumers—should demand it from the candidates.*

2. *The candidates should explain in detail their plans for getting the U.S. more involved in international organizations, treaties, and projects such as the global fight against AIDS, the International Criminal Court, and the Kyoto Protocol on global warming. The war on terror is not the only global war, not even the most important one.*

3. *The candidates need to explain their policies towards*
   South America, our neighbor to the south; towards
   China and India, the world's two most populous
   countries which are changing our economy
   profoundly; and Africa, which this year is sending
   record levels of refugee immigrants to the U.S. And
   what do they have to say about the humanitarian ca-
   tastrophe in Haiti right now, where some 300,000
   people are homeless and starving following Hurri-
   cane Jeanne?

If we allow the war on terror and the war in Iraq to to define our worldview and priorities, we will continue to see the
world in terms of "us vs. them." Indeed, we will see the whole
world in terms of war.

Yet most of us today say we need to see the world more
as "us." Not as a frill or luxury, we believe, but as a matter of
national security. Kerry's remarks at the Mayo Civic Center
suggest he sees the world in terms of global citizenship, instead of in the exclusive frame of war.

Security is *us.* Which candidate believes that more, and
will enact it more through personal leadership and policies?
That's the question that we need to be asking candidates frequently and forcefully, on Election Tuesday and every day. ●

Presidential Innocence Abroad

Among the handful of human skills that voters look for in presidential candidates—how good a spouse they are, how good a parent, how good a patriot—should be added how good a global citizen.

Foreign policy experience is the yardstick normally used to measure a candidate's skill at handling potential challenges from abroad. But in reality this measurement is limiting. Whether a candidate has ever lived abroad and shown skill at living in a foreign culture is the best test of global skills.

Living abroad is a tough life-challenge right up there with leaving home for college, getting married, or becoming a parent. Whether a candidate has sought this severe challenge; how they've coped with it; and how their worldview matured as a result are all important ways to judge the character of a presidential candidate.

In the present field of Democratic presidential candidates, only three—Wesley Clark, John Kerry, and Howard Dean—have lived abroad for significant periods of time. And among these, General Clark is by far the frontrunner in terms of years spent living overseas and of having demonstrably mastered critical international skills.

Wesley Clark attended Oxford College as a Rhodes Scholar and then spent the majority of his 34-year military career abroad, first in Vietnam, then in Europe in a succession of posts culminating as Supreme Commander of NATO in 1997.

The experience transformed Clark into a patriotic cosmopolitan—firmly and deeply American, yet comfortable with many kinds of people and cultures. His successes as a leader in NATO, during which time he often bucked his superiors in America in the service of global humanitarian aims, is the main proof.

The time comes for every American who lives overseas that the worldview of the "foreigners" you live with clash with those of your bosses and friends back home. In other words, you begin to feel more like "them" than like "us." You are plunged into an internal crisis as your loyalties and even your sense of self is tested.

Clark performed brilliantly at this juncture. While keeping American casualties low and international standing high, he led a coalition military campaign that halted two attempted genocides—one in Bosnia, and one in Kosovo.

John Kerry, a Vietnam War hero, went to boarding school in Switzerland and owns a home in Brittany, France. He also lived for a time in Oslo, Norway, where his father was in the Foreign Service. But with the exception of Vietnam, his overseas experience was in privileged expatriate quarters, and his record as a U.S. Senator is not distinguished by international accomplishments.

Joe Lieberman has never lived abroad but his immigrant parents and Orthodox Judaism has given him a strong internationalist outlook. His religious training stressed the tradition of serving God by serving other people, as well as the practice of "tikkun olam," or literally taking upon oneself the task of "healing the world" as a religious duty.

John Edwards has not lived overseas for significant periods nor mentioned in any of his official biographies any international experience that's been deeply meaningful to him.

Howard Dean didn't collect the global skills that Clark did during his years abroad, but he has what I consider a minimum requirement for any aspiring U.S. president: he lived abroad and came back a better man.

Between high school and college, Dean spent a year attending school in England. There he was exposed for the first time in his life to smart, articulate, passionately political people who disapproved of the United States. A shocker!

Equally important, Dean hitchhiked around Europe, visited northern Africa, and twice crossed the Iron Curtain on trips to Turkey.

Dean's family says that he left the U.S. as a longhaired, bright, aimless student, and that he came back as a goal-driven, patriotic, community-minded family man.

A good long look at the real world will do that to a person. It turns every liberal into a conservative, in the sense of realizing what a miraculous thing we've got going here in the United State—and wanting to conserve it.

As a whole nation, we should take that trip. ⬤

The Saudi Royals, By George

If George W. Bush truly leveled with southeast Minnesotans about his feelings about the war in Iraq—in the same way that he levels with Dick Cheney, Donald Rumsfeld, Paul Wolfowitz, Condoleeza Rice, and others in his inner circle—he would say something like this:

"My fellow Americans, thank God we won in Iraq, because at long last we can begin to extricate ourselves from our lose-lose, co-dependent, morally degrading, and mutually destructive relationship with Saudi Arabia.

"How I hate those photo-op sessions with the Saudi royals. I have to clench my teeth and smile every time, because I know what they're really doing. They're using their billions in oil profits to protect and prolong their corrupt regime. They spend hundreds of millions each year to keep every member of the extended royal Saud family docile in their palaces and their yachts, instead of scheming to take down King Fahd and Crown Prince Abdullah.

"Worse than that, the Saud family funnels millions of dollars every year to support hard-line Islamic fundamentalists, especially the Wahhabis. This is nothing but a desperate attempt to bribe and divert the extremists' attention away from Saudi Arabia—where the Wahhabi sect was founded—and toward other countries like Afghanistan, Egypt, Kenya, Bali, Yemen, Morocco, and, of course, the United States. King Fahd's and Crown Prince Abdullah's greatest fear is that they will meet the same fate as Anwar Sadat, the Egyptian prime minister assassinated by Muslim fundamentalists in 1981.

"To avoid that fate, the Sauds bankroll the Wahabbis, in the same way tobacco companies finance stop-smoking organizations. They want to blunt what would surely be a fatal attack. The Wahhabis, led by Osama bin Laden, hate the corrupt and materialistic Saud family even more than they hate Americans! But as long as they are getting millions in Saudi oil money to fund their terrorist training camps and global operations, the Wahhabis will probably wait a while before attacking King Fahd or Crown Prince Abdullah directly.

"But not forever, as the bombings in Riyadh last week show. Today, the target was Americans living in Riyadh. Tomorrow, it will be the Sauds.

"The fact that our family, a Texas oil family, has extensive business and personal ties with Saudi oil men and ministers —just as many other major Texas oil families do—hasn't made my plight any easier. Look, drilling for oil is an expensive proposition, and who's got the money and the expertise to invest in those deals? Could I really have done a background check on every single investment dollar I took in 1979 from a businessman representing Salem bin Laden, one of Osama bin Laden's brothers?

"In 1987, my company got into some financial difficulty and I had to sell a chunk of it to a Saudi investor. How was I supposed to know that those shares would end up in the hands of Khalid bin Mahfouz, who was a principal in BCCI, the bank that defrauded customers of $12 billion in the 1980s and was linked to money-laundering and terrorist funding?

"I was hoping that, once I became president, I could send Rummy to all the photo-ops and disentangle from the Saudi royals. Instead, thanks to OBL and 9/11, those old ties get dredged up again and again.

"Our country's deep reliance on Saudi oil—they are our second-biggest source of imported oil after Canada and they have a stranglehold on world oil prices thanks to their bottomless reserves—is now clearer than ever. So even today, I still need to clench my teeth and smile with the Saudi royals. Because a single spike in prices at the pump could send our economy even further into the dumps—and I'd be looking for another job in 2004.

"So thank God we won in Iraq, which has the world's second-largest proven reserves of oil after Saudi Arabia. We're going to make doggone sure that if nothing else happens in postwar Iraq, the United States will form a good working relationship with the new oil industry that arises there.

"Because once we do, we'll never have to worry about the Saudis tightening the oil price noose around our necks again. Best of all, we'll finally be able to target Saudi Arabia as the major state sponsor of international terrorism that, in fact, it is. Remember, 15 of the 19 terrorist hijackers on 9/11 came from none other than Saudi Arabia. By rights they should be included in the axis of evil. As soon as I'm able to swing it politically, I'll do it.

"And once all this happens, I'll never have to do another one of those grin and bear it, clenched-teeth photo ops with the Saudi Royals ever again." ●

Let's Not Get Jay-Walked

Jay Leno, in one of his trademark TV interviews with Americans, chatted on a Los Angeles street with a cheerful young man decked out in blue jeans and a head of frizzy blond hair.

"Who was the leader of Germany in World War II?" Leno asked.

"Hitler?" the young man ventured.

"What was his first name?"

"Just Hitler, wasn't it?"

"Hitler Hitler? He didn't have a first name? Was it Robert?"

"He was just known as Hitler. Like Cher."

American ignorance of world history, geography, and politics is an all-too-accurate cliché of our times. Not only Jay Leno but the National Geographic Society confirmed it last year with a study showing that among Americans aged 18 to 24, almost 30 percent could not identify the Pacific Ocean on a map. More than half could not locate India, and 85% could not find Iraq. The young people of America ranked next to last in the nine countries surveyed.

What are the causes of this appalling ignorance and what are its possible consequences in economic, cultural, and homeland security terms here in southeastern Minnesota?

Randy Nelson, the Rochester public school official in charge of curriculum, says that 9/11, the war on terrorism, the homeland security initiative and the war in Iraq have all made school officials more acutely aware of the need to better educate Rochester's young people about the world.

"Sometimes I'll say 'globalization' or 'competitive economy' to parents, and they say they think that's bogus," Nelson said. "They think we shouldn't teach that stuff. That must change. We need to be able to explain to kids and to parents that we are going to study this or that foreign culture, not only because it's in the textbook but because it has a very specific impact on us locally. Sometimes that component is missing."

Lack of such knowledge will translate into greater security risks, cultural wasting, and lost economic opportunities in our community, Nelson said.

For example, Irish entrepreneurism has already resulted in that country taking up to 60 percent of the business in the processing of U.S. health insurance claims, Nelson said. Grabbing that competitive niche could have be a no-brainer in a medical town like Rochester.

Despite the heightened sense of urgency brought by 9/11 and more recent global developments, however, the local public school curriculum hasn't yet changed. There is still no graduation requirement to take either geography or foreign language classes at the Rochester public schools.

There are many other roots of America's ignorance of the world, of course, than the failings of our public schools.

Our history as a nation of immigrants, surprisingly, is one. Historically, many immigrants to the U.S. consciously tried to erase their memories of their home countries, their native languages, and their troubled pasts. That has tended to increase our national amnesia about America's international history and connections.

Yet by sharing their deep knowledge of foreign lands and trends, immigrants have often played a powerful role in the opposite direction, too.

As a community where one in ten local residents was not born in the United States, Rochester is an ideal place to ask which of these trends dominates here. Are new immigrants in this community trying to forget their pasts? Or are they taking on the responsibility of teaching us what they know?

That is, are they sharing with us their treasure? Have we even asked them to?

Do we consider the vast foreign knowledge of our immigrant neighbors as a valuable public resource to be widely shared? If not, why not?

"It's a question that is under-considered," said Ron Buzard, director of the Intercultural Mutual Assistance Association, which offers legal and other services to immigrants in southeast Minnesota. "Too many times we look at immigrants only in terms of what help they need from us. In fact, they have much they can teach us such as foreign languages, human survival skills, and important human values we may lack here in the U.S."

The national news media, which over the past decade has cut back on international news, is often criticized for failing to meet its public obligations to educate an able democratic citizenry. It's fair to ask whether our local TV anchors, radio announcers, and print journalists are meeting the same set of challenges at the community level. Are they making a point to seek, to reveal, and to analyze the local effects of global causes? The local opportunities of global trends? The local dangers of global threats?

The man and woman on the street play a big role here too. Sure, we need our local public schools and our local media to do a better job educating us. But don't we as individuals also have a responsibility to educate ourselves?

Lest one day we embarrass ourselves before an international audience, if nothing else. With the Mayo Clinic and IBM here, we are truly a global town. It might pay to get smart about American history and world geography before Jay Leno flies into Rochester and starts asking questions. ●

The Round Goby and World Peace

Up at Wolf's Marina in Stillwater, the talk on the dock was all about the season's first citing on Lake Pepin of Bighead and Silver Carp—the strange fish that jump like giant fleas out of the wake of outboard motors, sometimes hitting folks on board smack on the head.

But the Asian carp is only one division in an army of invaders that has already infiltrated Minnesota, the boaters agreed. There was also the Round Goby, a bottom-dwelling, pollution-loving, fish-egg-eating menace from Eastern Europe; the Zebra Mussel from the Caspian Sea in northern Iran; and the Purple Loosestrife, a tall plant from Europe that is exceptionally pretty but has a rotten personality, as its name describes.

The summer invasion of exotic species has begun. And with it a reminder more poignant than ever that in our biological and environmental, as well as our political habitat, the porous borders of freedom come at a heavy price.

The ballast tanks of Great Lakes tankers, Mississippi cargo boats, and other commercial craft were years ago identified as the source of many foreign plant and animal species entering Minnesota's water systems.

Thanks to economic globalization, even faster pathways are now introducing new species into the state's natural habitats —especially the multi-billion-dollar global horticulture industry, much of which is conducted over the Internet.

"The Internet provides quick access to potentially invasive species," says Doug Jensen, coordinator of the University of Minnesota's Sea Grant program for improving the state's coastal waters. "An order to Singapore could arrive within days in a brown paper bag, unprotected and undetected by federal agents. These species may be highly problematic."

Liberal trade and immigration policies hasten the introduction of invasive species into the United States. Altogether, they have speeded up the rate of non-native species introduction into the U.S. by 3,000 times the natural rate, Jensen estimates.

Since 1970, he said, 1.4 new species per year have been introduced into the Great Lakes, a vastly higher than natural rate.

A Minnesota naturalist can sound like an anti-terror specialist at the Department of Homeland Security, in these strange days. Sometimes it's not just a similarity in language but a complete merging of actual policy goals.

"What species in other countries could decimate our agriculture, it's something we think about but don't talk about that much" for obvious security reasons, said Jay Rendall, coordinator of Exotic Species for the Department of Natural Resources.

Water gardening, one of the fastest-growing garden trends in the U.S., is now one of the state's top priorities in monitoring non-native species imports, according to Barbara Liukkonen, a water resource specialist for Sea Grant. Of the 140 non-native plant and animal species in the Great Lakes region, Liukkonen says, 42 percent were introduced in the past four years via the horticulture trade. Many of the imports were to supply water gardens.

Nine out of ten shipments of aquatic plants imported by nurseries come with "hitchhikers," small animals like Koi carp or Chinese Mystery Snails, which may themselves potentially introduce dangerous elements into the Minnesota ecosystem,

If we figure out a good solution to the problem of non-native plants and animals coming into this country, we'll learn something about how to handle the problem of nation's porous borders in other areas, too.

For example, naturalists always emphasize the need for

extremely careful discrimination among classes of non-native species—especially between the ones that are invasive and the ones that are not. There are a hundred times fewer invasive species than perfectly safe species. Among the latter, some may add to our quality of life and in no way harm it.

All the naturalists I spoke with gave a clue to their highly practical and sensitive perspective on life in their vocabulary, by always saying "non-native" and not "foreign" or "alien" to describe invasive species.

They did that not out of political correctness, I believe, but because they had totally internalized a global perspective. The plants and animals from Asia and Iran and Eastern Europe were simply not foreign or alien to them—they were of the planet earth, the one earth we all share. ●

The Siberian Tigers of Minnesota

More wild tigers now live as pets and in roadside zoos, breeding kennels, and privately-run wildlife attractions in the U.S. than live in the wilds of Asia, according to certified zookeepers and wildlife conservationists.

Estimates of the number of wild tigers kept as pets and in rural exhibition parks in the U.S. range as high as 10,000, while tigers remaining in the wild habitats of eastern Russia, China, India, Indonesia, and southeast Asia number less than 5,000, conservationists say.

A side-trend of globalization with an impact now clearly visible in Minnesota, the rise in privately-owned tigers, lions, and other breeds of wild cat is driving a dramatic rise in tiger-related accidents here and across the U.S. Increasing numbers of sanctuaries are also being built for wild cats abandoned by their owners or seized in raids of illegal breeding operations.

Small Minnesota farmers, looking to develop new sources of revenue after losing business to global agribusiness operations, sometimes turn to exhibiting exotic animals, or breeding them to sell as pets. Such business contributes to the health of rural Minnesota economies, they argue.

Conservationists say that breeding wild cats for such purposes is inhumane, environmentally unsound, and dangerous.

"It's more than a pet issue," said Tammy Quist, director of the Wildcat Sanctuary in Isanti County. "It's a public safety risk." In recent months, the sanctuary has taken in wild cats found in rural homes, amateur roadside zoos, and back-yards in Red Wing, Burnsville, Edina, and Golden Valley.

The sanctuary gets 30 calls a month from Minnesota pet owners who bought a tiger cub but can't handle a grown cat; from police who confiscate the cats; and from humane societies that pick up abused tigers and cougars. Filled to overcapacity, the Wildcat Sanctuary is raising money to build a larger facility to accommodate the growing number of wildcats in need of a home.

Two tiger maulings in Minnesota in recent weeks testify to the growing numbers of privately-owned wildcats in the U.S. In one of the incidents, a Minneapolis woman was seriously injured after being attacked by four tigers while cleaning their pen at a private property near Frontenac.

A month earlier, a teenager was swiped by a tiger at the Arcangel Wildlife farm near Underwood, and later developed a serious wound infection that required healthy skin grafts to heal.

In 2001, a tiger at a roadside animal park in Racine was euthanized after biting a Rochester girl. In 2003, another tiger at the site, called Bearcat Hollow, was killed after biting a woman on the wrist.

More than 600 tigers and other wild cats were confiscated in the U.S. last year, with roughly half that number euthanized to test for rabies or after no suitable sanctuary could be found for them, according to Ron Tilson, the director of conservation at the Minnesota Zoo. Four humans were killed and 40 were injured by tigers and other big cats that year, including 13 children. The year before, 33 such incidents were reported in the U.S.

Contrary to popular notions, virtually all privately-owned tigers in this country do not come from Asia, but are bred from parents here in the United States. Most wildcats are as easy to breed as house cats and have similar-sized litters. Cubs fetching between $500 and $2,000 apiece have lured many entrepreneurs into the business. Only later do the breeders find how difficult it is to maintain a safe and humane tiger breeding operation.

Rampant cross-breeding of species and mating parent-child pairs has degraded the gene pool of the five purebred tiger species in the world, and resulted in the U.S. wildcat population becoming a "genetic cocktail" that is entirely unfit for returning to the wild, according to Tilson.

"They are being bred for profit, for sale as pets and for their products, including their skins, bones, whiskers, and for taxidermy," Tilson said. "All of this is done on the black market, illegally or quietly."

Some wildlife groups say that U.S.-bred tigers are sold to "canned hunt" operations, mostly in Texas, where wealthy hunters pay to hunt tigers, lions, and other big game wild animals that are released on game farms.

A cross-breed between a housecat and the African serval wildcat, called a Savannah, has in recent years become a popular pet in the U.S., selling for between $4,000 and $10,000 a cat. Servals themselves have also become popular pets, but two attacks by servals against children have raised warning signals, and conservationists decry the breeding and cross-breeding of such cats as inhumane and ethically questionable.

The population of up to 10,000 privately-owned tigers in the U.S. began by mating a small number of parents from the wild who originally were smuggled into the U.S. from Asia, or illicitly sold from traveling circuses and zoos to unscrupulous entrepreneurs.

In the past decade, breeders found an eager market among people who wanted to boast that they owned a wild tiger.

"It's like buying a fancy car or a bigger house," said Leigh Henry, program officer for TRAFFIC, the wildlife trade monitoring branch of the World Wildlife Fund. "It's a macho thing. People want to be known for owning the biggest pet on the block."

Tigers start out as mewing kittens, but within a year can kill with a single swipe and need 20 pounds a day of fresh meat to eat. "It takes thousands of dollars a year to keep them," said Tom

Solin, a private investigator in Bellingham, Washington who helps law enforcement handle increasing numbers of wildcat cases. "Within a year they are in predator-prey mode."

Many private breeders say they are performing a public service by increasing a species that is endangered in its native habitat. But this is not true, wildcat onservation experts say.

"They create a lot of horrible genetic monsters," Tilson said. He said many deformed and mutant cubs must be euthanized along with the healthy ones that are born. But even the healthy ones could never survive in the wild.

"You lose significant genes through inbreeding," he said. "You start getting lower fecundity, more susceptibility to disease, and less ability to survive trauma. It's all about profit. Not a single organization would use these tigers in a recovery program." In such programs, animals bred in captivity are released into the wild to keep endangered species from going extinct.

The rise in tiger maulings in recent years, including the near-fatal attack on the Las Vegas performer Roy Horn in 2003, has prompted several states to pass laws prohibiting the private ownership of wild cats.

In May, 2004, Minnesota passed such a law, but present owners of own wild cats are exempted, as are breeders in compliance with the U.S. Department of Agriculture, which oversees animal breeding operations.

Fourteen states have comprehensive laws banning private ownership of wild and exotic animals; nine (including Minnesota) have partial bans; 13 have some form of regulations; and 14 states have no relevant legislation, according to Nicole Paquette, the director of legal and government affairs for the Animal Protection Institute, in Sacramento, California.

Opponents of such legislation, including the Feline Conservation Federation, argue that small zoo and breeding operations are on the whole safe and humane and are helping preserve endangered species for future generations.

In the debate preceding passage of the 2004 Minnesota

law, FCF spokesman Lynn Culver argued that family farms that raise exotic animals support many other local businesses including veterinarians, feed companies, and building supply stores.

"Not only are private, USDA-licensed breeders helping wildlife species, they are also important to rural economies," Culver said. ●

The Hmong Wisconsin Death Trip

Lee Cheng, a Hmong immigrant in Rochester, has replayed in his mind a hundred times what went so terribly wrong in the north Wisconsin woods—and he believes he knows what could have prevented it.

"The American hunter could have gone to the deer stand and said 'Hi, how are you? How is the family? Got any deer today?' And then after a little while he could mention to the Hmong guy that he was on private land but if he wanted to stay a while he could.

"The Hmong guy would figure it out. He would say to himself 'the guy wants me to go, so I go,' and he'd leave immediately. And that's it."

A mental health worker specializing in Hmong immigrant cases at the New Hope Counseling Center, Cheng said he was saddened and upset by the tragic deaths of six hunters, all apparently shot in cold blood by Chai Vang, a Hmong immigrant who became enraged after being told to leave a deer stand on private property near Dobie, Wisconsin.

But Cheng wasn't surprised. "Hmong men usually keep everything inside," he said. "They will keep all their frustrations inside until they explode. Probably this guy had been harassed many times in his life, which is common for Hmong living in America. If he had sought help for his anger, maybe all of this wouldn't have happened."

"Two Cultures Collide" has been the basic headline on innumerable articles attempting to explain the Wisconsin hunting death trip. Usually the articles focus on how northern

Wisconsin's citizens of European descent and Hmong immigrants have traditionally enjoyed hunting as an annual bonding ritual, while differing in their understanding of private and public property.

Yet cultures may have collided on a much simpler level than hunting rituals and land rights. The simple matter of how to communicate about a disagreement may have been the main cultural culprit in this case.

A little something called "saving face" is usually the first lesson taught in cross-cultural seminars for travelers heading to Asia.

I was skeptical of all the fuss made over "saving face" before I went to live in Japan and China. Boy, was I wrong. What I discovered during the eight years I lived in Asia in the 1990s is that saving face is far more subtle, more important, and more pervasive than I could ever have imagined.

In most Asian countries, saving face is not just about preventing public embarrassment in big situations such as closing a business deal or giving a speech, or in important family situations like weddings and dinners.

It's essentially about signaling one's respect for others—that one doesn't ever put one's own needs ahead those of others—in virtually all situations at all times, in public and private. It's a constant, ingrained behavior.

A small example is that while I was interviewing Cheng, he was cradling his infant daughter on his lap. At one point he wrinkled his nose and said "Oh, she has made a smell." I thought to myself, "the baby is due for a diaper change." But it wasn't until a few minutes later, when I remembered my Asian manners and said, "would you like to go change her diapers?" that Cheng, looking grateful and relieved, sprinted for the bathroom.

When he returned, I checked with him to make sure I'd read the situation correctly. "Yes, you are right," he said. "In America, when parents need to change diapers, they just announce this to the guest and get up in the middle of a conversation and go. That seems rude to a Hmong. Our way is first to say something indirect, and then say 'of course, our conversation takes priority,' and then wait for the guest to give permission to go."

It seems almost impossible that a small episode over diapers could have relevance to the Wisconsin shootings, but Cheng, after he had explained about the diapers, said "that's what I think happened in Wisconsin."

The two sides simply didn't know how to talk to each other.

What exactly happened in the North Woods may never be clear. But to Lee Cheng it is already clear enough. After one cultural misfire too many, all the frustrations pent up for years inside came violently out—round after round after round after round after round after round after round after round. ●

A Very Sudanese Christmas

I had myself a very Sudanese Christmas. In Stewartville.

From 6 p.m. to 6 a.m. last Saturday, a couple of hundred Sudanese immigrants gathered at the Stewartville Sportsman's Club to kick back and celebrate the biggest annual holiday in southern Sudan—Christmas.

Thanks to more than a century of missionary work, most of the population of Southern Sudan is Christian, and Christmas there has evolved into a hybrid holiday of Western religious ritual and African feasting and dancing.

So under the glass-eyed gaze of stuffed buck heads mounted on the Sportsman's Club's walls, young and old members of the Dinka, Bari, Shilluk, and a half dozen other tribes gathered to chat and munch on traditional Sudanese foods and boogie the Christmas night away.

Most arrived at the party after attending Christmas service at the Rochester Covenant Church, an evangelical congregation that holds a regular Sunday service especially for the area's recent Sudanese immigrants. Around 3,000 of the total 15,000 south Sudan refugees in the U.S. live in Minnesota, according to members of the Sudan immigrant community here.

"Christmas is a time when the people of south Sudan forgive themselves," said Khamis Dhien, one of the party's organizers, who fled Sudan in 1993 after his name appeared on a list of college students targeted for arrest or worse. His route to Rochester, where he works at the Crenlo truck-cab fabrication plant, wove through Zimbabwe and Kenya before he immigrated to Fargo, North Dakota, and finally Rochester in 1995.

In south Sudan, the Christmas holiday extends from December 23 to January 3, during which time everyone returns to their home village from wherever they live to reconnect with family and friends. Work in the fields and in the cities comes to a standstill as people make the rounds from house to house in their home village to visit with neighbors, to share news, and to party.

"It's like a big family reunion," Dhien said. At the Stewartville bash, visitors from as far away as Australia, England, and from many states around the U.S. had flown in to reunite with family members they hadn't seen for years.

Sudan has topped the list of countries suffering humanitarian catastrophes for most of the past 20 years. More than two million Sudanese, most in south Sudan, have died and 5.5 million been uprooted by war waged by the Islamist government in the North against the Christian population in the south.

The recent genocide in Darfur, in which government-backed tribal militias have killed more than 30,000 and displaced 1.5 million, is the most recent chapter in this long war waged by the Sudan government which is trying to impose sovereignty—and Islamic *shariah* law—across a country made of a patchwork of many tribes, languages, and customs.

Every person at the Stewartville party had lost close family members and many friends to the war, and many had bullet and machete scars testifying to their own close escapes. But, as Dhien said, it was a night to not only forget but also forgive, and so, to a thumping African beat, the dancers danced until the dawn's early light.

The moves on the dance floor varied from stately, to hips swirling in traditional African patterns that Elvis must have carefully studied.

And the clothes! The men in cream-colored suits and two-toned leather shoes, and the women in flowing tie-died dashikis with their hair swept up in blazing headscarves with silver-bangle earrings and shimmering necklaces.

Little children, born to their immigrant parents here in the U.S., bounced to the music right alongside their parents on the dance floor, while the teenaged boys and girls huddled around the periphery, preferring talk to dance.

One of the most active diaspora groups of the south Sudan resistance movement lives here in Minnesota. Leaders of the Sudan People's Liberation Army (SPLA), the de facto government of southern Sudan, travel to Minnesota frequently to explain the latest news to immigrants here and to encourage them to use the U.S. political system to influence the Sudan government.

There are two main tribes in the south, the Dinka and the Nuer, and decades of civil war have frayed relations between them badly. For the Stewartville party, Dhien, who like most of the party's organizers is a Dinka, invited every Nuer immigrant in Minnesota to come.

But only two did.

"We tried to get closer to them, but they kept themselves away," Dhien said. "Yet we keep up a spirit of hope. We accept them with open heart, open doors to everyone. We forgive. Christmas shows its best for everyone to love each other. It's the only way. We have to have a life in peace." ●

Globalization at Broadway and Fourth

"Globalization" is so fuzzy word, I need to visualize it residing at a specific address in order to understand it. For me, that address in Rochester is the corner of 4th Street and Broadway, smack downtown.

The shops and buildings on the four corners of that intersection tell the whole story of globalization in a nutshell—its possibilities and its pitfalls, the bounties it brings to our community but also the challenges.

On the southwest corner you have Rice & Spice, an Indian grocery and deli where customers line up six deep on late workday afternoons—Mayo Clinic and downtown office workers picking up curries direct from New Delhi, rubbing shoulders with Indian housewives dressed in colorful saris.

Across the street on the northwest corner there is Tejano Western Wear, a Mexican boutique that offers imported fashions ranging from sombreros and striped blankets to snakeskin boots, string ties, leather vests and tooled-silver belt buckles.

Catty-corner from Tejano Western Wear is the Rochester location of Rocco Altobelli's, the well-established Minnesota chain of beauty salons whose name bespeaks an immigrant success story somewhere in its past.

Across from Rocco Altobelli's on the northeast corner is a building that speaks as much about the challenges of globalization as the opportunities—the Union Labor Center—home to a half-dozen local unions including the Teamsters, the UAW and those unions representing laborers, painters and carpenters.

There are more winners than losers from globalization, they

say, but tell that to a factory worker whose job was exported to Tijuana. Whether in terms of lost jobs or the weakened state of unions caused by abundant overseas labor, every labor union today is coping with the pressures of globalization, often more than any other economic trend.

The northeast corner of 4th and Broadway reminds us to pause every time we hear a new economic development in the state being justified on the grounds that it will "make Minnesota more globally competitive."

Bit by bit—family farm by factory by retail shop, pine forest by river by prairie, city bus line by job zone by biotech corridor—our allegiance to this mantra is utterly transforming the economy, the culture and the landscape of our state.

But even when we succeed on purely economic terms in our global competition, are the overall changes to our state positive ones?

Each of us sees the changes differently. A union man sees "corporate globalism" pushing wages lower, destroying jobs and forcing painful dislocations. A medical researcher sees her job enhanced because her colleagues, immigrants from Japan, teach her skills that increase her expertise. A farmer grits his teeth and plants more row crops, which are bad for the land but good for his pocketbook at least in the short run.

Success as well as failure can rend a society. Too-sudden and too-great changes can open social and political vacuums that demagogues and tyrants can exploit. In China, which has been growing at more than 10 percent a year for several years, the government's biggest worry now is that the poor and the unemployed, whom the boom has left behind, will trigger a violent revolt.

The writer William Greider described globalization as "a wondrous new machine, strong and supple, a machine that reaps as it destroys. As it goes, it throws off enormous mows of wealth and bounty while it leaves behind great furrows of wreckage."

There is a saying, "You become what you resist." Thus, if

we compete in the wrong way with China, such as by joining an endless race to the bottom on prices, we'll inevitably become more like China and our other "race to the bottom" competitors in our values and every other way.

So what is the right way to compete? My suggestion is by remembering that as we slug it out in the global marketplace, our ultimate competitive strength lies not in our low prices but in our high values —of democracy, community, unity and equality.

At the corner of Fourth and Broadway, Rochester has become more like India and Mexico than ever before, to our benefit.

But only for some of us. How do we make sure that every tenant at the intersection enjoys the rewards of globalization?

L'Affaire de Janet's Breast

It's plain as day that not a single newspaper columnist in America has been able to resist the urge to write about The Breast.

Today, I finally surrender to the urge myself. I hasten to add that while I admit to abjectly caving, it is only because I've found a worthy and redeeming international angle to the story.

At first I skirted Janet's naked publicity stunt because I believed it was all about Americans' hypocrisy and prurience in matters of sex. I didn't want to write about that because what in heaven's name else is new?

The United States wields potentially apocalyptic military power across the globe. And our pop culture also stomps heavily across the planet via satellite feeds and CDs and films and videos that are rank with violence and pornography.

And yet on Super Bowl Sunday, we Americans howled in outrage at a two-second peek at a lady's nipple. That's childish and strange, but not new.

Then came my epiphany. I recalled seeing similar explosions of public outrage in Japan and Spain that both involved the nation's royal families. And reflecting on these similar incidents made me conclude that the Super Bowl mammary moment had very little to do with sex. Instead, a bitterly frustrated desire for national identity and unity was the culprit.

First the Japanese example. In June 1993, Crown Prince Naruhito, a shy and awkward young man who'd taken his sweet time finding a woman to marry, finally wed Masako Owada, a 30-year-old career diplomat from Tokyo.

In the moments after the wedding ceremony, the Prince and

Princess faced a gaggle of Japanese press photographers. In a moment of unguarded concern for her husband's appearance, the Princess reached out to lightly brush a lock of hair from his eyes. A photographer captured the moment and when the next day's papers published the photo a national scandal erupted.

How grossly ordinary! How much like plain old human beings these Children of Heaven, as Japanese tradition has it, were made to appear! How undignified and especially how un-Imperial and un-Royal!

As in every country with a monarchy, the Japanese royals are supposed to project the best and highest in the nation's soul and psyche. Ordinary is not good enough because the Japanese, as a nation, want to be better than that.

In Spain only one month ago, a similar outrage occurred and it once again involved the country's Prince and Princess, Felipe de Asturias and Leticia Ortiz. This time the happy royal couple was giving their first interview to the Spanish press to announce they were a couple and were engaged. As the cameras were rolling, the star-crossed Leticia made the mistake of brushing her hair back with her hands several times—very coquettish and un-Royal!

The papers killed her for it. Even worse, in the interview she wore an Italian designer dress instead of a Spanish one, and she snapped at Prince Felipe, who had begun to say something while she was talking, saying "Let me finish!"

That last transgression was the worst. It was a sudden moment of exposure of the reality beneath the façade, that was just too much for the Spanish people. Of course, Spaniards know the Prince and Princess are only human. They just don't want to see proof of that on national television.

What the Spanish want from their royals we Americans want from our Super Bowl—a few delicious moments of feeling unified as a nation and good about ourselves.

More Americans watched this year's Super Bowl game and half-time show (130 million) than voted in the 2000 presidential election (105 million). Once upon a time, Americans had fireside chats with President Roosevelt, and the Amos and Andy radio show, and the Ed Sullivan Show.

Now our national life is fractured into a million pieces and timeslots. No politician unites us. No celebrity unites us. No elections unite us.

Only the Super Bowl unites us. Only this year, a plain old ordinary breast divided us. Like the stinging paradox of a plain old King or Queen in Spain, or an ordinary human Empress in Japan, this was the source of our outrage.

It was the disappointment to be reminded in the very midst of our one remaining national celebration of oneness and uniqueness, how divided and common we are. It was not an exposure so much as a self-exposure.

We acted outraged. In reality we hurt, because we want to be better than that. ●

A Seasonal Song of Spam

My international ruminations turned to Spam this week.

That's right, the oversalted, dripping with fat, pink hunk of spiced pork meat that somehow became a great food icon in our United States.

With the scents of eggnog and peppermint now in the air, my attention couldn't help but turn this week from weighty matters to matters that make me weighty, i.e. food. (And shopping. At the Galleria Mall, I heard the "Jingle Bells" muzak playing and found myself softly singing "Spend-spend-spend, spend-spend-spend, spending all the way...")

With the sentiments of the season now upon us, I started to think, why couldn't we find evidence of our commonality and influence across borders in the commonest of things. And the humblest of foods. Our own Spam!

Right on cue, two news items broke last week, that Minnesota's "special parts of animal meat" ("spiced ham" is how the company phrases it) is going international. Thanks to America's declining reputation in Europe, Hormel is now marketing Spam in Britain as a British food. And in the Philippines, already one of Spam's biggest overseas markets, the company has just opened several "Spam Jam Cafés," with Spam burgers on offer.

I did a little research into Spam as a global phenomenon. The company has sold more than six billion of the blue 12-ounce cans since 1937, when the concoction was invented in Austin.

The stuff is produced in three foreign countries (Denmark, Korea, and the Philippines), sold directly in 41 countries, and is trademarked in more than 100. There are only 193 sovereign countries in the world, so we are talking one truly global product here. Software and Spam, covering the world.

But what truly hit me about Spam, upon reflection, was how this quintessentially American food, gastronomically crude yet culturally beloved, widely yet lovingly ridiculed, reminded me of many similar types of foods I've run across while living in other countries.

Every country, it seems, has a special corner of its cultural pantry stocked with weirdo dishes that everybody loves to hate. Or, more precisely, with foods that everyone in that country professes to love—while loving even more the fact that everyone else in the world seems shocked—shocked!—that the people of said nation could actually eat anything so awful, so vile.

Take for example the dish called *natto*, in Japan.

"Natto" is rotting, excuse me, fermenting soybeans. It looks like a pile of something you left in the refrigerator last week, and tastes like it too. A handful-sized serving is eaten with a dash of hot yellow mustard. But the really interesting thing about natto is that it has decomposed to precisely the point where long sagging strings of white mucus stretch from the dish to the chopsticks you are using to take in a brave mouthful of the stuff.

This spectacle greatly increases the mirth of one's Japanese hosts, who have served you natto for the pleasure of watching you eat it for the first time.

In Scotland, you have *haggis*, which is ground sheep lungs, heart, liver, mutton suet, and oatmeal all mixed together and served in a lamb's stomach. The locals insist they love it. Most definitely they love the deer-in-the-headlight looks that cross the faces of visitors when being served haggis the first time. Ditto, in England, being served blood sausages for breakfast.

But for sheer boldness of effect, nothing in my experience beats durian, the horrendously malodorous fruit that's native to Singapore and Malaysia. The smell is so bad and so easily permeates the atmosphere that all throughout Southeast Asia, hotels post at their front doorways the universal symbol of a circle with a red slash through the middle, crossing out a durian fruit.

To say the smell is similar to dirty socks would be a gentle euphemism. Normally, anything with such a smell is immediately taken outside, burned at the dump, or flushed. And yet, as with natto in Japan and haggis in Scotland, the locals say they love the stuff. (Did someone say lutefisk?)

Durian is so omnipresent in Singapore and Malaysia, so talked about and so joked about and so lovingly reviled—with the clear implication being that only a great nation could embrace so cruel-smelling a food—one wonders why they don't just put a durian on their national flags.

Now Spam is no durian, and I like our flag just the way it is. Yet it feels rousing and patriotic to sing of Spam, of everlasting love for our very own salt-and-pork crud, so easy on the palate, so hard on the arteries. I ate Spam sandwiches as a kid, so I'm a fan forever. And if more people around the world intensely disliked Spam, I would love it even more. ●

Sex on a Human Scale

For a few scandalous days back in 1967, the old Time Theater in downtown Rochester showed a movie whose heroine was a young woman dedicated to deeply exploring every aspect of her life—political, social, and sexual.

It was called "I Am Curious Yellow," and my most vivid memory of the film—which I wasn't actually allowed to see as I was 12-years-old at the time—is of the urgent whispers the adults in my life used to discuss it. And discuss it, and discuss it. In the mysterious way kids have of grasping essentials, I gathered that the lead actress, Lena Nyman, had done some very adventurous things on her personal journey.

Taboo things, of course, but this movie had magically been accorded a respectable status thanks to one crucial fact: it was made in Sweden. And it was understood that the Swedes were far more advanced in these matters than we were here. So we had things to learn.

All of which is a roundabout way of saying that Rochester, in its own special Mayo-on-Zumbro fashion, has for long been much more international in its outlook than would perhaps seem likely, here at the edge of the prairie.

Foreign films in particular have certainly played a key role in offering area residents a window onto the world. The Fellows Film Society, which showed international films at Mayo Clinic's Mann Hall throughout the 1960s and 1970s, brought vivid images and new information about foreign cultures.

I saw those films myself as a teenager and younger, catching my first taste of France via the 1964 movie "The Umbrellas of Cherbourg;" a flavor of China through a documentary on acupuncture; and many others.

Today, when knowledge of foreign cultures is no longer a luxury but—thanks to 9/11, Afghanistan, Iraq, and the war on terror—is acknowledged as a necessity for our long-term survival, the tradition of foreign films shown in Rochester continues in two main venues. One is the iFilm program of the Rochester Public Library, which presents foreign films on the second Wednesday of every month in the library's auditorium.

The other venue is the twice-a-year foreign film festival of the Rochester International Film Group, which began in 1996.

Alan Hoffman, a pediatric radiologist at Mayo Clinic, is the group's president. The spring and fall festivals each sell around 3,000 tickets to 800 unique visitors, or about 1 percent of Rochester's population, he says.

"That gives us a lot of room for improvement," Hoffman says.

The value of the films lies not only in their spicy exoticism but something deeper, Hoffman says.

"They bring viewpoints from other places," he says. "You live through a movie. For a couple of hours you live in another city, in another country. You identify with the characters and their situations."

A movie about a peasant living in Iraq might thus influence one's opinions about America's military presence in Iraq. The ravishingly beautiful movie Kandahar, set in Afghanistan and shown at last year's festival, gave many southeast Minnesotans a vivid sense of the nature, the history, and the sufferings of Afghani people living under the Taliban.

Practical life knowledge that is important yet overlooked by an American media obsessed with youth and celebrity, is offered in a bountiful buffet in foreign films. A Mongolian Tale, the first film shown when the international festival began in

103

1996, left a deep impression on Dr. Hoffman.

"The movie's main character was an old woman full of dignity," he said. "How often do you see that kind of portrayal of any older person in a Hollywood movie?"

At this year's festival, audiences especially enjoyed the Japanese film Lily Festival, which portrayed geriatric sex with tenderness and a gentle humor.

Ah, we are back to sex again. Now that the United States is awash in pornography, we don't need foreign films to tell us all the latest techniques. Or even to tell us that sex is OK.

Yet foreign films still play an important role. They typically delve into corners of life that are more human-scaled and real, and thus more useful in purely human terms, than average Hollywood fare.

After all, when it comes to the challenges like child-rearing, caring for aged parents, the struggle to live off the land, the search for God, and geriatric sex, we aren't going to learn what we need from Terminator 3. ●

III **UNITED DREAMS OF AMERICA**

Just Plain Smart

The night shift at the Schmidt Printing plant in Byron looks like Little Cambodia most times, but even on a Friday afternoon there's a strong Asian flavor on the shop floor.

These names topped the overtime sign-up list last Friday when I stopped by for a visit: Sang, Hassan, Pisoth, PJ, Sem and Sokem. Out on the floor, finishing up 12-hour shifts at the paper folding machines, were Bunna, Peau, Meng and Nisai.

And Sherab Bjorngaard, also at a folding machine, a Tibetan whose parents fled Tibet with the Dalai Lama in 1959, when the Chinese invaded the country. Her parents settled in Bangalore, India, where she grew up. She eventually married a Norwegian fellow and then settled in Rochester, which makes her a Tibetan-Indian-Norwegian-American.

It's just another day at Schmidt Printing, a 92-year-old company that has lived through a great many immigrant waves in its history but none, perhaps, as diverse and booming as the one it is living through now. Since the late 1970s, when Hmong and other Southeast Asian refugees starting settling in southeast Minnesota, Schmidt has been hiring them—and continues to do so.

In 2002, the last year for which statistics are available, more legal immigrants came to Minnesota than in any year since 1982, when large numbers of Hmong and other Southeast Asians settled here. Immigrants from Africa accounted for 70 percent of the increase, with 13,522 total legal immigrants moving into the state during the year, according to Barbara Ronningen of the Minnesota State Demographic Center.

Since it began hiring Southeast Asian immigrants, Schmidt has gained a reputation as an employer that's unusually sensitive to the needs of immigrant employees. Especially, of investing time and effort in training at the front end, and reaping rewards in low turnover and high employee loyalty down the line.

Over the past couple of years, interviewing dozens of Hmong, Lao and Cambodian immigrants in the Rochester area, I'd heard the same thing over and over from them—"Schmidt is a great place to work." Those words are so rarely spoken about any employer by any type of employee—immigrant or not—that I had to go see for myself what the company was doing right.

Theresa Whitcome, the company's human relations manager, said the company doesn't have any written policy on immigrant hiring. "What drives our hiring is the core values of the place," she said. "And our core value is to believe in the significance and the potential of every individual."

About 15 percent of Schmidt's 425 employees in its Byron and Rochester plants are Asian, she said.

The fact that immigrants often work at entry-level jobs that are hard to fill with longtime Minnesota residents is, of course, a major reason why many Asian immigrants work at Schmidt Printing. Entry-level production jobs at Schmidt pay $8 to $11 an hour, with more skilled operation jobs paying $9 to $15 an hour.

Still, if a large number of immigrants in entry-level jobs is common in Minnesota, Schmidt's low turnover and golden word of mouth is truly unusual.

"Immigrants helped to shape the values of this company," Whitcome said. In the mid-1990s, with employee morale sagging a bit, the company undertook a top-to-bottom series of conversations, meetings and shared writing that involved every employee, in order to define the company's main values.

Two of the four key values the company settled on—"family" and "respect"—are strongly dominant values in most Asian cultures and, as a result, got a fuller discussion and clarification within the company than would have happened without the Asian employees, Whitcome says.

In quick chats on the shop floor, Asian workers said their loyalty to Schmidt was strengthened by its flexibility on issues such as parents taking breaks or leaves to help sick children. They said the company also allows Asian employees to return to Asia to visit families for six or more weeks, with a job waiting for them when they return to Minnesota.

Monica Meng and her partner, Nisai Sath, both from Cambodia, say the company has shown flexibility by encouraging them to work as a team. Monica, having lived in the United States longer, has good English, while Nisai, who's got good calculating skills, still needs to go slow when speaking.

"Nisai's good at math and paperwork, and I'm good at English," Monica said. "Our supervisor gives us the time we need to work as a team."

That sounds like strong core values getting not just lip service, but being put in action. With immigration levels in Minnesota continuing to increase, it sounds like something else as well: just plain smart. ●

A Rabbi Who Loves God and the Vikings

You see him sometimes flying down Second Street, heading from Saint Marys to the Mayo Clinic with the tails of his long black coat flapping behind him, a calm smile on his bearded face, a lidded cup of Starbucks coffee in one hand, a black fedora on his head and a Torah under his arm.

He is Rabbi Dovid Greene, and he stands by himself as striking proof that Rochester, far from being the "flyover country" we say to ourselves we are (almost hopefully), is in reality super-cosmopolitan.

Because Rabbi Greene is no ordinary rabbi. He is an emissary to Rochester of one of the fastest-growing Jewish organizations in the world, the Chabad-Lubavitch, based in Brooklyn, New York. The group descends from a mystical branch of Judaism that started in Poland in the late 18th century.

Brought to America by a handful of European Jews fleeing Nazism in the early 1940s, the Chabad-Lubavitch has since grown to number more than 200,000 worldwide—a number that's had an outsized influence due to the group's zealous focus and global reach.

In Rochester that takes the form of Rabbi Greene himself, who with his wife Chanie runs the Chabad House at 730 Second St. S.W. That's the house with the 10-foot menorah—the nine-branched candelabrum that symbolizes the role of Jews as a "light to the world"—planted in the front yard.

The Chabad House was opened in Rochester in 1988, when the Lubavitch community realized how much global traffic, including Jews from all over the world, came through the city seeking medical help. Between 15,000 and 20,000 Jews a year visit Mayo Clinic, Rabbi Greene estimates, of which the Chabad House makes contact with about a thosuand.

"We try to imitate Abraham who was known for two things —visiting the sick and welcoming guests," Rabbi Greene says. Many mornings thus find Dovid and Chanie making rounds to the Methodist and Saint Marys hospital suites carrying brown paper lunch bags filled with kosher sandwiches, challah bread, and a small bottle of grape juice.

Those services are free, and Rabbi Greene supports the House with donations and from his work for local dairy farms that produce kosher foods, prepared under a rabbi's supervision.

A second part of his mission in Rochester, he says, is explaining Judaism to non-Jews or gentiles in the area. In this respect especially, the Chabad-Lubavitch break the mold of most orthodox Jewish sects, which see the secular world as a diversion from piety and thus emphasize retreat.

The Chabad-Lubavitch, by contrast, retain the intense piety and inward look of other orthodox Jews, yet stress that a full engagement with the world, including with non-Jews, is essential. While many orthodox Jewish sects have fought hard against assimilation into American culture, the Chabad-Lubavitch by contrast professes a twofold path—retaining religious identity within the context of a fully engaged civic life.

Therefore Rabbi Greene spends a lot of time in local schoolrooms. The goal is not conversion, he stresses, but simply the revelation and explanation of himself as a devout Jew. He has spent many class hours answering young children's questions about what his various items of clothing mean.

The small black skullcap called a yarmulke that he wears, for example. "We wear that to remind ourselves that there is always a higher power above us, something greater than our mind or our bodies, that is God," he explains.

And what about those white tassels hanging from his belt?

"Those are called tzitzis. In Hebrew every letter has a number, and the word tzitzis adds up to 600. Then there are eight strings and five knots on the strings, for a total of 613. The tzitzis reminds Jews of the 613 commandments they must follow."

As the gasps subside, Rabbi Greene adds that the seven laws God gave Noah are the essential ones, and are recommended for people of all creeds. (For those who are interested: no idolatry, no blasphemy, no adultery, no murder, no theft, no cruelty to animals, and the creation of courts of justice.)

Zealous God-consciousness is the hallmark of all "Chabadniks," as they call themselves. There are prayers and readings and reminders of God's earthly presence made incessantly throughout the day.

But take a closer look at Rabbi Greene's yarmulke. There you'll find cosmopolitanism mixed with piety, as I mentioned earlier. Right there on the side, stitched in loud purple as big as the Metrodome, is the Vikings logo.

"Oh, I'm a big fan," the Rabbi says. "Let's not talk about the disaster last Sunday, OK? I was asked once to move to Australia to run a Chabad House. But I looked into it and I finally said 'thank you, but I just don't understand Australian Rules football. Just can't figure it out. I'm culturally Minnesotan, so I'd better stay right here.' And I'm glad I did." ●

A Kazakh Artist's American Vision

"I found my art career in the garbage," says Serik Kulmeshkenov, from his cozy studio in northeast Rochester, nestled in a crook of Highway 63 North between a liquor store and a car dealership.

He's an artist of international stature despite his modest claims for his beginnings, about which more later. His studio walls are hung with awards from competitions in Poland, England, Russia, the Czech Republic, and Japan.

Serik's (pronounced sir-EEK) works fill an entire chapter in an encyclopedia of top international etchers and engravers, whose editors call Kulmeshkenov "an artist of kindly disposition well known to the general public" whose works revolve around "cosmic, historical, literary, and medical themes."

Serik's clean and classical style is whimsical and even surreal at times, mixing elements of the German master engraver Albrecht Durer, the Dutch visual illusionist M.C. Escher, and the droopy candy-cane trees and hats and highways of Dr. Seuss.

"The craftsmanship is extraordinary," says B.J. Shigaki, the director of the Rochester Art Center. "There is a fine narrative about his work, a story-telling. It's drawn with great intimacy and detail. It's so rare these days, when everything's done on computer, to see the hand still involved."

He's a cartoonist, too. Don Quixote figures prominently in his cartoons. One shows the hapless Spanish knight demolishing pictures of windmills on a computer with a click of the mouse. He's drawn a series of cartoons illustrating American idioms, those brilliantly imagistic phrases, with drawings of people who are "going bananas," "have a screw loose," and are "telling white lies once in a blue moon."

And Serik Kulmeshkenov, 46, is legally blind.

This cruel irony is closely tied to his claim to have found his career in the garbage. But to understand the linkage exactly, one needs to start at the beginning.

A native of Kazakhstan, the central Asian republic best known for its vast oil reserves, Kulmeshkenov is the son of a railroad conductor. A slight, round-faced man, he had an artistic bent and so, after a two-year stint in the army, studied architecture. Upon graduation he went to work designing hospitals and school buildings at Kazakhstan's state-run Architectural Institute.

Then, at age 26, he went blind.

The diagnosis was Behcet's Disease, a rare and incurable illness that causes inflammation of blood vessels. In Serik's case, the disorder affected his eyes. A three-week regimen of steroids would restore his vision, after which he'd have ten days of sight, and then it was back to the hospital again. This went on for 12 years, during which time he lost his left eye completely and most of the sight in his right. He lost his job as an architect, his income, and he very nearly lost his life.

"It seemed my future was destroyed," the artist says. "My soul, my inner space, was empty." This was the metaphorical pits, the "garbage" that Kulmeshkenov speaks of. But he means "garbage" quite literally, too.

On one of his ten-day furloughs from the hospital, Kulmeshkenov was at his mother's house taking out the trash. A newspaper article in one pile caught his eye, just before the final toss. He fished it out and discovered it was about bookplates, a special style of engraving stamped "Ex Libris" ("From the Library of ..."), an art form that in its long history has attracted artists of technical virtuosity, thematic diversity, and who often incline towards an M.C. Escher-like fascination with making visual puzzles and puns.

The bookplates fired Kulmeshkenov's brain. As the real world faded from his sight, he grabbed onto the vivid flashes the bookplates gave him of their magical world. Bookplate engravings often depict everyday items depicted as totems and icons—smoking pipes, acorns, planets, nudes, snowy mountain peaks, waves and clouds like a girl's flowing hair.

"It's a magical world," Kulmeshkenov says. He absorbed the images hungrily, knowing his sight would dim within days or hours or minutes. He started making engravings himself, self-taught, one by one. When he went blind again and back to the hospital for another round of steroids, his memories of the bookplate images focused his mind.

"I would be in the hospital for three weeks and I would think, 'there is an engraving at home waiting for me to finish it.' During this time I was able, by writing to artists around the world, to make friends with them and to share my art. So you see I was very lucky. Sometimes when a disease like this happens a person will use alcohol or drugs to solve the problem. But through bookplate engravings I found my art and I was able to keep my soul quite fresh."

Hard work brings luck, or so it's said, and it surely seemed providential when, after his dozen years of the grinding home-and-hospital routine, Kulmeshkenov won a visa to move to the United States in Russia's "green card lottery" of 1999.

Knowing that Mayo Clinic doctors could treat his Behcet's Disease possibly better than anywhere, it was to Rochester that he decamped.

So now, Kulmeshkenov, his wife and his three children and his cat named Angelika, are Minnesotans for life. With the help of a handheld magnifying glass and a closed-circuit TV drawing device, the artist is back at his table. The profusion of bookplates, engravings, etchings, and cartoons are starting to flow once again.

Given the view from his studio window, perhaps he will

one day render Andy's Liquor or Domaille's Buick-Mazda-Mitsubishi in some fantastic way.

More likely he will be telling visual stories about our frozen winters, our governor, our fishing habits, our Norwegian bachelor farmers, our football teams. In sum, he'll be drawing pictures of our dreams. But not, this time, for the trash. ●

From Russia With 800 SATs

Six fat envelopes from three of the most prestigious universities in the U.S. recently dropped one by one into the mailbox of Ghennadiy and Nataliya Batrachenko, a Russian immigrant couple who moved to Rochester from Moscow in 1999.

Harvard University. The Massachusetts Institute of Technology. The California Institute of Technology. Thump ... thump ... kabump. First to arrive were three envelopes for the Batrachenko's 18-year-old daughter, Anastasiya, who graduated from John Marshall this spring. The envelopes contained acceptances everywhere, with generous financial aid.

Then came three envelopes for 16-year-old Pavel Batrachenko, who applied to the same three colleges as his sister, and who also graduated this spring from John Marshall. A winner of Minnesota math and science competitions the past three years, he graduated the same year as Anastasiya because he tested into her class when the family first arrived in Rochester.

"Wow!" was Anastasiya's reaction to her goods news—understandably so. After only four years in the United States, she and Pavel, with their parents' unstinting support, have climbed one of this country's highest educational summits, an achievement to be savored for generations.

How did they do it? Putting in homework hours was one way.

In an online autobiography he wrote for the 2003 U.S. Physics Team, of which he is one of the top five members, Pavel lists fishing, biking, hiking, Frisbee, and reading books as hobbies, although "I don't have a lot of time to pursue these interests" due to the time spent studying physics and mathematics. Anastasiya recalls having seen only three movies in the past four years in Rochester, with the rest of the time devoted to homework.

Both got perfect 800 scores on the mathematics portions of their SAT tests.

But Pavel and Anastasiya's strong study habits and supportive parents only partly explain their success. Ultimately energizing were the values and traditions of the former Soviet Union, fanatically devoted to scientific achievement. It's a commitment that all of the Batrachenkos are energetically continuing today—only now to the great benefit of their adopted land.

The Soviet Union lavished resources on science until the Cold War ended in 1989. The government funded vast programs in physics, engineering, mathematics and the applied sciences. Scientists like Andrei Sakharov were national heroes, and "Science Olympiads" discovered and elevated the country's brightest young people to top spots in Soviet universities.

Ghennadiy rose through the Science Olympiads during this period, and both he and Nataliya ultimately gained good jobs as military research scientists in Moscow.

After 1989, the roof caved in on the sciences in Russia—and the Batrachenkos. With commercial and not military prowess now paramount in the world, the government slammed its funding priorities into reverse.

Russian government funding for science dropped from a high of 2% of GDP during Soviet times to less than one-third of one percent in the 1990s—a disastrous 85% drop—according to a Harvard University study last year.

Viktor Kalushkin, the chairman of the Russian Academy of Sciences, told a Moscow news conference in 2002 that more than 500,000 Russian scientists left the country in the 1990s, most of them never to return. He said the average monthly salary of a Russian scientist was $100 a month, compared to between $3,000-$7,000 in Western countries.

Most scientists in Russia were forced to take jobs as taxi drivers, office workers, and business people—or to emigrate.

"We did well during the Cold War," Nataliya remembers with a chuckle. "We both had good jobs, we defended our country, we were proud, and we made good money. Then one day it all ended, and we had to find other jobs."

The Batrachenkos took odd jobs while Ghennadiy put his resume on the Internet. By 1998 he was working for the Mayo Clinic as a computer programmer, a job he still holds. A year later, his whole family joined him.

"There is no stability in Russia and we wanted to give our children a chance to achieve their goals," Ghennadiy said. "Because I am sure that in this country they can have more success."

The Batrachenkos all hold U.S. permanent residency permits and plan to become U.S. citizens.

How does Ghennadiy define success for his children?

"I'd like them to like their jobs, and for their colleagues to appreciate their work," he says. "That would be enough." ●

Minnesota's Uighur-American

A complete list of the victims of 9/11 would include Amina Tursun, a St. Paul graduate student, although she was nowhere near New York City or Washington on the day of the attack.

She was living in St. Paul at the time. But in the months following the attack, the Chinese government discovered it could use America's war on terrorism to intensify a repressive campaign against a little-known minority group in Western China to which Tursun and her family belong.

"I am at high risk for being spied on by the Chinese," said Tursun, a member of the Uighur minority of western China. "The U.S. government will protect me here, but who will protect my family still in China?" The name Amina Tursun is, in fact, a pseudonym so that the Chinese authorities cannot use this article to locate her relatives.

The Uighur (pronounced WEE-gurr) are a Caucasian Turkic people who weave beautiful carpets, grow 60% of China's cotton, and farm some of the world's finest grapes, melons, and pomegranates. Most Uighur are Muslims although very liberal ones, and most Uighur women do not wear a veil.

The Uighurs look like Turks, speak a Turkic language, eat Turkic food, sing Turkic songs, and dance Turkic dances.

Nevertheless, they are Chinese citizens because their land, on China's remote western border, was annexed by China and called Xinjiang Province after the Communist Revolution of 1949. China covets Uighur territory because it contains enormous proven oil reserves; is agriculturally fertile in many places; and is sparsely populated.

Poor and overcrowded everywhere else, China for more than twenty years has thus resettled millions of ethnic Han Chinese into Xinjiang Province, which Uighurs call East Turkestan. In recent years, as the Uighurs have become a minority population in their own land, more and more of them have vocally protested the takeover of their region by China.

Things worsened after 9/11, when China stepped up repression of Uighurs in the name of "rooting out radical Islamic terrorists." For example, a national "Strike Hard" campaign aimed at common criminals was targeted at Uighur activists in Xinjiang. Today, fear of arrest for even casual promotion of Uighur nationhood is at an all-time high, as China has recently jailed hundreds of Uighur patriots, and executed dozens.

In August, 2002, the U.S. government added to the Uighurs woes when it placed an obscure Uighur Muslim group on the State Department's official list of global "terrorist organizations." Despite strong evidence that the group has no ties whatsoever to Al Qaeda, China used the listing as an excuse to increase surveillance of Uighur groups, expand its programs to "re-educate" Uighur imams, and broaden attacks on Uighur "terrorists."

In 2002, China outlawed use of the Uighur language in all schools and public places such as courthouses, sports arenas, and government offices.

The Uighur community in the U.S. numbers around 500, with Amina probably the only Uighur living in Minnesota. She knows most of the Uighur refugees in the U.S. but knows none but herself in this state.

Tursun's journey to America began at precisely the moment her radicalization against China began—when she applied for a passport to study Russian in neighboring Kazakhstan in the late 1990's. Russian is widely spoken in East Turkestan and is helpful in getting good jobs.

"I'd spent three months getting a special letter written, and the passport officer tore it up," she recalls. "The officer yelled

121

at me, 'You know why I am not giving you a passport! You are a Uighur! You know we have a separate policy for the Uighur people. Why do you want to go to Kazakhstan? It's because you want to go and join the separatists, the splittists, the terrorists!' When I objected, he called the police.

"When the police came, seven of them jumped me. They beat me on my chest and chopped at my head and my arms. They tore my shirt, which was under my jacket, and they broke one of my fingers. We were on the second floor and they grabbed me by my arms and legs, bent my head down, and they carried me down the stairs and threw me on the street."

"I felt like a homeless dog. For the first time I cried in public, I was so enraged and I felt so ashamed. I went home and I cried for two days. And I said 'One day, I'm going to take on you people.'"

In St. Paul, Tursun's dream is to start her own company. "My goal is to have a business for my people," she says. "I want to build an import-export business in Uighur carpets and silks. If I only buy from Uighur I will create jobs for Uighur people and help preserve Uighur culture."

"It will be very difficult," she adds. "Where will I find the funds? And everything has to go through China. I have very big dreams. But sometimes I think of a Uighur saying, 'We are the egg, and China is the stone. If the egg hits the stone, which one will break?'" ●

"No Cows Here!"

The kid has a sharp eye for shoes.

"How are your Rockports treating you?" he called out from across the Tradehome shoe store at Apache Mall, where he's working this summer.

I'd gone in to buy a new pair and the kid had me fitted within seconds. He had great sales banter, friendly but not too, and the whole store pulsed to his energy. He'd grabbed a new customer before I'd even left.

But not before I discovered, chatting at the register, that this sandy-haired 16-year-old Mayo High School junior is foreign-born—a "resident alien" in our government's strange parlance.

Behind his winning All-American façade, Kevin Strehler, fluent in teenager English down the last muffled "you know," is as worldly, as well-traveled, and as truly exotic as our Somali neighbors who brighten Rochester in their brilliant chiffons.

In other words, he's a global citizen.

Born in Zurich, Switzerland and still a legal citizen of that country, Kevin moved to Rochester as a child but spends a month each summer with relatives in his homeland. His first language, which he speaks at home with his parents, is Swiss German, the dialect of German spoken by 60% of Swiss. It has the remarkable distinction, considering it is a German dialect, of using the French word "merci" for "thank you."

His bi-national outlook influences every facet of his life, down to the unusual way his mother, named Marie-Antoinette, quickly dispatches unwanted telemarketing calls.

"In Switzerland, if there is no name after the hyphen, Marie is the name of a girl cow," explains Kevin. "So when the tele-marketers call and ask for Marie, my Mom always says 'There are no cows here!'"

The invisible and yet the most powerful thing about the kid is, simply, his international outlook. He carries it easily and unpretentiously. It's darned easy to miss in a shoe store. But make no mistake, he's a European.

We went for a coffee and I asked how being born and raised partially in Europe affects his political thinking. Bearing in mind that political thinking, like learning a second language, is not a skill that American teenagers automatically acquire as most European teenagers do.

"It leads me to try to harmonize conservative American and liberal European thinking," he says. "With the war in Iraq I had friends who said 'Let's get Saddam out of there, we'll amass a huge army and wipe theirs out and nothing will happen to us.' And I said, 'Are you willing to send family members over there? What about the money you need to spend? And what about the future of Iraq once the war is over?'"

The rap on global citizens is they're not patriotic, either to their native country or their adopted land. I throw that challenge Kevin's way.

"I'm patriotic both to Switzerland and the United States, and I'm proud to be from both places," he said. "By placing your loyalty too much in one place you cause problems. If your country is doing something wrong with the right intention, you might not accept that it might be wrong.

"As a Swiss I'm proud that such a small nation has been able to think for itself and have such a say in international affairs. As an American, I'm proud there are many freedoms and opportunities. You have to earn it, but once you do you can say 'I achieved this and America is supporting me.'"

Does his global perspective give him power?

"Absolutely," he says. "I have an advantage because of my multiple perspectives and sometimes I get hassled for it. A person may disagree with me and have a valid point, but not argue from a wide perspective."

As we drained our coffees, Kevin explained the European take on American child rearing, public transit, cohabitation before marriage, and how folks in Zurich look on their neighbors compared to how folks in Rochester do.

"Here people look at what you are and form an opinion, whereas in Europe you let them do what they do, and you don't judge so much."

My favorite was his take on the Minnesota legal drinking age.

"The idea here is when I'm 21 I can go into a bar and order a drink on my own and get piss drunk. Whereas in Europe you already know by that age there is no point to just doing that."

Now who said global citizenship was impractical?

Go for it, kid. Thanks for your view—and the shoes. ●

Wishing You a Very Prosperous 1383

I got an e-mail three days ago that caught my attention. "Happy New Year!" it pronounced. "We want to wish you and your family members a very wonderful and prosperous 1383!"

A typo, I wondered? A delayed e-mail delivery? Noticing that last date, make that a very delayed delivery?

Then I got another New Year's e-mail card, and another, and then I saw the pattern—all from Iranian friends living in Rochester and around the United States. (When you write a column called Global Rochester you make friends in faraway places.)

Many ended with this cryptic sign-off including the last name of the Egyptian President: "Nowruz Mubarak!"

A few phone calls and a Google later, I'd gotten to the bottom of this.

"Nowruz" is the Iranian New Year and it's still celebrated by most of the 83 Iranian-Americans who live in Rochester, and the 1,568 who live in Minnesota. And the President of Egypt, it turns out, has a last name that means "congratulations" in both Arabic and Persian—so "Nowruz Mubarak" is roughly translated "Happy New Year."

Lynne Karimi, an associate principal at the Sunset Terrace elementary school in Rochester, celebrates Nowruz even though she is not Iranian—but her husband is. Born in Minnesota mining country (Virginia, Minnesota), she married Assad Karimi, an international services administrator at Mayo Clinic. They lived in Teheran the first three years of their marriage.

During those years she learned to how to celebrate Nowruz,

a mélange of rituals that mixes elements of Christmas, Easter, Halloween, and that quasi-religious fever known as spring cleaning.

At the Karimi home, a special table called the "haft seen" is set as it is in every Iranian home for Nowruz. It is heaped with plates of pastries and candies and seven mysterious ritual objects including a mirror with an egg on top, a fish bowl with a live goldfish in it, bright-green wheat sprouts, and a bowl of clear water containing one orange and one rose leaf floating on top.

"I wouldn't consider Christmas without a Christmas tree, and I wouldn't consider Nowruz without a haft seen," said Karimi, whose three children—Sawra, Sonia, and Majid—grew up bi-cultural and have grandparents in Iran. "I want my kids to know about their father's tradition. It's part of who their father is, just like Christmas is a part of me."

In Iran, families huddle around radios and television sets to hear the announcement that Nowruz has begun—that the sun has crossed the equator and the Vernal Equinox, and the first day of Spring has sprung.

For Farhad Kosari, an Iranian-born medical researcher at Mayo Clinic, the Nowruz season stirs pangs of nostalgia for his home town of Isfahan.

"It's one of those times that I wish I could be home," he said. "On Nowruz eve, everyone eats fish, and the next day they go house to house to visit relatives. It's also a tradition that the housewives must clean house for Nowruz. It's no casual thing. The phrase in Persian literally means to 'shake the house.' My Mom used to start a whole month in advance."

The Halloween-like part of Nowruz is called "qashoz zani," during which kids drape themselves in body-length veils and go door to door in their neighborhoods, banging wooden spoons on pots, into which the neighbors drop candies. On the evening of the last Wednesday of the old year, another ceremony has people lighting small bonfires and ritually leaping over them.

As they leap, they chant a sentence to the fire which translated from Persian means "Give me your redness and take away my pale winter look!"

"I like what Nowruz stands for," Karimi says. "It's all about a rebirth—goodbye bad luck, and hello New Year."

She noted the similarities between Nowruz and American holidays and found one more likeness that is Rochester-specific. On the 13th day of the New Year comes "sizdah bedar," when everyone flees their cramped homes and apartments to picnic in the parks and the country. Iranian cities on this day are like ghost towns, and the parks fill with picnickers.

"Iranians love picnics," Karimi said. "They take blankets, and they have a full course meal of meats and bread and fruits and veggies. You cannot believe their picnics. It's like sitting down at Michaels." ●

"What's it going to be in my life?"

The day after Jorge Solis, then an illegal Mexican immigrant living in Seattle, married an American citizen in 1979, he went to apply for a Social Security number. The clerk listened to his story, picked up the phone and called the police, who came and put Jorge in jail. They charged him with marrying just to get legal immigration status, a violation of U.S. law.

His new bride came down the next day, swore they'd married for love and posted $500 bail. But during his night in jail, Jorge spent hours of sleepless anguish reviewing his life. He thought of the many years in Mexico he'd spent planning and saving and studying English to prepare for life in America. Now, after less than two years, it seemed the dream was over.

"I said, 'I guess I'm going back to Mexico,'" Jorge said. "I'm trying real hard to make a living. But at this point, I still have nothing—no job, no money, nothing. I thought, 'What's it going to be in my life?'"

Today, as the owner of two of southern Minnesota's most popular Mexican restaurants, the Fiesta Mexicana in Rochester and Red Wing, Jorge Solis has answered that question resoundingly and positively. His days on the run from the Immigration and Naturalization Service are long over—he employs more than 30 workers and has three children in local schools. He puts in six days a week at the Rochester restaurant, and splits the seventh day between the St. Francis Catholic Church and the soccer field, where he co-sponsors, with Tejano Western Wear, another Mexican-owned business, a B-league soccer team.

Most important, though, is Jorge's unofficial position as a role model, a personal adviser and "padrone"—Spanish for leading male figure—in Rochester's community of 1,500 Hispanic immigrants.

There are no figures on how many of this group are illegal —without a valid visa, Social Security number or permanent resident status validated by a "green card." But Rochester immigration attorneys, such as Michael A. York, say their practice helping illegal Mexican immigrants is brisk, and nationally, the INS estimates about half of the total illegal immigrant population in the United States is Mexican.

Not that the United States minds this; just the opposite.

Before Sept. 11, President Bush was close to granting amnesty for the 3 million to 4 million illegal Mexican immigrants living in America. Lax enforcement of deportation rules against those immigrants is America's de facto guest worker program that keeps inflation low, fills jobs many Americans wouldn't touch and makes U.S. exports competitive in world markets.

Yet the effect of so many immigrants, many of whom take years to learn English, has become one of America's most complex and controversial civic debates. For many years, debates about bilingual education, amnesty for illegal workers and ethnic-related crime and poverty rates have raged in Texas and California, where most Mexican immigrants live.

Now many other states, including Minnesota, are grappling with similar issues as increasing numbers of Mexican migrant workers, such as those who follow the annual corn harvest, settle here instead of moving on. In addition, immigrants who first emigrated to the Southwest are now moving, as Jorge did, to states farther north and east of California to build their lives.

Jorge's story begins in Cuautla, a poor farming village of 2,500 in central Mexico, about 175 miles west of Guadalajara. One of eight children, Jorge's mother had a second-grade education, and his father was illiterate. During the growing season, his father planted, plowed, and harvested corn for a daily wage; off season, he chopped wood and sold it to a local bakery. Beans and tortillas were the family's daily staple, with dinners occasionally supplemented by roasted squirrel or rabbit bagged with a muzzle-loader.

At age 14, in the seventh grade, Jorge came to his first major crossroads and a decision that ultimately set him on a path to the United States. His father wanted an extra hand in the field and encouraged him to quit school. But Jorge had seen a handful of Cuautlanese men who had emigrated to "el norte" and returned to the village bedecked in consumerist glory.

"They came back with nice clothes, driving a car. They could buy some land or a house. You saw those things and you said to yourself 'I want to go there.'"

The avuncular priest of Cuautla's Santo Santiago church saw the ambition in Jorge's eyes, took him aside and warned: "You think you're going to sweep dollars up off the street in the U.S.? No, you'll have to work hard, and you'll need an education. Stay in school. Learn English, then go."

Which is just what Jorge did. Grades seven to nine, he worked the fields in the mornings to pay his school tuition. He learned English words and phrases, and he stayed put when one of his brothers crossed the border and headed to work as a dishwasher at a Washington restaurant.

At age 18, his brother wired him $300 to pay "el coyotes," the smugglers who would sneak him across the border from Tijuana to San Diego. In 1977, he made the break—a 36-hour bus journey from Cuaulta to Tijuana. From there, he was taken to the U.S. border, where he climbed a chain link fence and made a mad dash for a waiting car on Interstate 5 in San Ysidro. The smugglers stuffed him and two other illegals into the trunk where, after two hours of suffocating heat and dark and carbon monoxide, he arrived in Los Angeles.

That was for starters. He spent his first three months in virtual imprisonment in a Los Angeles apartment. The "coyotes" kept him around to sweep the floors and go out to buy pizzas and cigarettes. On one such trip he called a contact whose phone number he'd gotten in Mexico; they picked him up, and he made his getaway.

Next stop was Tacoma, Washington, to join his brother, but his lack of papers kept him jobless for six months. Then he got a position washing dishes at a restaurant for $1.50 an hour, six days a week, 13 hours a day. Home was an upstairs apartment where his fellow restaurant workers had claimed all the sofas and beds. "I'd go home exhausted and sleep on the floor all night," Jorge says.

"I said, 'God, this is the U.S.? It's too hard. It's too much. This is the dream?' But I stayed. I wasn't going to go back."

The day when all hope seemed dead came in late 1979. In less than a year, Jorge had worked his way up to cook, the most important restaurant job, and he was earning $800 a month. He had responsibility, respect, a paycheck, and a fiancée. Then, one evening after the restaurant closed, seven immigration officers swarmed the place. Guns drawn, five of them blocked the doors while two others searched the darkened space with flashlights.

"I jumped under the counter at the bar," Jorge said. "One guy jumped into the garbage. He didn't get caught, but three of us did."

Unable to produce a green card, Jorge and his two co-workers were loaded into a bus and driven south through Oregon and California. At the U.S. border town of Calexico, the U.S. immigration officials dropped them off and watched until they'd walked back into Mexico.

It was a cat-and-mouse game, and within a few days, Jorge had made it back to Washington. This time, he stayed, and married his fiancée. What saved him was steady work in a network of Mexican restaurants run by Cuautlanese who had emigrated to Washington in the early 1970s. Jorge worked his way up in these restaurants, smallish eateries that sold inexpensive Mexican taco and tortilla meals and which went by names like El Matador, Torreros, Jalisco, Zapatillo, El Toro, Azteca, La Costa, and El Marinero.

These restaurants were Jorge's Harvard and Yale. In them he learned the Mexican restaurant business from dishwasher up.

As grinding and difficult as the work was, he absorbed from the restaurants a set of skills that worked in America. In 1999, the Cuautlanese restaurants of Washington employed 10,000 people and had made such an impact on the Washington economy that Gov. Gary Locke, the first Chinese-American U.S. governor and himself a child of immigrant parents, visited the town of Cuautla on a trade mission to thank the town and celebrate its relationship with his state.

By 1992, Jorge and his wife, Annee, had saved $19,000, enough to buy their own first restaurant, La Cabana, in Oregon City, Oregon. Only a few months after their opening, however, disaster seemed certain when another Mexican restaurant announced it would open on a street directly between La Cabana and the neighborhood where most of Jorge's customers lived. Despair set in until Jorge realized that a growth spurt in Oregon City would allow him to sell the place at a tidy profit. He was offered $55,000 for the place and he sold, netting a $36,000 capital gain on the property.

One day during this period, a customer came in, sat down, and told Jorge that Money Magazine had just rated Rochester as the best place to live in America. That was all Jorge needed to hear.

After a couple of scouting trips, he found a vacant building on the frontage road of U.S. 52 near Sixth Street Southwest, bought it and settled in. The building will be torn down later this year for the U.S. 52 widening project.

Jorge, having sold the place to the state, is moving the restaurant to a spot in Northbrook Shopping Center. The new restaurant will open in late August.

How long does it take to become an American? For Jorge, more than 25 years. He applied for U.S. citizenship only last summer, and when the United States played Mexico in the World Cup recently, he rooted for Mexico.

"I've lived more of my life here than in Mexico, and I know this country has given me more than Mexico, but still, inside, I feel…" his voice fades away.

Getting his three children to go to church is a major fault line in his cross-cultural life.

"I have to beg my kids to come to Mass with me," he said, shaking his head. "My mother always dressed me up in nice clean clothes for Sunday Mass, and we sang songs together. Religion keeps a family close. It helps the community and it helps teenagers when they start to have experiences in life. But my kids would rather be playing Sega. And with all these scandals, it's even harder. They say, 'Why should we go? These guys are devils.' I tell them that religion is not about you and the priests, it's about you and God. It's something that nobody can take away from you. It's something I really want to pass on to them, but they're not interested."

The difficulty of keeping the family together is the hardest thing about American life for Jorge.

"The mother and father in America both work, and the kids are raised by day care. Then at age 18, they move out to start a new life. In Mexico, the family is much stronger and more supportive.

"But if you work hard in America, you get ahead. You get a home, a car, have some money in the bank. There are jobs everywhere. If you want to work, there is a job. In Mexico, even if you want to work, there are no jobs."

At Fiesta Mexicana, Jorge is forced to require all employees to present a green card and a valid Social Security number before they can work. He also knows many Mexicans in the United States, especially migrant workers who follow seasons of work including the corn harvest in Minnesota in the summer, that have dubious credentials. He was in their place 20 years ago.

He wishes average American citizens, as well as U.S. corporations, were more keenly aware of the benefits that Mexican immigrants bring to this country.

"Most Americans wouldn't touch the jobs that immigrants do—in the fields, in construction, in restaurants. So I don't think that immigrants are taking jobs away from Americans. They are taking the low-pay, hard-work jobs. They are helping the United States to be strong." ⬤

Sugar Stirred into Minnesota Milk

On the outskirts of Stewartville, in a roadside motel snuggled between a frozen cornfield and chiropractic clinic, there is a man who begins each day by lighting a candle and bowing his head in prayer.

In a whisper, he says words of thanks into a small shrine stuffed with drawings of deities, including a dancing elephant, an emaciated monk, a monkey god, a four-armed goddess who pours a stream of gold coins from her open palms, and a 15th-century Sufi poet whose crowned head radiates sunbeams.

The poet wrote this man's morning prayer, which he recites out loud:

"God, you gave us eyes to see good things, ears to hear good things, and a tongue to speak honesty and truth. You made the sun, the moon, the stars and everything in the universe. Thank you for that. In return, God, I will try hard to be a good human being. I will pray to you, and if a hungry person comes to my house, I will feed him. Amen."

The praying man is Champak Bhakta, and his house is the AmericInn just north of Stewartville on U.S. 63. He has owned and operated the motel since 1995, when he moved to Stewartville with his wife, Mina, from Biloxi, Mississippi.

It would be easy to overlook the AmericInn, unless you were in town perhaps to visit relatives and needed a bed for the night. Overlooking it would be a loss because Champak and his wife, Mina, offer a good strong cup of tea and make visitors feel at home. They are a living example of a mighty wave of U.S. immigration that has brought 1.6 million of the best, brightest, and the most ambitious citizens of India to the United States to pursue their American dreams.

The lobby hardly looks Indian. Poinsettias and white-flocked ornaments decorate the foyer, and a Christmas tree still stands by the fireplace. On a coffee table lies a book of Mark Twain short stories, the Gideon Bible, and the Alcoholic Anonymous BigBook.

Yet if you sit down by the fire for a while, India appears vividly in your mind's eye as Champak recalls the 24-year journey from a small village in the Indian province of Gujarat, through a dozen towns throughout the American South as he raised a family, saved money, looked for opportunity, and ended up in Stewartville.

Throughout his journey, Champak, like most Indian-born citizens of the United States, has become thoroughly American while also retaining his essential Indian roots, especially his Hindu faith.

He always spoke Gujarati, the Indian language of his home province, at home to make sure his American-born children grew up bilingual. He's a vegetarian.

If you ask him to explain the secret of his family's successful grafting into modern America while preserving his rural Indian roots, he tells you the story of the Parsi in Gujarat.

A devout religious people of the ancient Persian Empire, the Parsis fled persecution by Islamic marauders around 600 A.D., many of them arriving in Gujarat. There, the local Indians looked on them initially with fear and skepticism. To allay those fears, Parsi leaders, unable to speak Gujarat, are said to have poured a cup of sugar into a container of milk.

"That showed the Hindus that the Parsis intended to make India sweeter by merging into the mainstream," Champak says. "That has always been our goal as Indian immigrants."

The couple's biggest accomplishment, he says, is having found ways, while raising three children and running their businesses, to stir their Hindu and Indian cultural heritage into American life, like sugar into milk.

"There is freedom and opportunity in America," he says. "The laws are good, and they protect you. It's true that India is a poor country, but that's not all it is. An Indian is never afraid to do a job, no matter what. If a room has to be cleaned, somebody has to do it. Why not me? It's an honor to work. So long as you work and praise God and live peacefully, God will reward you. That's our religion. It's guided our lives in America, and it's worked."

Born in 1956 to a farmer of cotton, rice, and sugarcane, Champak grew up in a "joint family," a common living arrangement in India in which brothers, their wives and children all live under the same roof. In his home, there were three brothers, their wives, and 13 children.

At age 16, he moved to the nearby town of Vidhyanagar, literally "Education Town," where, at age 20, he received a bachelor's degree in industrial chemistry. Yet, his prospects for getting a job in India were basically none. Being a member of the Bhakta caste, which ranked around the middle of India's several hundred castes ranging from Brahmin at the top to Harijans (outcasts) at the bottom, didn't make things easier. The Bhakta caste tended to be farmers or workers in the trades, not the professions, so finding connections to land a job was impossible.

Meanwhile, the beacon on the hill—America—beckoned. Since 1965, when quotas that had long restricted Asian immigration to the United States were abolished, hundreds of thousands of Indians had jumped at the chance to leave. Among them was the oldest of Champak's siblings, a sister, who emigrated in 1970. One by one, at the rate of about a sibling every two years, the sister sponsored all five of Champak's brothers and sisters to come to the United States.

"All the kids moved to America because, in our village, it was a struggle just to live, to get food, to get money," he says. "In the U.S., we knew you could feed your family without such terrible struggle."

His elderly parents remain in the Gujarat village of Syadla, where they are supported by their five children, now all U.S. citizens, who also visit them at least once every year.

Champak, the fourth sibling to emigrate, did so in 1978. He arrived with $20 in his pocket and went directly to Hollywood, California, where an older brother, Hasmukhbhai, ran a motel.

Champak remembers his first days in the United States, taking walks around his brother's neighborhood.

"The department stores and grocery stores were so neat and clean," he says. "And I never saw so many cars before in my life. There was just so much of everything, and I knew that if I worked really hard in America, I would have a good chance to succeed. It was like going from earth to heaven."

So began Champak's American journey, jumping from job to job and town to town, seeking better opportunities and the best place to raise his growing family. After three months of working at his brother's motel, he moved on to another Indian-owned motel on Sunset Boulevard. In 1978, he moved to Coleman, Texas, to a $2.75-an-hour job at a brick factory, and in 1979, he relocated to a motel in Huntsville, Texas, where Mina joined him from India with one child. She'd been pregnant when he'd left to set up a home for them in the United States.

In 1979, the family moved to Houston, where Champak worked as a machinist and Mina as a cook at a Jack-in-the-Box. By then thinking of owning a motel one day, they were saving money. Their extended network of Indian friends and family, both here and in India, knew the couple had reached the stage in life where they needed to buy a stake in a business. So when Champak asked them to pitch in to help him buy the 287 Motel in Quanta, Texas, a 12-unit place with RV parking for eight, they quickly did. A thousand dollars here, two thousand there, plus his savings, and soon Champak had the necessary $15,000 down payment.

The 287 Motel thrived for a few years, riding a Texas oil boom, and Champak quickly paid back his no-interest loans. Then the oil boom went bust, and so did the 287.

"I couldn't even sell the place," he says. "There we no buyers, so I gave it back to the owner. When we left, I didn't have a penny, and I was just as broke as when I first came to this country."

A dry cleaner in nearby Altus, Oklahoma, offered Champak a job, and having no other offers and three children by now, he accepted. A year later, a cousin in Biloxi asked Champak to become a partner in a dry-cleaning place next to the Keesler Air Force Base—$75,000 down on $200,000. Once again, friends and family stepped forward with loans.

Dry cleaning military uniforms was his business for the next eight years until one day, when his kids were their teens, the city of Biloxi let casinos come in. Everything changed.

"I didn't want them hanging around in that atmosphere," Champak says. "I realized that if I didn't pay attention to them, they might be with bad people and be influenced by them. I wanted to protect my children, and to protect them, I had to spend time with them. And to spend the time, I had to move."

Champak moved his family to Stewartville in 1995. Since then, Champak says, he's come to realize why so many Indian immigrants from the Bhakta caste have chosen to make their living as moteliers.

There are, of course, the practical reasons, such as the chance for ownership and to increase one's net worth and set one's own hours.

But there is a deeper reason, Champak says, that connects to the Hinduism practiced by his caste, which venerates the Sufi poet, Kabir, as a prophet of the Hindu god, Ram. Several times each year, Champak meets with fellow Indian immigrants of his own caste from the Midwest who workshop Kabir, to read and sing Kabir's verses and songs. When members of his caste greet each other they say "Ram Kabir" as a hello.

What connects Kabir to the motel business is the main character of many of his poems, a mysterious stranger called "the Guest." The Guest usually arrives unannounced and in disguise in a person's life. Knowing how to recognize the Guest and how to welcome him generously is the tricky but much-desired goal that Kabir describes in his poems.

As in this poem:

> *The Holy One disguised as an old person at a motel,*
> *Goes out to ask for carfare.*
> *But I never seem to catch sight of him.*
> *If I did, what would I ask him for?*
> *He has already experienced what is missing in my life.*
> *Kabir says: I belong to this old person.*
> *Now let the events about to come, come!*

And this one:

> *The night is dark and long ... hours go by ...*
> *Because I am alone, I sit up suddenly,*
> *Fear goes through me.*
> *Kabir says: Listen, my friend,*
> *There is one thing in the world that satisfies,*
> *And that is a meeting with the Guest.*

Champak has little doubt as to the identity of the Guest.

"It's anyone who comes to the motel," he says. "Whoever comes, we help them, we respect them, honor them and try to make them feel this is their second home. That's what Hinduism is all about, and it's also what Kabir says. The two most important things in life, he tells us, are first to pray to God, and second, that if anyone comes to your house who is hungry, feed him. That's why I'm in the hospitality industry."

Sometimes, in his prayers, Champak thanks his adopted country for having shown him and his family such hospitality.

He asks his deities to keep showing him new ways, here in the frozen cornfields of America, to pass it on. ●

Lakes + Snow + Cold = Home

Konstantin Kulikov is a Russian immigrant with an American dream.

He works out of a sprawling woodshop on U.S. 63 South, a labyrinth of rooms stuffed with every imaginable type of wood saw, piles of lumber, walls hung with architectural designs, and floors sprinkled with sawdust.

In one of the rooms stands the monster machine he brought with him from Ozersk, Russia, to make his American dream a reality. This is the "Kul." It's a computerized wood lathe that spits out mile after mile of pine board molding carved in intricate designs to exact specifications.

A broad-shouldered man with pale blue eyes and boyish dimples, Kulikov, 47, invented the Kul in Russia as a way to speed the production of wood moldings with non-linear designs. The Kul carves wood into paisleys and diamond shapes, waves and peaks like cake frosting.

Today, Kulikov is one of 250 Russians in Rochester, an entrepreneur who represents both the new face of a region growing ever more diverse, and the age-old American dream of hard work and freedom leading to fulfillment.

He couldn't quite make it happen in Russia, although after the collapse of the Soviet Union in 1989, things looked hopeful for a while.

He borrowed money and got the Kul built. "It was a beautiful time, when the finished machine came into our shop. We put in the first board and it worked! The guys ran out in the street to celebrate. They thought the product was so beautiful that someone would immediately put in a substantial order."

But problems cropped up. The 160 percent interest Kulikov had to pay on his loan made it hard to support advertising and marketing for the Kul. Russia's growing economic problems made daily life, not to mention running a business, nearly impossible. Paper money changed colors from week to week, and the ruble was devalued to almost nothing.

When Kulikov won a visa lottery to visit Rochester, he didn't hesitate. And the Kul isn't the only thing he brought with him. At the Ultimate Wood Design woodshop, he is hatching plans for several dozen inventions he dreamed up in Russia but never got a chance to build.

There is an anti-theft device that would foil any car thief in the world. There is a device that "offers human transportation but is fun at the same time—all-terrain except for water." There is a gadget that helps athletes train for track events so effectively it guarantees their success, he says.

"In Russia there are thousands and thousands of good ideas, but they stay in the air, and no one can make them work," Kulikov says. "The bureaucracy is a country within a country. Here in America, I've never met one official who didn't give me a straight answer and let me go on my way."

Living in Rochester since 1997, Kulikov and his wife, Valentina, both remarried, have between them two parents, three siblings, and three daughters who remain in Russia. The Kulikovs live in a northeast Rochester apartment, tend a vegetable garden near U.S. 52 North, and spend much of their free time studying English. Kulikov has shown the Kul in trade shows around Minnesota and is looking for a good salesman to spread the word.

"In America, if you have a good idea, work hard, and lead a simple life, you can build and build, go up and up and up."

"A friend once complained to me that American food is not right, American women are not right, the streets are not right, nature is not right. I told him, 'I miss Russian food, I miss

Russian nature. I don't like the American police car sirens going off so much, I don't like this, I don't like that. All those things together are wrong, definitely. But you know what? Put all those things together, combine them, and it's beautiful. America is beautiful."

He's a patriot with cosmopolitan tastes. He likes Russian novels, French movies and Led Zeppelin played loud while he works. He's got a quick smile, a sly wit and a notch in his right thumb taken out by a joiner.

His hometown is Ozersk, on the thickly forested eastern slopes of the Ural Mountains, which divide Russia like a cleaver. Kulikov says he feels at home in Rochester because it's so much like Ozersk, where it snows heavily and is freezing cold for six months each year. Ozersk, which imeans "Lake City," has a population of 85,000.

Like Rochester, Ozersk is also a one-company town, although its business is darker than healing the sick. A complex of factories, the Mayak Combinat, reprocesses plutonium, the fissionable fuel used in nuclear weapons and nuclear power plants. It also stores nuclear waste.

You won't find Ozersk on a map. It was built from scratch in greatest secrecy in the late 1940s, in response to America's successful detonation of the atom bomb. Today, Ozersk is a well-known part of Russia's nuclear weapons industry, like Los Alamos in the United States, but remains a highly classified national security facility.

"It was a wonderful place to grow up," Kulikov says. "It was in the middle of nowhere, but we had the best food in Russia, a sports stadium, a skating rink, a movie theater, a library and everything was free. But there was barbed wire around the place, deep in the forest, and only the government knew we existed."

In Russia, Ozersk is called a "closed city." It was a tough decision, Kulikov said, to emigrate to the United States.

"As a Russian patriot, I tried my best to build my machine

there," he said. "But we failed to find a reliable partner." The collapse of the Soviet Union gave him and his team hope that things would turn around. But the ruble's repeated devaluations in the early 1990s delivered blow after blow.

"You went to bed with enough money to buy a car, and you woke up with enough for a pair of shoes," Kulikov remembers. "If you could prove you had earned the money you could get it back, but if you had slowly built your savings year after year, you had no proof and it was just suddenly gone."

The years of struggle tipped the scales for Kulikov. "If you don't have money, you have nothing to lose," he said. "And I had no money. The point of life is not to drink beers, to go to the movies, these types of things. It's to find out who and what you are. And if you are able to build something like the Kul, you are obligated to try."

On his first day in America, a friend took him to a barbecue picnic in Lake City. "It was a Saturday. It was so clean and friendly. I looked at the Mississippi River, and I thought of Tom Sawyer, a book I knew well. I heard a noise from the road, and I asked my friend, 'What is that?' He said 'It's a Harley Davidson.' A Harley! I said to him, 'I can't believe I am in America, in this clean park, eating this delicious food, with these friendly people, across the world from where I was only yesterday. It's impossible."

Kulikov immediately enrolled himself in the Adult Literacy program of the Rochester Community and Technical College, where he sat in class with immigrants from Somalia, Sudan, Mexico, and China, to learn a new language at age 43.

"English sounded like 'wa-wa-wa-wa-wa-wa-wa,'" he recalls. "I couldn't separate the words." After masterinag four levels of English as a Second Language, he was able get by on his own. He is intensely grateful to the English teachers at the RCTC.

His big break in America was meeting Karim Esmailzadeh. A Rochester businessman, Esmailzadeh owns the Ultimate Wood Designs workshop that Kulikov uses as his base.

A native of Iran who emigrated to the United States in the 1960s, he recognized in Kulikov, and Kulikov recognized in him, a kindred spirit.

"He understands me better than anyone," Kulikov said. "He's an inventor and he came here 40 years ago and he knows what it's like to be in the middle of nowhere with no support, no language, not knowing the country, and then to try to survive and be successful. He knows how hard it is."

Having no common language, the two men communicated for months "by making little drawings on pieces of paper," Kulikov said.

Since he came to Rochester, Kulikov has written a regular column called "Love Your Homeland" for his hometown newspaper in Ozersk.

In the column he writes about his life in Rochester, whom he meets and what he sees, and offers observations about American character and society.

At first he wrote a lot about food: how Americans love barbecues and enormous grocery stores, and the paradox of the sheer abundance of food in America yet the difficulty of getting juicy red tomatoes and other fresh vegetables. He spent one column describing in loving detail each dish served at the massive hot table in the Old Country Buffet in Barclay Square.

He wrote about the baby-changing tables in public bathrooms —even in the men's rooms! "Americans love to spend their free time with their children," he wrote. "They can also have fun without alcohol."

"In America, the music is great, but the lyrics are too simple," he said another time. "In Russia, it's just the opposite. You don't listen to Russian pop music for the music but for the great stories the singers tell."

He was smitten by Minnesota's "right turn on red" law.

"How wonderful it is! How many months and years it would take for that kind of reasonable law to get passed in Russia!"

After a while, Kulikov noticed more about American society and character. To his surprise he discovered that it was far easier in Russia than the United States to get access to foreign books, movies and music.

"In any Russian town, you can go into a video store and get movies from all countries of the world," he said. "My favorites are French comedies, and I love movies with Jean-Paul Belmondo, Pierre Richard, and Luis de Funes. But I can't find them in video stores here. And the library and bookstores have only a few Russian books."

The biggest problem in American society is loneliness, he said.

"If you go to a bar and talk to a woman, it can become a sexual harassment lawsuit. If she has a strong enough lawyer, she can do it. Many people seem to be going into a cocoon. You want to protect yourself. But the cocoon becomes so hard that finally other people can't get in."

Yet the amount of freedom to become what you want to be in America still dwarfs that in other countries, he said.

"There are difficulties, but I am strong. Everything I have ever dreamed has come true. And this dream will also come true. Give me some trees, some lakes, and some cold, and I am at home." ●

Education is the Sun and Moon

Phengta Phetsarath began her journey to Rochester by sewing $100 into the waistband of her skirt, saying a prayer to Buddha and giving her husband a hard choice. It was 1980. She had decided to flee Laos and its communist government, which had abducted her sister in the middle of the night.

The only problem was that Phengta had an infant son. And her husband, who had a steady job, hadn't yet decided to make the escape. It would begin with a short but dangerous boat trip across the Mekong River to Thailand.

It was a deeply desperate moment. Phengta had decided, firmly and finally, to flee for herself. But would her husband and her son choose to come with her? Or would she make her journey to her new life alone?

If she debated the pro's and con's of escape with her family at home, she knew she would never leave Laos. So on her own, she paid a Mekong River boatman enough for passage for three, and one morning, only 15 minutes before the boat was to leave, she turned to her husband and said:

> *"Sir, I am leaving in 15 minutes. Are you sure you*
> *want to stay in Laos? I offer you two options. One is*
> *divorce. The other is to please come with me and*
> *our son. If we stay in Laos our entire life, we won't*
> *be able to build our future, and our son won't get*
> *a good education. Let's think of our son."*

Ten minutes later, the whole family was on the boat.

Today, Phengta, a woman of 52 with preternatural optimism, a shy smile and a silver-toned laugh, is an American citizen, and one of Rochester's busiest civic activists. A paralegal at the state-funded Southern Minnesota Regional Legal Services, Phengta is a key person in Rochester responsible for helping immigrants, refugees, and political asylum applicants through the first phases of becoming American.

Many courthouses, police stations, hospitals and schools in southern Minnesota have Phengta at the top of their Rolodexes, to call on for help as a translator during a crisis.

Besides her professional services, she works indefatigably as a mentor and guide for several hundred immigrants and their families in Asian social networks and through active participation in two local churches—the Wat Lao Buddhist Temple in Farmington, and the Emmanuel Baptist Church in Rochester, which has many Asian immigrants as members.

She's also an entrepreneur. From her first days in the United States, Phengta has run businesses to support her family in America and the extended family she left behind in Laos. Working with a crafts shop based in Vientiane, Laos, Phengta sells Lao and Hmong embroidery and appliqués, story quilts, baskets, batiks, and other crafts out of her Rochester home. She sends home between $300 and $500 every three months.

She's proudest of a business she calls the "Cow Bank," which she started with a $5,000 investment in a cooperative run by two brothers who live in Laos. The company bought heifers because they offered a return on investment in three ways: they calved, they produced milk for sale, and their manure could be sold as fertilizer. Now the coop manages all three businesses and maintains many acres of mulberry leaves, which it sells and uses on its own silk farm (silk works eat the leaves).

"I don't have a million dollars, but I do have ideas," she says.

As one of approximately 9,000 immigrants who live in Rochester, Phengta is a standout success at assimilation in a rapidly diversifying ethnic community. She is at the vanguard of that community because she exemplifies the last generation of immigrants to assimilate in the region, while also helping to guide and shape the next generation.

Phengta is crystal clear about one idea. She teaches this idea to her clients every day. To Phengta, this idea is synonymous with the promise of Rochester and of America itself. It's captured in a word that for her rings with the promise of fulfillment that she has sought from the day she crossed the Mekong River in a smuggler's boat.

The word is education. To Phengta, the word education means something magical.

To understand this better, consider a story. In Laos, Phengta's oldest sister was a fortune teller. She told fortunes to make extra money in a country fast falling to ruin under the Communist Party. After 1975, when the Communists took power, people who publicly disagreed with the government began to disappear. A co-worker of Phengta's husband who was indiscreet with his opinions was absent from work one day and later was pronounced dead.

The Communists' paranoia went much further than aversion to criticism. Anyone who knew, or who gave the impression of knowing, anything at all beyond what the Communists knew, was suspect. This included teachers, students, and professional people. Educated people.

And fortune tellers. Because Phengta's sister claimed to divine a person's future using flowers, candles, and prayer, she was labeled a danger to society. One night she disappeared.

"A policeman and a party leader came and banged on our door," Phengta recalls. "They asked for my sister. My mom said, 'She is upstairs.' So they ran upstairs, handcuffed her, and took her away."

Six months later, she wrote her family a letter from a "re-education camp." Five years later, she was released, but by that time, Phengta had fled Laos with her husband and her son.

The moral of this story, to Phengta, is that the root source of violence is ignorance. Pure and simple, lack of education breeds senseless killing.

"The Communists had been in the war, but they were never educated," she says. "Their re-education camp wasn't college or university, it was just a place where you learned how to gather food in the forest and cut bamboo."

"Education is like the sun or the moon," Phengta says. "It brings a sparkle to our lives. How can you even see the world if you don't have an education?"

Anger is one source of energy for Phengta; compassion is another. But gratitude is the strongest energy source of all.

When recounting her most dire moments, Phengta always remembers an angel who tipped the scales, ever so slightly, in her favor.

There was the time at the Nong Kai Refugee Camp in Thailand, when night after night drunken soldiers came to her hut and yelled, with her husband and son present, "You want to have a good time?" The soldiers' nightly visits became more rude, rowdy and demanding, until Phengta was fighting panic all day long. The angel who appeared that time was a distant relative who had some standing at the camp, who mentioned the fact of her relationship to Phengta to the soldiers. The nightly visits stopped.

Another time, the angel turned out to be a United Nations official who began a crucial interview at the refugee camp by snapping at Phengta: "Why do you want to live in America? The Americans bombed your country and killed many of your people." With the fierce self-composure for which she is still known, Phengta responded: "Sir, you are correct. America made the war, but that doesn't mean that I hate the American people. America is a good place to hope and to get an education."

The official stamped her immigration papers "Approved."

It was nighttime when Phengta's flight to the United States

arrived in San Francisco. From the airplane, she saw the lights of the city sparkling underneath her, and she said to herself: "I survived. Thank God who brought me here."

When the plane landed and was taxiing to the dock, her son, Osah, asked over and over: "Are we in America? Are we in America?" And Phengta said: "Yes we are. Why don't you get some sleep?" The angel that time presented himself, of all places, in the San Francisco airport elevator as Phengta and her family made their way to the customs desk.

"I saw the electric light in the elevator, and I said, 'This is the spirit that is shining over me. Thank you for giving me life in the United States.'"

From her first days in America, Phengta took every chance to take a class, to learn a lesson, to go for a degree. In Austin, where she was sent after a three-week layover in San Francisco, she dived into nighttime "ESL"—English as a Second Language. Later she took reading and composition classes at the Austin Community College.

Daytimes were spent cleaning houses, flipping burgers at Hardee's, and waitressing. After four years, she moved with her family to St. Paul, where, after a few months, she got her first big break: a data entry job at Norwest Bank. Six months later, she was promoted to assistant supervisor, a job she held for six years. It was the only period in her life when school was put on the back burner. With Osah now going to high school, she had time only for her Norwest Bank job and, at night, more part-time waitressing at a Chinese restaurant in St. Paul.

In 1991, the family of three moved to Rochester. Two years of entrepreneurism followed, during which Phengta worked fulltime on the "Cow Bank" and her import-export business. In 1994, she became a case worker at the Intercultural Mutual Assistance Association, Rochester's main immigration service agency. And in 1998, she started working as a paralegal at Southern Minnesota Regional Legal Services.

Osah, who worked for Domaille Buick in Rochester until last year, is now a manager at Burnsville Toyota. And her husband, Paul, works at Mayo Clinic in the maintenance department.

An American citizen since 1987, Phengta remains an in-between person in many ways—not fully of one or another culture, but rather a translator between one and many cultures. That role has its good and bad points. Among the good points is a richness of life, a never-ending challenge that draws on her multiple energy sources and pays out well in terms of intellect and spirit and soul. Among the bad points is a nagging sense that she remains misunderstood in both of the worlds she inhabits.

"It's the Asian way to be strict with children, but our kids are growing up in America," Phengta says. "I tell the parents, 'You must listen to your kids. You must go to the PTA. You must give your kids a second chance. Or would you rather see them in jail?' Sometimes the parents say I am too Americanized. 'Phengta, you don't know where you came from.' I know they hate me sometimes, but do I get mad at them? No. Because I know what I'm doing. I only want to help them. One day they will understand."

Her biggest challenge goes in the other direction—educating Americans about immigrants and refugees. Phengta remains frustrated that amid their affluence and freedoms and good fortune, Americans often remain ignorant about people from foreign countries who are now their colleagues at work, fellow churchgoers, and next-door neighbors.

"Sometimes American people say 'Go home and don't take my job. Don't take my money. Don't take my land.' These people may not realize that immigrants pay taxes when they work in the U.S., just like a citizen does. So in this case, the American may not have the education.

"Also because we come from a country with different laws, we may act in a different way. We might dig up worms on somebody's front lawn, because in our country that is OK.

"So all we ask is: Americans, please remember that we are all human beings. We immigrants are not perfect. But we are willing to learn. So, Americans, please be willing to learn. Please be willing to learn a little bit about us." ●

The Best of Two Cultures

Ping Yang learned quickly how important it is to master the tiniest subtleties of a new language—lest one be horribly misunderstood. She learned the lesson from a fellow Chinese student shortly after arriving at Johns Hopkins University in Baltimore from Beijing in 1984.

"My friend was trying to tell everyone how important her adviser was," Ping said. "But she put the stress on the wrong syllable." And how. The friend was baffled by the loud guffaws that greeted her gushing announcement that "my adviser is a very, very impotent man."

From the hilarious to the tragic, from the strange to the sublime, Ping Yang, a Mayo Clinic researcher and principal of the Chinese Language School in Rochester, has experienced it all in her journey from China to America, where she is now a wife, mother, doctor and citizen. She's lived through a revolution that killed 3 million Chinese; she was one of the first Chinese students to live in the United States after 30 years of frozen relations thawed in the middle 1980s; and she was stranded in the United States, unable to return to China after the Tienanmen Square massacre in 1989.

Presently, Ping Yang divides her life between running the Chinese School, directing Mayo's world-class lung cancer research program, religious attendance at a 6 a.m. aerobics class ("it's my drug and my remedy"), and the most challenging of all, being a full-time Chinese-American mom to two teenage daughters who were born in America.

Besides notching up their own impressive achievements

in piano, ballet and learning to speak Chinese, the daughters, Hannah and Shanna, are beginning to show interest in makeup, boys, Christina Aguilera, and other American ways that baffle and sometimes frustrate their traditional Chinese mom.

Ping and her family are part of a post-war immigration trend that is profoundly changing American society and culture. The Chinese Exclusion Act of 1882 limited Chinese immigration to the United States for nearly a century. But since 1970, China, including Hong Kong and Taiwan, has sent more immigrants here than any other nation but Mexico. Almost 1.5 million Chinese have become U.S. citizens in that time, with many more living in the country on long-term visas.

As important as their sheer numbers is the effect Chinese immigrants are having on the direction and quality of American life. An unusually high percentage of Chinese immigrants are highly educated and thus quickly contribute to the highest echelons of American society.

The effect has been transformative, especially in areas such as high technology, engineering, medicine, and scientific research, areas where China's education system is traditionally strong.

While in the middle 19th century Chinese immigrants helped to build America's railroads, in the late 20th century, super-educated Chinese immigrants helped build the world's information superhighway, mostly from office cubicles in southern California. In Silicon Valley, one in four workers were born in Asia, and about a third of those are Chinese. Bringing with them strong values towards family, education, and work, Chinese Americans have raised test scores and set new standards in fields ranging from the movies (martial artist Bruce Lee) to architecture (I.M. Pei), from medical research (David Ho developed the "cocktail" strategy for fighting AIDS) to music (cellist Yo-Yo Ma).

Ping's journey to Rochester began in the early 1960s. She grew up in the rural town of Taigu, about 600 miles southwest of Beijing. The town's big employer was Shanxi University, an agricultural college, where her grandfather taught veterinary medicine. Ping was born in Beijing but was sent to Taigu because her mother and father, college students at the time, couldn't raise her, whereas her grandparents could.

As Ping tells it, being raised by her grandparents was a key to her life. She learned from them the values of traditional Chinese culture, especially the redemptive value of hard work, persistence, and sacrifice.

"In public and at school, our brains were washed by Maoism and Communism, which were our faith and our future," Ping said. "But at home my grandfather showed me and taught me about the old Chinese ways, about Chinese history, and Confucius. He read me the great Chinese literary classics like 'The Dream of the Red Chamber,' 'The Water Margin', and 'The Three Kingdoms.'"

From her grandmother, Ping learned even more.

"She taught me what a girl should be," Ping said. "She said, 'If your life is totally dependent on a man, you never know what will happen. So you need to learn all the skills you need to stand on your own—cooking, sewing, stitching, embroidering. And you need to learn your own professional skill. After you learn all that, if you want to act like a boy, that's OK.' From her I learned that you can be just as capable as a man, but people will always see you as a woman first."

Ping came face to face with history in the late 1960s when the Cultural Revolution, Mao Tse Tung's attempt to revive the communist revolutionary spirit in China, began to unfold. It was one of the bloodiest and psychologically most damaging events ever to be inflicted on a human society. Mao's idea was to elevate ordinary peasants and demote and denigrate all "bourgeois" intellectuals, professionals and, of course, anyone who had ever politically opposed him. Between 1966 and 1976, when Mao died and the Cultural Revolution ended, millions of educated Chinese were torn from their lives in the cities and sent to be "re-educated" in factories and farms in rural China.

Unfortunately, Ping's grandfather had belonged to the political party Mao crushed on his rise to power, not as a soldier or politician but simply as a party member. That was enough to put him squarely in the crosshairs of Mao's Cultural Revolution.

For having sided with Chiang Kai Shek, the other party's vanquished leader, Ping's grandfather was stripped of his professorship and sent to a pig farm to shovel manure for a living. He was frequently harassed and beaten by young Red Guard thugs as a "historical counter-revolutionary." Worst of all, he was routinely paraded in the public humiliation rituals known as "struggle sessions."

Sometimes, Ping witnessed these brutal events.

"He would be criticized by a big audience, on an evening or a weekend, at the school auditorium," she said. "He had to stand on stage with the other counter-revolutionaries. They put a dunce cap on him and a sign around his neck. He had to bend over so the sign hung from his neck.

"My heart was just broken. It was hurting so much. I was so totally confused, just 6 or 7 years old, and I had to watch this. My grandfather was such a sweet, nice guy. How could he be going through that?"

Ping didn't escape harassment herself. She was labeled a "little historical counter-revolutionary," another category of Red Guard victim, and was subjected to taunts and beatings while walking home from school.

She credits her grandmother with instilling the life philosophy that got her through that rough time and future ones. "She always told me, 'No matter what they call you, you are the same person, and heaven will not fall.' She said if you keep your eye on your own goals, you will be OK."

At age 13, Ping moved to Beijing, was reunited with her parents, and attended high school. Her test scores at graduation got her into a medical college, after which, armed with a Chinese medical degree, she took another test and, in 1984, qualified to become one of the first Chinese to visit the United States.

DOUGLAS MCGILL

During the next 12 years, she earned a master's degree in public health from Johns Hopkins University in 1985; a doctorate from Johns Hopkins in 1990; and worked as an assistant professor of medicine at the University of Pittsburgh until 1996. She moved to Rochester with her husband, Bosheng (or "Bo" as he's known to everyone), and their two daughters in 1996.

Ironically, Deng Xiaoping, the Chinese premier whose "Open Door to the West" policy made Ping's move to the United States possible, was also responsible for her staying here. Originally, Ping's plan was to return to China after she got her PhD. However, when she was ready to do that in late 1989, Deng sent the army to suppress several thousand pro-democracy activists in Tienanmen Square, killing several hundred of them. The country was plunged into chaos, and when Ping's letters seeking employment in China went unanswered, she chose to stay in the United States.

As principal of the Rochester Chinese School, Ping is able to address the imbalances she and other Chinese Americans experience between the two cultures, she said. The school, started five years ago, serves about 50 students, most of them the American-born children of Chinese-born parents. Some of the Chinese-born students are the adopted children of American-born area residents, and a sprinkling of American, Vietnamese, Cambodian, and Thai adults also attend the school.

The raison d'etre of the school is to teach the Chinese language and culture to the American-born children of Chinese parents. The parents want their children to understand their family ancestry and be able to communicate with their grandparents and other family members who still live in China.

"We want to teach the best parts of both cultures," Ping said. "By learning the Chinese language they can learn to love the best traditions and values of Chinese culture."

The school also organizes occasional parties and festivals, especially Chinese New Year's, when traditional food is served and students put on a talent show with humorous skits, an opera and poetry readings—all performed in Chinese.

Being a mom to two teenage American daughters often brings Ping into conflict with the traditional values she learned from her grandparents.

"Kids in America aren't taught that real accomplishment requires hard work and sacrifice," Ping said. "Young women want to be like Britney Spears and Christina Aguilera. It looks so fun and so easy. Of course it's hard work to succeed at what those women do, or to succeed at anything else. It's a strength of Chinese culture that it teaches those important lessons."

Ping went to Working Mother magazine (her kids had bought her a gift subscription) recently for some tips on American family life. An article about how to deal with your in-laws shocked and angered her.

"One of the tips was that if your in-laws live close by you and drop by often without notice, change your locks. Another was to break all ties with your in-laws. But what if your in-laws are poor, and they need your help? Do you just cut off ties? Can you really advance yourself in life and enjoy 'success' without thinking about and helping others, especially the people in your own family? It made me really angry, and I canceled my subscription."

Infrequently, Ping has encountered racism. When a grounded U.S. spy plane was held captive in southern China for several weeks in early 2001, vandals in Rochester knocked over mailboxes at the homes of several Asian families, including the Yangs. That reminded Ping of the harassment her family suffered during the Cultural Revolution.

Her overwhelming experience of Americans has been that "they are a genuinely warm and open and welcoming people. And there's freedom here. You can do the work that you want to do in this country."

When Ping and Bo named their daughters, they put their philosophy of "joining the best of both cultures" into action. The name Hannah, given to their first born, comes from the

Chinese phrase "Hai Na," which means "across the ocean." Shanna, born three years later, comes from the Chinese "Shan Na," which means "over the mountains." The Yangs were living then in Pittsburgh, in the foothills of the Appalachians.

A Chinese saying, "The mountains and the sea depend on each other," added another value that Ping wanted to pass on to her daughters.

"Because Bo and I grew up in a different culture from them, maybe we can't support them as strongly as our parents and our grandparents supported us," Ping said. "So they'll have to be each other's strongest support.

"I want them to be in harmony. I want them to care for each other and to support each other all their lives. Whether they are in China or in this country, Bo and I wanted them to know the meaning of their names, which is also about the meaning and purpose of their lives." ●

A Better Life for the Kids

Two distinct moments made Zakaria Gaal, a Somali immigrant who works at a Rochester law firm and is prominent in the Somali community here, decide once and for all to leave Mogadishu, where he was born and raised and worked as a lawyer. Both of those moments involved guns.

After Somalia's strongman president Siad Barre was toppled by warlords in 1991, the country quickly disintegrated. One after another social service—schools, police, hospitals, courts, public transport—had ceased to function in the country's capital, Mogadishu. Gaal decided to stay as long as he could, hoping that stability and peace would be restored. Instead, life got worse as the once-beautiful, Italian-colonial streets of Mogadishu were transformed into a bullet-holed landscape occupied by warlords and their roving gangs of thugs. The rat-a-tat of automatic machine gun fire, sometimes near and sometimes far, became a background noise of daily life.

"One day I was taking a shower, and a bullet fell right out of the ceiling," says Gaal, a slight, soft-spoken 44-year-old. "It came from a long way away, maybe from someone firing an AK47 into the air. It fell right into my hand."

That surreal moment was disconcerting. But a truly harrowing moment later clinched Gaal's decision to flee his homeland. By early 1992, he had lost several friends to stray bullets and random robbery-killings carried out by the dreaded *moryan*, machine gun-toting gangsters who chew qat, a leaf with a stimulative effect like cocaine, while preying on innocent citizens for food, sex and money.

One day in 1992 while driving in Mogadishu with a friend in the back seat, a moryan approached Gaal's car with his pistol drawn. "I didn't know it, but my friend had a gun, too, and he pulled it out," Gaal recalls. "Now I am stopped at the intersection, the moryan and my friend pointing their guns at each other, screaming they'll shoot. Finally another moryan appeared and pulled his buddy away. It was too much for me. All the time we lived under such risk. You could never tell what would happen the next day. It might be the end of your life. So I started to think, what is the best way to get out?"

A decade later, Gaal is among the 3,500 Somalis who have immigrated to southeastern Minnesota in recent years. He has thrived in Rochester since arriving in 1997. With his Somali law degree worthless, he quickly landed a job on the hard-drive assembly line at IBM to support himself, his wife Halima, and his three young children. More than two years followed of 18-hour days split between the IBM assembly line and classrooms at Rochester Community and Technical College, where he received an Associate of Arts degree in 1999.

Today, as a homeowner and legal assistant at the Klampe Delehanty & Morris law firm, Gaal has risen to a leadership role bridging the two worlds he inhabits, the predominantly Muslim Somali immigrant community and the mainly Christian native-born American community.

A Muslim who declares "my faith is my way of life," Gaal prays five times a day, putting his prayer mat down toward Mecca in his law office for a few minutes, or walking a few blocks to the Rochester Islamic Center mosque on North Broadway. Yet his leadership role in Rochester, where he works as a volunteer for the school system and for the courts on behalf of troubled children, is mostly civic and secular. For the public school system he serves on the District Integration Task Force, finding ways to assimilate immigrant children into classrooms.

As a volunteer legal guardian in Olmsted District Court proceedings, he prepares recommendations for judges sentencing young Somalis who get in trouble. And as a paralegal at Klampe Delehanty Morris, he offers pro bono personal injury, family and criminal legal aid—and lots of informal advice—to the area's Somali community. .

Indeed, a commitment to absolute neutrality in the public sphere is a paramount value for Gaal. It's one that he learned originally from his father, who was a school principal and a pro-democracy activist in the 1960s and 1970s in Mogadishu. He spent a lot of time in jail for his troubles but he never, Gaal recalls with pride, taught his children to find refuge in hate-generating identities of any kind—religious, national, or tribal. He politely but firmly declines to mention the name of the Somali clan to which, by birth but not by choice, he belongs. Clan rivalries fuel the violence that has ruined Somalia, and they sometimes complicate relations between the Somali refugees who have settled in the U.S.

"My father was liked by people in all clans because he worked to stay neutral," Gaal says. "That's what I want for myself. My clan is not important, not in Somalia and especially not in America. Here, I am an immigrant who is trying to become an American citizen." Now a permanent U.S. resident, Gaal plans to test for his American citizenship later this year.

When the exodus of Somalis began in 1991, tens of thousands of refugees poured into overflowing camps in Kenya, just across the southern border. The civil war had ruined the economy, but Gaal had saved some U.S. dollars and was able to escape by commercial airline to Nairobi. He did so carrying only a change of clothes and an envelope containing his birth and marriage certificates, his university diploma, and the worthless deed to his abandoned property in Mogadishu.

His journey to America was a matter of hope and waiting, mostly in Cairo, where he and his wife stayed with relatives, jobless, for five long years. He chose America as his goal because in 1984, he'd had a good experience as an exchange student at Boston University. "I saw so many different types of people, and I realized it's a country where you can participate in the economy, you can take part in life," he recalls. "Also I had Somali friends who were making progress in their lives here. I saw it was a country where, if you are organized and work hard and have a target, you can reach it."

A pair of twins, Mohamed and Mekaiel, were born in Cairo in 1995, putting added pressure on Gaal to create a stable home with an income. The family was existing on the goodwill of friends and relatives, with Gaal paying back by helping other immigrants with their legal problems. Year after year, he applied for the U.S. visa lottery for refugees. Then one Sunday morning, there was a knock on the door, and it was the mailman with a big white envelope. I open it up and I said 'Wow, Halima, we won the visas!'"

Gaal chose Rochester while still in Cairo. While doing legal research at the American Library one day, he picked up a copy of Money magazine. "It said Rochester was the top city in the U.S. for economic opportunity, for safety, and for raising children," Gaal recalls.

He might have stayed in Minneapolis, where his plane first landed, if it wasn't for a Rochester Direct shuttle bus driver who was friendly and made a good impression. "I sat in the front seat and I told him I was a new immigrant and that I wanted to live in Rochester," Gaal recalls. "He was a friendly guy and he told me it was a good place, a good town. He gave me his business card. He gave me good, positive information. In fact, he's the one who told me that IBM was hiring, and that became my first job."

For obvious reasons, the past year was not an easy one for dark-skinned, youngish Muslim men in the United States, including Gaal. After 9/11, he spoke at local churches, at the Rochester Islamic Center, and elsewhere to explain the basic ideas of the Islamic faith. He explains that the word Islam means "peace," and that Osama bin Laden "doesn't represent the Islamic community in the world, and he gives a bad picture of Islam." Gaal hasn't experienced serious outright racial discrimination in Rochester, he says, but he "gets calls every day" from other Somalis with such complaints.

His strategy for personally coping is the same one he uses with regard to his clan: he refuses to draw any part of his self-identity from his skin color.

"If there is an incident and you think to yourself, 'This is a racial thing,' you have to be intelligent about your emotions," he says. "You have to have self-control. You have to be able to react and respond in an appropriate way."

Coming from a country that affords zero protection to its citizens, Gaal says that no matter how bad a situation may get in the United States, he can stay confident and calm. "There is a legal system in this country," he says. "There is a Constitution. There are laws and government agencies that exist to protect your rights."

Gaal reached into his briefcase and took out a book he is reading, entitled "A White Teacher Talks About Race," by Minnesota schoolteacher Julie Landsman. The book recounts her experiences trying to understand and to serve American citizens and soon-to-be-citizens of other races whom she teaches in her classrooms.

"Color really doesn't make any difference," Gaal said. "We are all living in this nation. Americans always have to keep in mind what makes them American. One of those things is the diversity of the people."

Gaal also produced a dog-eared sheet of paper that he always keeps close by for inspiration and to share with others. It's a quote from Federal Reserve Chairman Alan Greenspan that reads in part: "We have always been a country where everybody, except for a very small few, has roots in other countries. I have always thought that we should be very carefully focused on the contribution which skilled people from abroad, and unskilled people from abroad, can contribute to this country, as they have for generation after generation."

Gaal's mother, who he helped to flee from Somalia to Cairo, and was hoping to help emigrate to the United States, died in Cairo in 2000. His father, the Somali schoolteacher, patriot and democrat, died in Mogadishu five years earlier.

"Dad spent his last cent to give his kids an education," Gaal says. "It's the only way to become self-sufficient, to get knowledge, to make progress, and to help other people. That's what I want for my kids. I'm working hard in the hope that my children will have a better life than I do now." ●

The Heroism of Hospitality

In a town that receives 1.5 million visitors annually and where one in ten citizens was born in a foreign country, it's worth spending a moment to consider the ethical practice of welcoming newcomers and strangers into our homes: hospitality.

My theory is that hospitality is the greatest of all the human virtues and the one that's most needed in today's world.

It's the greatest human virtue because it's selfless, it's touched by grace, it's humble but necessary, and it's hard. It's a kind of social glue that makes friends of potential enemies. A single dinner of sharing can sow a friendship of years and years.

It's most needed in the world today because, in a way unique among human practices, hospitality brings us into direct contact with those cultures and happenings about which we normally say "I know it's important to understand what's going on in the world, but it's hard to keep up as long as I'm living here in little ol' [fill in the name of your hometown]."

I believe that hospitality requires more courage, more determination, more imagination, and more moral commitment than does altruism, physical heroism, or any of the other more celebrated virtues.

For example, you can become a hero in a matter of minutes. If there's a baby in a burning house, your adrenalin kicks in, you go on autopilot, you save the baby, and you're a hero. You're front page stuff.

However, to be hospitable means that day in, day out, year after year after year, quietly and without gain or glory, you seek out people who are strangers and different from you, very often people who are less fortunate than you. You make the effort to get to know them and to bring them into your life. You have them over for dinner. You may struggle through long confusing conversations where it seems that neither of you understands a word.

But hopefully you share smiles and you keep at it and you develop trust, and after a while you understand a few more words, and then a few more, and then a few more.

People who are hospitable probably offer just as much to their communities as one-time heroes do. Probably much more, because hospitality to strangers and newcomers invites new attitudes, beliefs, skills, knowledge, and other treasures that can add to the spice of life and to community a survival kit.

Where are the odes and the epics to hospitality? Well, where are the odes and epics to decency and common sense? Where for that matter are the statues to hospice nurses, adoptive parents, refugee aid workers, inner city high school teachers, big brothers and sisters, Alzheimer's spouses, and the millions of other living angels who hold the world together with unsung grace?

But hospitality does have some heroes.

Christianity has the tradition of Jesus as the stranger ("I was a stranger and you took me in," Matthew 25:35) and the Good Samaritan. The great Hindu sage, Kabir, puts the mysterious figure of the "Guest" at the very center of the moral universe: "Listen, my friend, there is only one thing in the world that satisfies, and that is a meeting with the Guest." And the Golden Rule is all about hospitality.

"Hospitality," said Immanuel Kant, "signifies the right every stranger has of not being treated as an enemy in the country in which he arrives. One speaks here of a right founded upon that of the common possession of the surface of the earth."

It's logical that there are only two ways to learn about, and in so doing make a measure of peace, with the world. One is to go out into the world by literally traveling there, or by imaginatively traveling through, say, books or movies.

The other way is just the opposite—not to leave home to travel the world, but rather to invite the world into your home. In Rochester, it's no cliché that the whole world is right on our doorstep, waiting to be invited in. We could be heroes. ●

"Teacher Bill, Do You Like Beer?"

Bill Adler, who trains health inspectors for the Minnesota Department of Health in Rochester, just got back from a ten-month visit to China.

He's got a sports bag filled with memorabilia from his trip —knick-knacks bought at curiosity shops, bigger items like a portable hanging scale that Chinese use to weigh vegetables at the market, and above all, photographs.

Hundreds and hundreds of photographs. In many of them, Bill, who taught English to students at Hunan University in the south-central city of Changsha, stands surrounded by Chinese students and neighbors, all of them beaming widely as they surround him, a treasured American friend.

Other photographs show oddities of China today with captions in Bill's neat handwriting. A picture of a busy downtown intersection with a red traffic light hanging over it is annotated with "Everybody drives through red lights in China." Another picture shows a spanking new seven-story building with the words "Women's dorm, no elevators."

"I'd go back in a heartbeat," said Bill, who has worked for 26 years as a health inspector here. He started taking Chinese language lessons in town after mainland Chinese immigrants started opening new restaurants and he couldn't communicate with them.

"It's vital to know the culture of the businesses we regulate," Bill said. "That's what the language lessons were about. They introduced me to a lot of the culture I wouldn't have understood otherwise. Only then could I start to understand the problems they were having, and start working with them."

At the Saturday morning school of the Rochester Chinese Culture Association, Bill sat in classes with the six-and seven-year-old children of Chinese immigrants who came to Rochester to work at Mayo and IBM.

He started a company called Safe Foods in Different Languages, and published a Chinese-language guide to safe food practices. But still something was missing. "I needed to go deeper," he said. Friends at the Chinese school lined him up with Hunan University, and off he went.

From last September through June of this year, he taught English to 48 Chinese college students while living in a spartan campus apartment, in a building with chronic plumbing problems, in a city where the sun is almost never seen thanks to the heat haze, construction dust, and air pollution.

He loved every minute of it.

"It is amazing to see China change," he said. "It is struggling and modernizing. My students were so eager and grateful and they worked so hard. I felt that what I did every day was truly valued, and that is a real opiate. That, and the very close friendships I made, make me want to go back."

A few conversations he had with students still stick with him.

"In one class I asked 'If you could be anything for 24 hours, what would you want to be?" And one female student said 'Blind.' 'Why?' I asked, and she said 'Adversity brings change and I want to start the process.'"

"Isn't that incredible?" Adler recalls today.

Another time a young man asked him, "Teacher Bill, do you like beer?"

"I said 'Yes,' and he said 'You're fat.' Well at first I was taken aback, and I didn't know what to feel. But then I realized he was just trying to learn English. Those were the few words he knew and he used them. So it was okay. I was so happy he had the trust in me to open up and be that direct."

Now isn't *that* incredible? Isn't that a pretty deep story about learning tolerance and patience and understanding, about rising above surface appearances that might easily engender conflict and defensiveness?

That's why I think of Bill Adler, and other Americans who put their comfortable lives here on hold for a little while, as modern explorers, contemporary Columbuses.

They come back with a treasure called wisdom. It's more valuable than anything material, like antiques or ancient art or any tourist treasure, because it's a key to human relationships and harmony across great divides.

"There was a place called English Corner on campus where kids came each weekend to practice their English," Adler said. "They would crowd around. Some teachers did it once or twice and then quit, because the students always asked the same questions like 'What's your name?' and 'Where are you from?' They got bored, and at first I did too."

"But then I realized 'Hey, English Corner is not for me, it's for them. They ask those questions because they need the repetition to learn. So I went back, and after that, everything got better. I started asking them questions too, simple ones, and they started answering. And I started to make friends."

That's the kind of moral turning point it would be great to see repeated at all levels of society, from America's reconstruction effort in Iraq, to the way our own community welcomes our new citizens who speak foreign tongues. Thanks, Bill. ●

Teaching Beyond Arrogance

Jerry Hrabe starts his high school geography class at Lourdes every year by giving three tests—the T-shirt test, the newspaper test, and the company test.

For the T-shirt test, students must examine every T-shirt in their homes and note down the countries where they were made. Then, moving through each room in the house, they're assigned to turn over every serving dish, peek behind every computer, and take notes on every pillow and stuffed toy and other object made in a foreign country and tally the results.

The newspaper test does the same thing with the day's paper —students make a note of every foreign influence in every local story. A John Marshall basketball star from Sudan? That counts. An article noting that Thailand, like southern Minnesota, is struggling with a methamphetamine epidemic? You bet. Job outsourcing, Asian bird flu, SARS, WMDs, deployments to Iraq? Check, check, check, check, check.

The company test is the most demanding. Students go to local companies (Mayo Clinic and IBM not allowed) and interview the owners, asking them for total foreign sales, component parts they buy from abroad, specialized positions they've hired from abroad, and low-wage jobs they've sent abroad.

The final result of all three tests combined? The creation of a kind of Global Interdependence Index (my phrase) for Rochester—a rough measure of just how interconnected our town is to the rest of the world, and just how dependent it is economically, culturally, and for physical security.

"If you took away foreign products and personal connections, many Rochester companies would simply fold," Hrabe said. "It's not just the foreign restaurants and grocery stores, either. The big grocery stores, the Hyvees, would have to close too. So would several local technology companies working in computer parts and fiber optics."

Not to mention that without our foreign-made clothing we'd be mighty cold in the winter. And if every "Made in China" item magically disappeared we'd be late to work (no alarm clock), unhygienic (no toothbrush), grumpy (no electric coffee grinder), and out of touch (no telephone).

"I try to teach a philosophy of life," said Hrabe, whose schoolroom is hung with art and crafts and maps of the world. "We need to get past the American arrogance that we are the most important people in the world. We have a lot to learn from other countries and other people."

A native of Rochester (and a graduate of Lourdes), in his early 20's Hrabe had never traveled further than to his father's home in Pukwana, South Dakota, a dot on the map where I-90 crosses the Missouri River.

He signed up for two years in the Peace Corps, which he spent in Kota Kinabalu, the capital of Malaysia's Sabah province, next to Borneo.

"I lived with them, sat down with them for two years, ate their food," he recalls. "I played ball with them. I became enmeshed in their lives, which is a totally different thing from being a tourist for a week or two. I learned that 'they' aren't any different from 'us.' Internally, there's no difference. It made me much more tolerant at an early age of people of other ethnicities."

The Peace Corps years set his course for life. Back in Minnesota he attended graduate school in history and in 1969 joined the Lourdes staff, where he's taught geography and history ever since. In recent years, he and a colleague have organized annual trips abroad for students and parents—jam-packed 10-day teaching tours through China, Spain, Europe, and Greece.

This year Hrabe's class is raising money to help farmers in developing nations buy livestock such as chickens ($20 each), goats ($50), sheep ($150), and heifers ($500). The idea is that livestock provide a regular source of food, relieving hunger while affecting the environment minimally.

Hrabe encourages students to get involved in the Channel One Food Bank and Community Food Response, two welfare services in Rochester. He directs them to a web site where, thanks to a roster of commercial sponsors, one click of the mouse pays for a cup of staple food added to giant aid deliveries sent to more than 25 developing countries.

"I tell my students 'You don't have to spend money. You can spend time. You can volunteer. You can write your Congressman.' I'm trying to impart that even as students they have some responsibility, and also some wherewithal, to do something to improve the world." ●

Little Johnny on the Top of the World

Well, I'll be darned. Johnny Fleming, the pudgy little boy who hung around our house when we were kids, has become one of the most powerful businessmen in the world.

A Wal-Mart press release tells the story: "Wal-Mart stores, Inc. today announced the promotion of John Fleming, 46, to Chief Marketing Officer for the company."

John was my kid brother's best friend, one of a tight gang of classmates who hung together from elementary through high school carousing, bragging, planning wild exploits, telling stories, and generally kicking up teenage dust.

Now little Johnny runs the global marketing and advertising efforts of the world's largest corporation with 1.7 million employees, working at 5,170 stores in nine countries, that last year sold $285 billion worth of stuff.

That's more than eight times the size of Microsoft in sales. If Wal-Mart were a country it would rank in size just behind Saudi Arabia, and far ahead of Sweden, Greece, Switzerland, and Austria.

John, wherever you are, my sincere congratulations.

We dropped out of touch for a few decades, but word always came through of your rise in retail from Dayton's to Target to Walmart.com (where you were president and CEO), and now to this job where, according to your press release, you will run all of Wal-Mart's marketing, advertising, and consumer communications worldwide.

It's that last word, *worldwide*, that catches my attention the most, John, and it's why I'm writting to you today.

When we were growing up together here in Rochester, where I still live, our world was bounded by 6th Avenue (the street we both lived on); by the Soldiers Field Golf Course where we played golf by day and furtively collected lost golf balls from the water traps by night; by Edison Elementary School and Mayo High School; and by the various countryside spots we picked for our Friday night beer bash "keggers."

These were the four corners of our world—our north, east, west, and south.

But now, John, you're at the tip-top level of a company with operations in China, Brazil, Germany, England, Mexico, Canada, England, South Korea, Argentina, and Puerto Rico. In some of these places, like England, War-Mart is the largest company in the country.

In every country you operate, Wal-Mart is, de facto, intimately involved with that country's economy, politics, and culture.

I saw you on CNN the other day, John, and you looked spiff in your wet-look hairstyle and shiny gold tie. You looked relaxed and confident and were quick with the latest Wal-Mart growth numbers and marketing spiels.

But dude, some friendly advice: You're *beyond* all that now. You need to be. You've always thought of yourself as a businessman, and you're a damn good one, but for this new job you need to grow and change more than ever before.

You're on the world stage now, Johnny boy. You're a leader of men and women in many countries you have never visited, in whose homes you have never shared a meal, whose languages you don't speak. You need to be humble.

Even your great management skills aren't good enough any more to excel in your new job. You've got to be a diplomat now, and a global citizen.

I saw an interview recently with one of your new colleagues in the top tier at Wal-Mart, in charge of international and corporate affairs. The interviewer asked the executive whether

Wal-Mart's race-to-the-bottom pricing strategy exacts an overall cost to the world that's simply not worth it.

The Wal-Mart man kissed the question off. "This question almost belongs to a Nobel Prize-winning laureate in economics, rather than an executive from Wal-Mart," he said. "It's an issue that's far greater than Wal-Mart."

I hope you do better than this guy, John.

It'll be hard. You'll be pressured a million times now to give this same answer—"it's a bigger question than Wal-Mart" —whenever a journalist asks about Wal-Mart's impact on the world.

But what a cowardly cop out that answer is. Since when was it okay for anyone to willfully ignore the impact he or she has on the world around him—much less for the world's largest company to do it? To shuck off this vital moral question to the "experts?"

It's the Golden Rule, man.

To not deeply ask yourself about Wal-Mart's impact on the world, especially now as you take on these awesome responsibilities, John, would be a missed opportunity at the least. At the worst, it would be like the auto executives who still say that global warming is a mere "scientific issue."

Or, you'd become like the cigarette executives who for decades argued that smokers' health was a "medical issue."

Little Johnny Fleming from 6th Avenue in Rochester would never have said such things. I hope the new John, sitting on top of the world, won't either. ●

The Flag Lady of Rochester

Gwen Vilen, a nurse at Mayo Clinic, flew the American flag from her front porch on the Labor Day holiday. But on a separate 25-foot-flagpole standing smack in her front yard she hoisted another flag as well—the red, white, and blue horizontal cross of the flag of Norway.

"So many Minnesotans and Midwesterners come from Norway," Vilen explained. "And if ever there was a hardworking people with a strong work ethic, it's the Norwegians. It fits right into Labor Day."

Vilen's neighbors in southeast Rochester glance up each morning to see which flag from around the globe is flying that day. They've seen plenty, such as the Indian flag on August 15 for India's Independence Day; the Spanish flag on August 19 to mark the Spanish poet Federico Garcia Lorca's death; and the Canadian flag on July 1 for Canada Day, in honor of Canada's founding as a nation.

Vilen's passion and hobby as a global citizen is to fly the flag of every nation in the world on their national holidays, and on days when simple respect for our fellow human beings is due. Yesterday, she raised the Russian flag in remembrance of the slaughtered children of Beslan.

"I've always been interested in what's going on in the world, in history and politics," Vilen said. Her interest was bookish until last spring, when the U.S. invaded Iraq and she found herself overwhelmed with feelings of "alarm and sadness. I was especially shocked by our unilateral decision to go it alone and to ignore so many of our allies."

A Vietnam War protester, Vilen's life after the 1960's turned to studying to become a nurse, then working as a nurse and being a mother. After the Iraq War started, Vilen decided to make her first political protest since those long-ago days by visiting the Herold Flag shop on Second Street, buying the blue-and-white flag of the United Nations, and hoisting it over her home.

It flew there for more than a year. "The UN is a forum for nations to come together to talk," she said. "It's a place to get things on the table and talk about them, even if they are offensive. It's our obligation to talk about our problems peacefully to resolve them, rather than go to war."

In May, she bought and planted the 25-foot flagpole in her front yard and started the regular rotation of flags of the world. The response was immediate and thus far positive—even when she flew the flag of Iraq, which drew not a single protest or raised eyebrow.

"We are in that country now, and we say we've liberated it, so Iraq is now an ally," Vilen explains. "We shouldn't hesitate to fly their flag, any more than we'd hesitate to fly the flag of any of our nation's allies."

When she flew the Saudi flag, the result was even more wondrous. Christine Livingston-Alzarqa and her husband, Saleh Alzarqa, a Saudi, were moving to Rochester and looking for a good neighborhood to live, when by pure chance they noticed the Saudi flag in Vilen's front yard. "We felt like it would be a welcoming neighborhood," Christine said.

They rented the home directly across the street from Vilen's, and since then the two women have become best friends.

"It's hard to put into words my feelings for Gwen," Christine said. "Arabs are not real popular in the U.S. right now, and we were concerned about moving here. To see someone so courageous is really inspiring."

Yet Vilen says she acts not out of courage but self-interest. Many people, understandably, say they know the world is full of terrible problems and would like to help, but are busy with their lives and just don't know how.

How, I asked Vilen, had she been able to bypass this rationalization and find so active a channel for her compassion?

"It brings so many interesting people into my life," she answered. "So I feel a kind of fullness. As a nurse, you know, you see so many people who are so lonely, so afraid, and so alone. It's the result of a society that emphasizes individualism. I like to focus on community.

"Also, every flag is beautiful," she added. "I just love the way they look when they fly."

Learning from Strangers

So now all swarthy young men wearing turbans are the spitting image of evil. This is as basic a problem as how white people look at blacks and what they feel when they do.

It's a question of how we relate to strangers, to the exotic and vaguely threatening other.

We can make enemies of potential friends if we let our imaginations run wild. "All strangers and beggars are from Zeus," Homer said. In other words, the Gods appear among us mortals in disguise, and it's the strangest-looking among us who bring the precious gift of wisdom.

Strangers are even Gods, possibly. It's a very consistent message in the Jewish, Christian, Arab, and Buddhist wisdom literature: the stranger is the savior. The dusty, smelly, crippled, begging stranger bears celestial truth.

In the Christian story, God came to earth as a scruffy prophet wandering the desert. Arabs revere the principle of hospitality to strangers one meets in the desert, and Buddhists teach one route to enlightenment is to regard every person one meets along life's journey as the Buddha.

"Be not forgetful to entertain strangers, for thereby some have entertained angels unawares," the writer of Hebrews advises.

Angels would be good to meet, but I find another Bible passage even more helpful on the subject of strangers. King David cries out in Chronicles: "We are aliens and strangers in Your sight, as were all our forefathers; and our days on earth are like a shadow, without hope."

This makes it clear that our deepest fears originate not in

strangers, but within ourselves. What makes us quail is not Al Capone with a baseball bat, or Bin Laden with an M-16. It's the fear that our lives are without meaning or hope. That we ourselves are strangers in the world and in our own homes, strangers to our own husbands and wives and children, and strangers even to ourselves.

What would it be like to follow the instruction of the wisdom writings and open the door to the stranger? There are two answers, one religious and one secular.

The religious answer we've already covered: the stranger is God, and the reward is everlasting life. For others, such as me, there are the more down-to-earth rewards of simple hospitality that Francis Bacon, in his essay on Goodness, described: "If a man be gracious and courteous to strangers, it shows he is a citizen of the world; and that his heart is no island cut off from other lands, but a continent that joins them. If he easily pardons and remits offences, it shows that his mind is planted above injuries, so that he cannot be shot."

By "easy pardons" Bacon is not suggesting we pardon mass killers. Rather, he endorses the habit of forgiveness for the practical returns it brings. By hospitality we befriend others before they become our enemies. Swarthy or dusty or poor —we must let them in. We may have qualms about inviting strangers in for dinner, but we've got to risk it because the alternatives are even riskier.

What do the Greeks, the Bible, Buddha, Francis Bacon, and common sense teach on this topic?

That hospitality is a critical part of homeland security.

That learning from strangers makes us global citizens, lifts us above self-pity, and saves us from being shot. ●

A Red Stain of Bewitching Beauty

Amber Nicosia's idea of a perfect Saturday night is to invite over two or three of her girlfriends, mix a greenish powder with some lemon juice, black tea, and eucalyptus oil, and to paint the resulting mud on each others' bodies in psychedelic sunbursts, creeping vines, intricate labyrinths, paisley patterns, geckoes, stars, moons, and butterflies.

"It's a bonding thing," says Nicosia, a recent graduate of the Rochester Technical and Community College. "The designs are beautiful, but the important thing is being together."

This ritual, odd as it may sound, is increasingly popular in southeastern Minnesota, where hundreds of women have taken up the ancient art of *mehndi*, or henna body painting.

Once practiced only at Indian weddings and festivals, and during Muslim celebrations such as Eid, mehndi in our community is rapidly being adapted into such distinctive American festivals as Halloween, New Year's Day, the Fourth of July, and the Olmsted County Fair, which had a bustling mehndi booth this year.

There is no more ardent a group of new henna practitioners than teenage girls.

Carly Blazing, an eighth grader at Kellogg, has had several menhdi done by friends over the years. "It's cool, it's fun," she says. "It's like a tattoo but it's not permanent, if your Mom won't let you get a tattoo."

Carly's mom, Vicki Blazing, has had a couple of henna paintings done on herself, both for beauty and meaning. "It's not just a tattoo," she says. "It marks an event with some symbolism."

The orange-red stain of the henna paintings stays on the skin for two to four weeks, depending on how much was initially applied and how much you shower or wash your hands. The henna paste is applied with a tiny "carrot bag," like a frosting bag, and is worn until it dries and flakes off.

"It looks like goose poop when you first put it on," explains Vinisha Bhatia, a Century High School student who immigrated to Rochester from India four years ago and made many of her new friends in Rochester by painting them with henna.

The hypnotic spell cast by henna designs is legendary. There is archeological evidence of henna at Neolithic sites, circa 9,000 B.C., and paintings on pottery, fresco, fabric, and paper from virtually all of the ancient Middle Eastern, northern African, and Indian civilizations show elaborate henna designs used by women at weddings and festivals.

Super-fine henna patterns worn by Indian women at weddings, and the bolder floral designs of Arabic mehndi, are the two most popular mehndi styles even to this day.

But Minnesota henna artists like Lisa O'Hanlon, who does dozens of henna paintings each week for customers at Ananke Designs in Rochester, are rapidly morphing those two traditional forms into new directions with New Age moons and suns, and their own personal designs.

O'Hanlon's average customer is a 45-year-old local woman with a last name like Johnson, Smith, or Miller, she says. They often come in with girlfriends, or sometimes with a sister or daughter, to have the designs done together. The pain management unit at the Mayo Clinic sometimes sends customers who want a symbol representing "Courage" or "Patience" painted on. Other women buy kits to use at henna parties.

"Henna parties are like candle parties or Tupperware parties only more so," O'Hanlon says. "At a henna party you take off your shirt and sit there in your bra, getting stuff drawn on you by your best friends. It's very personal and it can be a very spiritual thing."

Very un-guy like, for sure. Most men don't have the patience for henna, O'Hanlon says. They prefer the permanent tattoos with the painful but once-and-it's-over rite of passage application. Or they want only "bitchin'" henna designs, like barbed wire around the biceps, which she refuses to do.

In the history of henna, it was ever thus. In my research, I could find only one solid reference to men using henna painting. That was Indian warriors who dipped their hands in henna before they went off to war—as a reminder of their wives who were waiting for them back home.

On her web site, O'Hanlon lists anniversaries, births, and birthdays as other times when customers like to stain themselves in red. She quotes a writer, Catherine Cartwright Jones, who says that women are attracted to henna "to appreciate each other's newness, awe, experience, terror, sexuality, and blood-borne responsibility for the continuation of humanity."

O'Hanlon states her own goals as a henna artist in bluntly Midwestern terms: "I want you to get a dark and exciting stain every time!" ●

Minnesota's Mensch

The indispensable Elmer L. Andersen played many roles during his long lifetime—traveling furniture salesman, liberal Republican, glue-company tycoon, dairy farmer, Minnesota State Senator, Minnesota Governor, serious book collector, and newspaper executive, to name just a few.

But if he were to choose just one name for himself—the role that he was proudest of and tried hardest to be—I bet he'd go with global citizen.

He often said that of all the many honors he received, he was proudest of a plaque that named him as a "mensch," the Hebrew word for useful citizen.

"That's what I've always wanted to be, an honorable, useful citizen," he wrote in his autobiography, *A Man's Reach*.

There are a hundred ways you could point to Andersen's undying passion not only for the people of Minnesota, but the people of the world.

As the son of immigrants from Norway and Sweden, he naturally saw no essential distinction between Americans and people of other nationalities, while at the same time seeing America as a blessed land of opportunity.

He said he loved the iron workers of northern Minnesota because he shared the immigrant heritage with them. "I understood why they were the way they were. I knew what it was like to work in a factory. I shared their values—family, hard work, education, each succeeding generation getting ahead."

When he scrambled up from traveling salesman to own his own company, H.B. Fuller, which he built into a multinational firm, he often stressed the potential for business to push government towards global cooperation.

"Industry has a wonderful opportunity to show leadership and use its muscle to bring the United States into close alliance with the world community," he wrote. He argued tirelessly for closer American involvement in the United Nations, even at the cost of some sovereign control.

"I liken the necessity of risking some of our sovereignty through U.N. participation to the risk the thirteen original American states faced as they formed a new nation," he wrote in *I Trust to be Believed*, a book published earlier this year.

When the constitution replaced state independence with federalism, "that was a big change for the people at the time, just as it's a big change now to think in world terms. But it's absolutely vital, and the sooner we get to it, the better."

Anderson's global citizenship was part of his philosophy of life. He found interest and beauty everywhere. "Aging is a wonderful thing," he wrote. "It is an extension of life." For him, beauty was beauty, joy was joy, a good idea was a good idea, no matter how humble or ordinary or for that matter how exotic or foreign its country of origin. He was open to life in all directions.

"The Quakers have a wonderful trait," this Lutheran wrote. "They never vote on anything. When people feel that their point of view is outside the consensus and a consensus is forming, they 'stand aside.' That is such a lovely expression: to stand aside. Let life go on. Let a person live his or her personal belief, without making an issue of it."

At a farm in Sweden, "I remember their strawberry patch. They cared for those strawberries as if every one was precious. Those Swedish farmers lived modestly, yet richly. Compared to them, we ricochet through life. The speed of American life and the gulping of experiences can be an unfortunate thing. Too much of life is gone before it is really lived."

Is it possible that so gentle a soul, one so subtly and joyously attuned to life, could ever have been our Governor, could have mastered the rough and tumble of politics, could have risen to the top of the corporate ladder?

He did. And perhaps his lesson to us therefore is that idealism is not so fragile, nor hope so naïve, as we may all think in these cynical times. Maybe one lesson we can take from Elmer Andersen is that optimism is not unrealistic, but in fact is inevitable given a true openness to life.

"Many years of living have given me a sense of confidence about the future," he wrote. "No matter how bad things seem to be on some front, they will change, usually for the better.

"A wonderful new century is dawned, and I am glad to be among those who greet it," he wrote in 2000. "There is so much to live for."

All the energy this state will ever need is encapsulated in those words. And all the love, too. Thank you, Elmer L. Andersen, our Governor, our mensch. ●

Whole Child, Whole World

At the Rochester Montessori School on Sunday, I discovered a secret to establishing peace on earth and goodwill among all men and women.

But first, a funny story.

Ronice Donovan, a teacher at the Montessori school, was telling me about an incident in one of her classes for children ages 3 to 6. The kids had cracked open a sand dollar and a star-shaped "dove of peace" had fallen out.

"What's that?" asked one little boy.

"That's God!" the other children in class all shouted.

"What is God?" the little boy asked, puzzled.

"God made everything!" the other children cried. "Don't you know? He made everything in the world!"

"Did he make the sky?" the little boy asked.

"Yes!"

"Did he make the earth?"

"Yes! Yes! And he made the ocean and the whales and everything!"

"The little boy thought about that for a while, then looked up at Ronice and said 'God must have a very big desk.'"

Maria Montessori was an Italian physician, psychologist and educator who thought that if adults could only learn to understand and respect the world of the child—a land as strange and faraway as Asia, Africa or the Middle East—then adults would learn something so essential about themselves that they might immediately see the futility of violence and stop war altogether.

The local Montessori school, started in 1968, has 160 students, a third of whom were born abroad or are the children of immigrant parents. The school is one of about 7,000 Montessori schools around the United States.

The school's annual Multicultural Day Celebration was Sunday. The auditorium was hung with brightly-colored "papel picata," or Mexican cut-paper decorations. In the back, a buffet groaned with Chinese dumplings, British scones, Korean kimchee (spicy pickled cabbage), Mexican tortillas, Indian bajji (fried potato slices dipped in lentil flour), and a yummy Swiss pastry, Zuercher Pfarrhaustorte ("Hey, try this," people called it).

On stage, the children sang and danced to a medley of folk tunes from 14 countries.

Moms and dads paced with their digital cameras, many of them dressed in traditional Indian saris, Indonesian sarongs, German lederhosen and dirndls, and Chinese silk cheongsam.

I asked some parents what the school's four-word vision statement—"Whole Child, Whole World"—meant to them.

"It means creating in these children a future that is based on the ideals of humanity versus corporate greed and insensitivity," said Stephanie Peterson, who has two daughters at the school.

"The school teaches how to appreciate the earth, and other people, and how to build on personal relationships," Janine Kamath said. Her husband, Patrick, added that "our two daughters knew there was an Asia and an Africa even before they could write or read. At age 5 or 6, that's more important."

To Yvonne Lee, a nurse with two kids at the school, the motto means "loving and caring." And to Jeff Piepho, the school's board president, it means "to make the children complete in themselves, and therefore prepared for the whole world."

"With all the doctors, lawyers and brainy people in the world, there is still something obviously awry," said Patrick Sheedy, the school's director. "Some common sense is missing, some knowledge about how to live with one another in a healthy community."

That's why the school starts a child's education not with reading and writing, Sheedy said, but rather with lessons on "grace and courtesy." These include lessons in "opening and shutting a door quietly, how to interrupt politely, and how to move around a classroom with care."

These are the very skills of peace, Ronice Donovan said.

"We work with the subtleties of what it means to be at peace," she said. "If children are whole from the inside out, with a belief system constructed from family and community, they will change the world and be peacekeepers."

One of Maria Montessori's books, "The Secret of Childhood," contains a passage that echoes Donovan's views and seems wise in an ultimate way.

"Adults have not understood children or adolescents, and they are, as a consequence, in continual conflict with them," Montessori wrote. "The adult must find within himself the still unknown error that prevents him from seeing the child as he is."

That last sentence, in case you missed it, is the secret to world peace. Achieve it, Maria Montessori said, peace will follow in the world. From the peace between parent and child will follow the peace between child and child, and man and man, and nation and nation.

At the Rochester Montessori School, they don't talk about teaching. They talk about creating an environment where adults stand back in order to allow children to be exactly as they were on the day they were born.

Which is a human being at peace inside. ●

Rainbows from Tibet

Every morning in a small Rochester apartment, Rinzin and Dadon, recent immigrants from Tibet, rise and fill seven small silver bowls with water, light some sticks of incense, and pray to heal the whole earth.

"We ask God to fill the world so everyone has enough to eat and drink and will not suffer," Rinzin explained. Both he and his wife have only one name, following Tibetan tradition. "We ask for compassion for every living being, including humans and animals, insects and trees. We say 'How happy I am, I want every being to be happy.'"

In the evening, the water is sprinkled over flowers in the front yard and the night prayers begin. "We say 'God, if I did anything bad towards other beings today, forgive me,'" Rinzin says. "Our religion is compassion. The Dalai Lama says that what makes us happy is to help others before we help ourselves, and to pray for others before we pray for ourselves."

It is something of a paradox that Rinzin and Dadon's own lives have seen a lot of suffering. Their life in Rochester, now that both are in their late 60's, is the latest step in an epic journey through one of the great historical events of the 20th century—the invasion and brutal subjugation of Tibet by China.

The invasion began in 1950 and by 1959, the Dalai Lama himself was driven into exile, being forced to walk through the Himalayan mountains to safety. Some 80,000 Tibetans followed him on that journey, Rinzin and Dadon being two of them. They were newlyweds then, with one child.

Rinzin had been a herder, living in a tent on the high north-

195

ern Tibetan plateau, tending 1,000 sheep, 400 yak, and 50 horses. As the Chinese tightened their grip on Tibet, more than 6,000 monasteries were destroyed, and ordinary herders were executed for owning an image of the Dalai Lama.

"We would be killed if we were caught praying," Rinzin recalls. "We wanted to be free to practice our religion. If the Dalai Lama is leaving for India, we thought it would be a good idea to follow him."

The perilous trek through the Himalayas killed many hundreds from cold and exposure. In Rinzin and Dadon's traveling group of 20, four died.

"It was colder than Minnesota," Rinzin said. "Our shoes fell apart and we had to tear our clothes and use the rags to protect our feet. We had no food and begged from villagers along the way."

Dadon's eyes brimmed with tears that spilled over as she recalled those days. "The worst part was having to leave my father behind," she said. "I wasn't able to find him to say good-bye. I remember like it was yesterday."

After walking for months they reached Kathmandu, Nepal. There they stayed until the Dalai Lama arranged, with help from Indian Prime Minister Jawaharlal Nehru, for the 80,000 Tibetan refugees to resettle in northern India. In return, the refugees promised to help India build the narrow, harrowing mountain road connecting India to Nepal—which Rinzin did for the next eight years.

Today, Rinzin and Dadon live with their daughter, Sherab, who won a visa lottery to immigrate to the U.S. in the early 1990s. A single mother, she helps supports her son, her parents and herself on a single income.

"My hope is to go back to see my home village once before I die," Rinzin says. But that is unlikely as long as the Chinese continue to dominate Tibet, which they now are culturally subjugating by the resettlement of tens of thousands of ethnic Han Chinese in Tibet.

Rinzin and Dadon brighten when the talk returns to prayer.

Rinzin chants "Om Mani Padme Hum" as he fingers prayer beads, once for each bead, 108 beads in all. It is the ancient "Jewel in the Lotus" mantra of Tibetan Buddhism, with each of the six spoken syllables said to contain the vibrations needed to purify the soul of pride, jealousy, desire, prejudice, possessiveness, and aggression.

Meanwhile Dadon, her head bowed, also is chanting "Om Mani Padme Hum" as she rhythmically spins a small silver "mani," a prayer wheel that contains within it a tightly-packed scroll of prayers asking for God's compassion to reach all beings in the world.

One is meant to see rainbows of energy thrown from the prayer wheel as it spins around, the bright colors spraying down upon the whole globe as healing rain. ●

No Jobs. No Money. No Life.

Even today, Muharem Dedic wonders what happened to Joni.

Dedic, a slim young man with jet black hair and a wide smile, runs the day-to-day business at the Sanus Bosnian Restaurant, which opened the other day in Rochester in the Broadway Commons shopping area.

The restaurant is a family business with Dedic's father, Smajil, a former grocery store and restaurant owner in Bosnia, doing the business strategy and bookkeeping; his mother, Sahiz, holding down the home front; and his two younger sisters, Murahema and Murisa, doing the daily shopping and the waitressing, the sweeping and cleaning and everything else.

Joni was the beloved pet dog they had to leave behind in 1992 when, warned by a Serbian neighbor that they must all leave within a day or be killed, the entire Dedic family joined a tractor caravan out of town with several thousand other Bosnian Muslims fleeing for their lives.

Besides Joni, the Dedic's were forced to abandon the grocery store and the restaurant the family had spent several decades building; their two-story home and every chair, bed, table, and appliance in it; nearly all the family photographs and albums and memorabilia and legal papers; their two cars; a cow; and several chickens and cats. With the family's bank accounts frozen on account of the war, they were also penniless.

"One day two guys came to their house and simply said 'Just leave. If you don't you will be killed,'" Dedic remembers. He was 11 at the time. Twenty other families in the Dedic's extended family joined them in the exodus.

It was the beginning of what came to be known as "ethnic cleansing"—the Yugoslav dictator Slobodan Milosevic's modern-day version of Hitler's "final solution." Milosevic saw his dream of a Greater Serbia as thwarted by independence-seeking and territories and republics like Bosnia, Croatia, and Kosovo. Above all, Milosevic saw Bosnian Muslims standing in his way.

His sick answer was to try to kill them all. His paramilitaries swooped across Muslim territories conducting sieges of entire cities and, in countrified areas, house-to-house arson and shelling and executions of Muslims.

More than 200,000 were killed from 1992 to 1995, and more than two million refugees, the Dedic family among them, were violently uprooted.

After long journeys through safe houses, relatives' homes, United Nations shelters and refugee camps across Europe, about 100,000 Bosnian refugees resettled in the United States, according to the 2000 Census. Of these, more than 2,000 came to Minnesota and more than 300 to Olmsted County.

The Dedic family journey traced a giant Zorro-like "Z" across Europe.

Starting from their home town Sanski Most (the Sanus Hotel there is the namesake of their restaurant), the family traveled by tractor, bus, car, animal freight car and on foot through the Bosnian towns of Bosanski Novi, Banja Luka, Doboi, and Brcko; then to the Croation towns of Slavonski Brod, Pozega, and Zagreb; then to a German military base on the Netherland border with the unlikely name of Shopping; and finally to the German city of Gelsenkirchen, where they spent the five years living as refugees.

In 1997, with the war in Bosnia over, the Dedic family returned to Sanski Most to try to start life anew. But they couldn't return to their old home which had been ransacked and destroyed by fire.

The city's economy was equally ruined. Within months, the family's savings from several years of work in Germany was gone.

"There were no jobs, and therefore no money, no life," Muharen said. An uncle who had fled Bosnia for Arlington, Texas, and then had moved to Rochester, told them that the Minnesota winters were cold but the economy was warm. So Rochester it was. The family arrived in 1999.

Since then everyone in the family has worked constantly, even as the children attended Century and John Marshall high schools. The jobs haven't been glamorous—mostly hotel cleaning and grocery store stacking on the overnight shift.

But they are jobs, and after four years, they've now led to the restaurant.

"Dobru Dosli u Sanus" says the chalkboard sign in front. "Welcome to the Sanus Restaurant." Inside, the menu features shish kebabs, raznjici (veal and onion in pita bread), chevapchicki (seasoned ground beef patties), palachinke (jelly crepes), and strong Bosnian coffee.

Muharen spoke calmly about all of the terrors his family has lived through, becoming emotional only once. That was when he talked about his father.

"He's my life, he's my everything," Muharen said. "Through these years, there was no life without him. Whatever we needed, no matter how hard it was for him, we just asked and he said 'Here.' I am so proud of my dad.

"He really knows how to spend $100. A lot of people, they can spend it in one minute and get nothing. He can make money go a long, long way.

"My dad owned a grocery store in Sanski Most, which was very popular. Today he is stacking at night at Hyvee South. When you see him there at night, you see he is not happy. All of his children see that. We would like life to be easier for him and for our Mom. So we will work hard." ●

Heirlooms for Africa

Sheiknor Qassim, who spins connecting webs between Rochester and Africa via art and finance, is spinning his newest webs with boxes of books.

Really big boxes, containing 25,000 books apiece.

After moving to Rochester from Somalia in 1994, Qassim led an effort to lobby Fannie Mae, the mortgage lender, to offer loans to Muslim immigrants whose religion prohibits the paying of interest. The result was the Fannie Mae Islamic Initiative, which structures mortgages that do not technically include interest payments but still allow new immigrants to buy homes.

Qassim's Kilimanjaro Gallery, in the Kahler Hotel Arcade from 2000 to 2002, displayed carved African masks, textiles, ritual objects, and voluptuous fertility sculptures.

His newest project, launched in collaboration with the St. Paul-based "Books for Africa," is to send 100,000 textbooks and children's books to elementary and high schools in northern Somalia. English is still the language of commerce and education in northern Somalia, a former British colony.

"Rochester can contribute a lot to the world," Qassim says. "The world contributes a lot to Rochester, such as patients who spend their money and doctors and scientists and computer specialists who bring their talent. So I thought, 'We receive a lot here, what could we give back?'"

Books, came the answer. "Books go into landfills in the United States sometimes, we have so many," Qassim said. "In Africa they have hardly any. Why not share?"

Mud brick schoolhouses containing rickety benches and

in some cases a cracked blackboard are common in African villages, without a book to be seen. Often the schools are built by hand by parents and may include a room called a "library," though the shelves of the library are usually empty.

"Many times an African family will own a book and people will come and visit the family and be shown the book as if it were an heirloom," says Patrick Plonski, the director of Books for Africa. "It would look like any old book to us, but to them it's a treasure, a symbol of knowledge and learning."

"Our goal is to end the book famine in Africa," Qassim says.

Founded in 1988 by Tom Warth, a self-made publishing magnate in Minneapolis, Books for Africa has sent about ten million books to 23 countries in Africa. That makes the St. Paul-based group the world's largest shipper of books to the African continent, Plonsky says.

The books are carefully chosen for quality and suitability for elementary and high schoolers. Textbooks donated by publishing companies, in unsold lots and slightly dated volumes, are the biggest category. Next are any kind of reference book from dictionaries, atlases, and encyclopedias to almanacs and any kind of "how to" manual.

Medical and health books are in great demand, as are books on basic bookkeeping and financial skills and small business manuals.

Working with Books for Africa, Qassim has gathered 100,000 books into four large containers that are now sitting in a St. Paul warehouse. They are packed and ready to ship to the northern Somali city of Hargeysa.

RISES, a Rochester immigrant services group, and the Rochester Rotary Club, have helped Qassim to raise the $6,000 per container it will cost to ship all four containers to Hargeysa.

Once the books reach Africa and are distributed, donors receive photographs via Books for Africa of the actual books in the schools and libraries where they are placed, and a report on how they are being used.

Besides the inherent pleasure of doing the right thing, there are practical long-term benefits to book philanthropy, Plonsky argues.

"Global stability and education is in our interest," Plonsky says. "We benefit from a stable world. Problems in other parts of the world invariably come back in some way to the U.S."

America's declining prestige in the world, a trend that has intensified after the war in Iraq, is also strongly countered by people-to-people humanitarian programs like Books for Africa, Plonsky says.

Supplementing the Koran, the only book that is allowed in some Islamist schools, with a full library portraying the worlds of science, art, religion, and politics, is another motivation behind the Books for Africa mission.

"Terrorism is about fear of the unknown," Plonsky says. "If no one else is there to provide another point of view, young people will accept the only point of view they are given. Books give those other views."

Qassim's own education was interrupted by civil war and famine in Somalia, which forced him to flee Somalia first for Italy, then for America. So for him the promise of education embodied in every single book is key.

"Poverty is a disease of ignorance, and education is the cure," he says. ●

From Kathmandu to Clarks Grove

In 1983, Durga Pokhrel changed her place of residence from a dungeon prison in the remote high mountains of western Nepal to the farmhouse of Earl and Beverly Thompson in Clarks Grove, Minnesota.

A democracy activist jailed on trumped-up charges of trying to kidnap Nepal's crown prince, Pokhrel had for years been in the crosshairs of the country's brutal secret police. She was unexpectedly released from prison in April 1983, but she knew she had to flee the country or face re-arrest, continued harassment or assassination by her political foes.

A tourist couple from Minnesota she had met once in Nepal had told her "please call if you ever need help." So now, just freed from jail, where she'd spent one year sleeping on bare bricks and straining drinking water through a corner of her sari, she called. Earl and Beverly Thompson, without a moment's hesitation, bought her a ticket from Kathmandu to Minneapolis.

Within two days, Pokhrel was walking through April snow in her sandals.

"It was a heavenly feeling," she says. "It was so quiet. I always imagined the U.S. to be so fast, with music playing, every place like New York City. Yet Clarks Grove was so peaceful. And the big sky. I grew up in the high mountains where you only see a little sky. Minnesota sky looks like the ocean.

"I slept for two days and nights, and the minute I woke up I felt, 'Life!' All the time I heard that word in my mind. 'Life!' I was still alive. In Nepal I was a kind of revolutionary, but now I said 'No, I want to live.' I felt how much I wanted to live, how much I loved my life."

Today, more than two decades later, Pokhrel is again living in Nepal, this time married with three children and still pushing for change in her country as a well-known journalist and writer, human rights campaigner, and as former chairperson of Nepal's National Commission for Women.

She traveled to the U.S. this summer to warn of Nepal's worsening crisis as the country's ruling monarchy battles a rebel movement that controls fully 80% of the country.

"It's getting worse in Nepal by the day, by the hour," she said. "It's a human catastrophe. You cannot imagine what is going on."

Pokhrel always stops in Minnesota first on her U.S. trips, to meet with her adopted American family in Clarks Grove. Last week I met up with her at the home of Jolyn Thompson, the daughter of her benefactors Earl and Beverly, in Rochester.

Dressed in a rainbow-colored sari, Pokhrel painted a dire picture of Nepal today and voiced a passionate plea for support.

"We look to America as a leading democratic country and we need help," she said. "We need to bring together Nepal's revolutionary Maoists, the King, and the political parties together at the negotiating table. If America facilitates this, it is possible. Otherwise it is not, and there will be civil war."

Civil war is exactly what some experts say has been raging in Nepal for nine years, especially in the impoverished countryside where the lack of government services has given Nepal's Maoist rebels a foothold.

In their early years, the Maoists won the support of villagers with campaigns against gambling, alcoholism, and government corruption. But brutal suppression of the revolutionaries by the Nepalese army in recent years has led to equally brutal reprisals and attacks by the Maoists.

Today the Maoists are virtually an entrenched opposition army controlling most of Nepal's rural areas, where they stage frequent blockades of food and medicines, assassinate political rivals, and have abducted thousands of civilians for recruitment in forced labor and "re-education programs."

A report released last month by Amnesty International documented the conflict's impact on Nepal's children and families. The Maoists have abducted tens of thousands of school children along with their teachers for 'political education' sessions, the report said.

Typically the armed rebels storm a school and force everyone to trek to a remote location for the sessions which may go on for days. However, many children never return, with boys recruited as soldiers and girls sometimes raped, murdered, and tossed aside. A large percentage of Nepal's 200,000 refugees are children, the reports estimates, with up to 15,000 Nepalese children likely to be displaced from their homes in 2005.

The impact of the violence on Nepalese families and culture has been profound. Families are now often female-headed as husbands are recruited by the rebels, are killed in a conflict, or disappear, and the children of fatherless families face intense social discrimination.

Rural schools have been transformed into garrisons, with classes ended. Private schools, opposed by the Maoists, have been bombed. Teachers are a particular target, forced to pay 10-15% of their income in tax to the rebels and tortured or killed if caught teaching non-revolutionary principles. So far 160 teachers have been killed and 3,000 displaced, Amnesty estimates.

More than 12,000 people have been killed by the violence in the past nine years, the report said. Many times that number have died from the indirect effects of the violence including hunger and disease, especially among children.

"Everyone at this point has emotional problems in Nepal," Pokhrel said.

Yet as gruesome as the bill of indictment is against the Maoist rebels, Pokhrel warns, labeling them as "terrorists" will only lead to greater tragedy. That's because such a labeling will further open the sluice gate of arms sales by the United States and its allies to Nepal.

"If you brand the Maoists the same way as those who blew up the World Trade Center, this is what invites people to more violence," Pokhrel says. "I am not defending them, but the Maoists are a political group. You need to treat political people politically, and terrorists in a terrorist way."

The Maoists, she points out, began as a legitimate widespread people's movement and that members of the Communist Party of Nepal (Maoist) held the third largest number of seats in Nepal's parliament following the democratic elections held in the country in 1990 and 1992.

The root cause of the conflict in Nepal, according to Pokhrel, is the non-inclusive nature of the country's governing system and constitution, which explicitly excludes women from obtaining citizenship at birth and which also discriminates against ethnic groups and castes.

"We don't have a functioning real democracy in the country," Pokhrel said. "The system is very much feudal and only a very few rich people control everything. The constitution limits the access of women and indigenous people to citizenship, and untouchables are nowhere in the picture."

Roughly half of Nepal's population has no legal status and thus is unable to obtain health services, education, open a bank account, apply for a passport, or receive government aid or services. The fact that the Maoists readily accept women, including in their fighting forces, is a major reason they've been able to consolidate power so widely, Pokhrel added.

The United States has for years been a leading supplier of weapons and arms to Nepal, providing $8.4 million in weapons from 1994 to 2003, according to the World Policy Institute. The weapons are transferred under a U.S. Congressional justification that gives high priority to providing the Nepal military with "capability to prevail against the Maoist insurgents."

Since 9/11, the U.S. administration policy of pursuing a global war on terror has notably increased American interest in militarily supporting Nepal's ruling monarchy. Foreign Military Financing (FMF), the largest U.S. military aid program, increased its aid to Nepal from $597,000 in 2001 to $22 million in 2002 and since then has averaged about $4 million in military aid per year

Heading to Washington, D.C. last week to meet with U.S. Representative Betty McCollum and other legislators, Durga Pokhrel had her message ready.

"Don't send more arms, because if you do there will be more killing and a real civil war," Pokhrel said. "I love America as my own second home, but if that happens the revolutionaries will say that Americans are the enemy, and it will be hard for Americans to be in Nepal. And that would be too bad."

Too bad in Kathmandu, and in Clarks Grove. ●

Foreigners Are Us

We have met the foreigner and he is us.

In Saudi Arabia, a strange and foreign land if ever there was, a recent terrorist attack was aimed not primarily at Saudi citizens but rather at European and American citizens who have chosen to live large portions of their lives, often raising children into their teen years, in Saudi Arabia.

More than 35,000 Americans are living in Saudi Arabia, many working for American oil and consulting companies, some for the United States military and some for the 100 percent Saudi-owned oil production company, Saudi Aramco. Expatriates are an unusual breed of American citizen who, after living for years in a foreign country, might think and act more like a "foreigner" than an American. When they come back to the United States they often feel culture shock as strongly as they felt when they first moved abroad.

Between 3 million and 6 million Americans, or up to 2 percent of the U.S. population, live as expatriates around the world, shopping and socializing and paying bills in foreign currencies, adopting foreign customs, making foreign friends, often speaking in adopted foreign tongues.

Even in highly protected enclaves such as those in Saudi Arabia, expatriates brush up directly against the disorienting strangeness of the "other" and quickly learn the skills needed to adapt, to make peace and to thrive.

In other words, this special two percent of the U.S. population has become expert at a set of skills the entire United States is badly in need of learning, and fast.

Expatriates are a rich but entirely untapped resource. As the sole global superpower and one that is not shy, under President Bush, about pushing its military weight around, those skills will be even more needed in the years ahead. We need to make friends as we try to increase the odds that democratic habits and institutions are adopted worldwide.

I received this Internet joke in my e-mail the other day from a friend in Hong Kong: "In New York City, the United Nations adopted a resolution to study the food shortage in the rest of the world. But three delegates raised objections. The delegate from Africa did not understand the word 'food.' The delegate from Europe did not understand the word 'shortage.' And the U.S. delegate did not understand what was meant by 'the rest of the world.'"

Is this how we want to be known by our global neighbors?

Expatriate Americans are like honey bees who buzz around the world collecting rich nectars and pollens. They are a valuable source of understanding of the very countries we are culturally, economically and militarily invading—if only we would use that resource. But we don't. When American expatriates return to the U.S. they usually run smack into a stone wall of ignorance and indifference among most Americans about the places they spent much of their lives.

Last week, I visited with a former Rochester, Minnesota kindergarten teacher who now teaches in Saudi Arabia for Saudi Aramco in an oil town near the Arabian Gulf. She is furloughed in St. Paul with her three children, waiting for tensions to subside so she and her kids can rejoin her husband in the Gulf. Is she incredibly relieved to be back safely in the United States?

Nope. She can't wait to get back to the Gulf. "It's our home," she said. "Our friends are there. We like it there, and I still feel safe there." She asked that her name not be used in order to avoid any political or visa entanglements.

Her eagerness to return seemed in part fueled by the lack of interest Minnesotans have shown in learning what she knows firsthand about Saudi Arabia, Arabic culture and Islam.

One of her youngsters rolled his eyes as he said: "When kids here find out I live in Saudi Arabia, they say 'Do you go to school on a camel?' 'Have you ever ridden a camel?' It's always camels, camels, camels."

When the camel questions stop, conversation shifts to more compelling matters such as skateboarding and the Minnesota Twins.

In these days of a global war on terrorism and homeland security alerts and suspicious sideways glances going to foreigners, doesn't it make sense to sit down with the true experts in our midst and to learn from them?

And who really is a foreigner these days, anyway? ●

Outsource Yourself

A terrific story in the Minneapolis Star-Tribune on Monday, about a young southern Minnesota man who moved to Brazil to become a farmer, brilliantly defines a powerful counter-strategy for Minnesotans who feel their jobs are threatened by foreign competition.

Outsource yourself!

The article by reporter Kevin Diaz, the second installment in a three-part series on how central Brazil is fast replacing the American Midwest as the world's breadbasket, focuses on Josh Neusch, a 22-year-old farmer who grew up in Fairmont, Minnesota.

When Neusch graduated from high school four years ago he had two options: to help his Dad and two brothers expand the family farm, or try to start a farm of his own. With farmland in southern Minnesota averaging more than $2,000 per acre, however, option two was well out of reach.

Neusch's solution: move to Brazil where farmland costs $150 per acre. Last year he bought 7,500 acres in the Mato Grosso region of central Brazil, where he now lives full-time growing soybeans and rice. He pays his workers twice the Brazilian minimum wage of $88 a month, compared to more than $1,000 a month in wages he'd pay in Minnesota.

The man is a modern pioneer following economic opportunity just as thousands of Scandinavian and German immigrants did when they settled the challenging frontier territory called Minnesota in the mid-19th century.

Here's the larger point: not just in agriculture but in manufacturing, software, engineering, and many other fields, one possible answer to foreign competition is the age-old advice that begins "if you can't beat 'em ..."

Starting life as an expatriate may sound like a radical solution to tough economic times, but examples like Neusch show it's a potentially appealing one. The federal government estimates 4.1 million American citizens presently live and work overseas, though expatriate groups and job agencies estimate the number is easily twice that large and growing.

A little-known secret about expatriate life is something I discovered first-hand when I moved to Tokyo in 1989, beginning a decade of travels there, in England, and in Hong Kong. The secret is that if you can put up with the stresses of living in a foreign country, the economic rewards can be big.

A little bit of risk on the front side can turn into big reward later on.

My first discovery came when I filed my 1989 U.S. federal income taxes and discovered that the first $70,000 that an expatriate earns while working abroad was tax free. (The amount is now $80,000.) Then I learned that my company, a New York-based news organization, used the standard corporate "balance-sheet approach" to determining my salary while living overseas.

The idea, followed by most companies with offices overseas, is to set a salary that ensures the maintenance of a "home lifestyle" for its expat employees. Because the American lifestyle is more luxurious than in many other countries, especially in Asia, expatriate employees thus very often live like Kings and Queens compared to their local surroundings.

Of course, not everyone works for a big corporation with offices overseas. Yet the economic disparity between the U.S. and other countries, especially in the developing world, is so great that the comparative advantage usually holds. For example, a Minnesota schoolteacher who takes a job teaching English in China might see her salary fall from $40,000 to $25,000 a year—a 37% decrease. Yet her cost of living would easily be 60% lower in China than in Minnesota, leaving good room for spending on comfort and savings.

I don't mean to minimize the hassle factor—if hassle is a big enough word for turning your life upside down. Being separated from loved ones back home for months or years at a time is tough. Neusch, in Brazil, has to travel 600 miles to the nearest fast food joint, a Domino's Pizza in a town called Goiana. His Brazilian girlfriend lives 120 miles down a bad road.

Did I mention you need to learn a whole new language?

As globalization rages on, though, more and more of us are going to feel its fiery tingle at our toes. Once upon a time the U.S. dependence on Middle East oil was almost the single area where the American way of life depended on the unbroken flow of a single strategic substance.

Today, there is an OPEC of commodity food goods rising in the world that is called Brazil. There is an OPEC of low cost manufactured goods upon which our economy is already utterly dependent, called China. There is an OPEC of software services called India—have you telephoned your American computer maker recently for technical support?

In each of these cases, there is a possible "join them" scenario like the one that Josh Neusch is living in Brazil. True, true, snakes keep getting into his house, and he hates snakes. But he's got the consolation of knowing that he's building something.

He's not living in the past. He's creating his future. ●

Patriot of Venezuela and Minnesota

Leon Topel is battling cancer, but he doesn't talk about it much.

He's too much in love and too desperately worried about his home country of Venezuela to dwell on his own travails.

Leon and Cora Topel started coming to Rochester in 1977. That was the year their daughter, also named Cora, got sick and needed better medical care than they could get in their home town of Valencia, Venezuela.

They got good news and bad news from their Mayo doctors. The good news was that Cora's sickness wasn't fatal. The bad news was that it would have to be managed from year to year, probably for her whole life.

Wandering through downtown Rochester back then, Leon Topel, an owner of real estate, publishing, and manufacturing concerns in Venezuela, looked carefully at the town he'd call a second home for years to come.

The gothic grandeur of the Plummer Building, piercing the Midwestern sky like a French cathedral, struck him. So did the relaxed pace and the high level of education for such a small town. So did the economic stability that IBM and the Mayo Clinic obviously lent Rochester.

"I realized that I would be related to the Mayo Clinic and to Rochester for the rest of my life because of my daughter," he said. "I liked Rochester very much. To me it's something like a European city. So instead of investing in another place, like many other Venezuelans do, I invested here."

He bought a red brick building on Third Street, downtown's "historic" mini-mall with Wong's Cafe at one end and Bilotti's

Pizza at the other. In later years, with local partners, he built 50 duplex homes in the Liberty Manor development in northwest Rochester.

He's living now in a short-lease apartment downtown as he receives chemotherapy at the Mayo Clinic. But if you sit down with Leon for a chat, as I did last week, he doesn't fret about his health.

The cancer of despotism and authoritarian government—in the person of Hugo Chavez, the Marxist president of Venezuela —is what's on his mind.

"Chavez is taking control of everything, from the Supreme Court to the National Assembly to Venezuela's oil industry, and also the Army," he said. "He pays them all through corruption. Our democracy is at stake. If this isn't resolved, there could be a civil war in Venezuela."

Like Fidel Castro's recent execution of political opponents and Robert Mugabe's decimation of Zimbabwe's democracy, the crisis in Venezuela is one of those conflagrations that's raged in an eery silence here in the U.S. It's like a movie with the sound turned off, as we've gorged on the war in Iraq.

In a country only a three-hour flight south of Miami, Hugo Chavez in recent months has jailed the union official who organized a strike to remove him from power; openly defied Supreme Court rulings to limit his power; imposed strict currency controls limiting U.S. dollars allowed in the country; and fired 17,000 workers at the country's largest oil company, the PDVSA. He replaced these professionals with industry neophytes and political appointees whose new assignment is "to help the poor."

Since Chavez was elected on the wings of such populist rhetoric in 1998, Venezuela's poor have suffered more than ever. The number of people living below the poverty line has soared to 80 percent from 67 percent, and the average annual income for Venezuelans last year fell 29 percent, to $3,835 from $5,385, according to Global Insight, a global economics consulting firm.

The crash has forced Leon to lay off workers at his companies, and Cora, who runs a small nursery and landscaping firm, has trimmed its staff to only three employees from the eight she normally employs.

"For us in Venezuela, the U.S. is our big neighbor and our protector," Cora says. "We have democracy and we value democracy. We are a Western society, not Islamic or Asian. And yet right now our democracy is in danger and it seems to us the U.S. is neglecting us while looking at other things."

A relevant metaphor here is metastasis—the way pathogens like cancer cells spread suddenly from one organ in the body to another organ far away.

Is there a better way to explain 9/11?

Now we've clearly got a problem even closer to home.

As I understand Leon and Cora Topel, passionate patriots of Venezuela and Rochester, they are asking "How can we get healthy together?" ●

A Love Letter (Unrequited, Alas)

The world sent us delicately worded letters asking for our friend-ship yet eager not to intrude, written in longhand and sent in the mail.

We sent back a flood of hateful e-mails in return.

Marina McCall of Uruguay sent us this ardent note:

> *"I remember sitting in my junior high school classroom in November 1963. "A nun came in to call us to the chapel to pray for the president of the U.S., who had been shot. I remember sitting for two days watching on TV and crying like I had never cried before, just like I cried on September 11 when the twin towers collapsed. I have loved America ever since, and it is because of this love that I write to you today. Because I'm saddened at what is happening to America's image abroad and the hatred I see all around me."*

Marina's is just one of more than 14,000 letters sent by people who live outside the U.S. to swing voters in Clark County, Ohio, before last week's national election. The letters were sent as part of a campaign organized by the Guardian news-paper of London, which encouraged people in Europe, South America, the Middle East and Asia who felt their lives would be affected by the election, to express their feelings to people with a vote.

Ms. McCall urged her Ohio correspondent to vote for John Kerry because "dialogue is what Mr. Kerry is offering and that is what the world needs now. I would please beg you to vote for all of us who cannot, but whose lives are affected by the decisions take by the leader of the free world."

As a result of setting up a channel through which non-Americans could reach actual voters in Clark County, Ohio, the Guardian was deluged with thousands of vicious e-mails from Americans all over the country.

It would be unseemly to print here the worst of the e-mails that the Guardian published. Wishes that sudden death, bad luck, and tooth decay be visited on the Guardian's editors were numerous. Every act of human elimination was invoked in capital letters. Grave threats were made.

"Keep your noses out of our business," read one of the milder notes. "As I recall we kicked you out of our country back in 1776. We do not require input from losers and idiots on who we vote for in our own country."

When I lived in England in the middle 1990s, I was amazed how both the Brits and the Irish invoked centuries-old battles with the freshness of a recent grudge. Now I am hearing the same thing here.

When is it going to sink in that we all live together on this one beautiful earth?

"Our most basic common link is that we all inhabit this planet," said President John F. Kennedy in a commencement speech at American University in 1963. "We all breathe the same air. We all cherish our children's future. And we are all mortal."

History can sometimes reach such a point that the noblest aspirations we've ever managed to articulate can come to sound outdated and naïve. Have we really become so cynical that Kennedy's call to common humanity no longer moves us?

In this election, the world was for John Kerry by 8 to 1.

That certainly doesn't mean that John Kerry should have been elected. The campaign was enlightening, the election was fair, and we got the president that most of us wanted and that we as a nation therefore deserve.

I'm just saying, we can't tell 7/8 of the world to shove it.

Already our foreign policy has made us unpopular around the world. Of course, governments sometimes have to take unpopular positions.

But the role of individuals can be different. Even when governments clash, on a personal level there can be peace. Hospitality can thrive. It's not easy but it can be done. It's one thing that individuals who otherwise feel powerless in the face of great world events, can actually do.

Kennedy also said in his commencement speech: "What kind of peace do I mean? Not a Pax Americana enforced on the world by American weapons of war. I am talking about genuine peace, not merely peace for Americans, but peace for all men and women; not merely peace in our time, but peace for all time."

He didn't specify how to attain that peace, but here is my suggestion for a good start: politeness by politeness, kind word by kind word. ●

What is Immigration For?

When a person goes to college, gets married, or makes a large financial investment, some prior discussion aimed at defining the purposes of the venture is obviously a good idea.

Why not with immigration?

Yet this is not our national practice. Look at Rochester, Minnesota, for example. I set out to discover why the community of Rochester—the town of 81,000 where I live—has changed its ethnic color from all-white to multi-hued in recent years.

What policy, or national or local purpose, drove the waves of immigration behind the color-change in my town?

The change has been startling. In the years I grew up here in the 1960's and 70's, my friends ran the gamut from Johnson, Enquist, and Olsen to Plunkett, Skinner, Judge, Vanderheyden, Uhlenhopp, and Pine. In other words, it was not a wide gamut at all. We were Scandinavian Protestants or German Catholics; we ate hamburgers and hot dogs; we went to summer camps; we were Boy Scouts and Girl Scouts; we put up Christmas trees.

Today, one out of ten people in Rochester is an immigrant. They've come here from every continent in the world *except* Western Europe. These people are every color *but* white and they celebrate holidays like *Eid* and *Dewali* and *Cinco de Mayo*, and they wouldn't know *Oktoberfest* from a hole in the ground.

Somalis, Cambodians, Mexicans, Serbs, Hmong, Vietnamese, and Chinese are Rochester's major immigrant groups and they've left an indelible mark on life here. In some schools as many as half of the children speak English as a second language, and Rochester now has food shops, gift shops, restaurants, soccer teams, language classes, churches, temples, and law and medical offices that offer specialized products and services to ethnic groups.

Some of our 8,000 immigrants came as humanitarian refugees (Bosnians, Somalis); some came as political asylees (Hmong, Laotians, Vietnamese); some came under work-related visas (Europeans, Iranians, Indians); and others came under the so-called "diversity" provisions of the INS, which awards a quota of visas by lottery each year to nationals of Eastern European, former Soviet, and other countries.

Finally, many of our newest 1,500 Mexican neighbors are here illegally—that is without a visa or "green card" allowing them U.S. residency. Yet they are allowed to stay because our de facto national policy is to enforce deportation only rarely so as to give our businesses a source of cheap labor.

Rochester has been stable and prosperous enough to accommodate this influx so that new human energy, outlooks, and skills have been beneficially extracted to the benefit of all. Local business such as the Mayo Clinic and IBM have kept the local economy growing steadily for many years. At the same time, two traditional sources of labor for low-wage jobs—part-time farmers and women—have been steadily shrinking. New immigrants are taking those jobs and thus have enabled Rochester's economic growth to continue.

Many other U.S. communities, however, and indeed the U.S. as a whole, haven't been so lucky. A lax official view on immigration and visas was at least partially responsible for 9/11. What's more, there is evidence that a shift in the popular notion of immigration—from the old ideal of assimilation to the newer one of multicultural mosaic—has had a harmful effect.

In many communities, rates of income, home ownership, and citizenship have all declined among immigrants since 1970, reversing more than 100 years of the opposite trend. More immigrants than ever before never learn English, and retain their old cultural identities. Assimilation is faltering.

In California, where in many places people live and die speaking only Spanish, demographic trends are on track to make as much as half the population Latino within 20 to 30 years. Some Hispanic identity groups are rallying around the notions of "La Reconquista" and of Aztlan, a sovereign state merging Mexico and the U.S. Southwest. Can a divisive and draining Quebec-style secessionist movement be far behind?

What's missing from this picture is an articulated purpose for our national immigration policy. Currently the INS hands out visas on a case-by-case basis in response to the demands of three groups: people living outside the U.S. who want to live here; people living inside the U.S. who want to bring their family members to join them; and of U.S. businesses who want to attract cheap labor.

These are the forces that drive our national immigration policy. There is not a mention of U.S. national interest there.

In the absence of articulated national interest, chaos reigns. Our national immigration policy is a cluster of policies, each with its separate rationale and its own gaping loopholes open to abuse and fraud.

The most egregiously obvious example is the difference between U.S. policy, and U.S. practice, towards illegal immigrants. We let in more than a quarter million illegal immigrants a year and deport only a tiny fraction of them. Why? Because our economy, especially in the Southwest, is dependent on cheap labor.

Another example is the "family reunification" provisions, which account for two-thirds of legal immigration into the U.S. As many as four million people around the world are already approved to immigrate under these provisions, but will have to wait up to 40 years for their number to be called.

The theory is that stable families provide a base from which all of its members can assimilate more easily into U.S. society. Yet in practice the system is abused, with distant cousins and other relatives coming in as brothers and sisters. As a result, rather than providing a base for assimilation into America, large extended families formed in this way provide an insular culture-within-a-culture, in which the original foreign language can be spoken at all times and no assimilation is ever accomplished.

Of course, there are important humanitarian reasons to make family reunification a priority in immigration. Separation from family members is a painful and debilitating emotional experience. Yet there are far more family reunification visas granted each year than refugee visas, and surely the humanitarian case is stronger for refugees, who risk not discomfort but death due to war or drought or famine.

The point is that every immigration category—humanitarian, refugee, employment-based, and lottery visas—are shot through with similar contradications and inconsistencies. The root cause is that U.S. immigration laws have proliferated and been amended so many times over the past decades that U.S. immigration policy is just a messy hodge-podge entirely unsupported by a rationale based on our national interest.

How might such a rationale be worded? Should we say that the purpose of immigration is to bring the greatest good to the greatest number of people? Should we define it narrowly, to say its purpose is to improve our economy? Or broaden it, to include the improvement of our national quality of life?

Is humanitarian immigration important to maintain our self-image, and our reputation in the world, as a caring and humane people? Then we should say so. Maybe we should consider how immigrants bring into the U.S. certain types of global linkages that translate into real value. For example, such linkages make our country both more prosperous, by virtue of widened access to global markets, and more secure, by virtue of our relationship with immigrants deepening our friendship and our tolerance of other peoples.

Maybe we should go whole hog. Maybe we should say that the purpose of immigration is to make Americans.

Maybe we should say that the purpose of U.S. immigration

policy should be to shape and mold people who come to this country into citizens who possess a common base of cultural and language skills; that is, a set of skills that will allow them, working collaboratively as citizens, to interact more productively and more humanely with each other, so as to further the way of life and values we hold dear—freedom, pluralism, democracy, capitalism, and equality of dignity and of human rights.

Whatever we decide, at least at that point we will have chosen what kind of a people we want to be and how we are going to get there. ●

Fix Immigration Now

As with parenting and motorcycle maintenance, the first rule of national immigration policy should be "If it ain't broke, don't fix it." Even after 9/11, many people still argue that our present policy of essentially unchecked mass immigration is a wonderful idea.

I beg to differ. My liberal friends think I'm cracked to say so, but the thing looks broke to me. Here are six reasons why, and therefore, why our national immigration policy should be fixed:

1. *Our existing immigration policy does not flow from a national sense of identity and purpose.* Instead it is an ad hoc assemblage of civil rights, big business, and Cold War-era policies that have resulted in the greatest immigration wave in U.S. history. There has never been an effort to update our national immigration policy despite its having added 24 million people to the population—three New York Cities, or about one-tenth the country's total—in the past 10 years.

2. *It's inhumane to bring so many people into the U.S. with no plan to educate them or their children.* Today's global economy depends more than ever on high-level skills and thus a high level of education to succeed. However, our present high tolerance for accepting illegal immigrants is based on their usefulness as low-wage workers. A low-wage job can be a stepping stone to better jobs in the future, but that's true only as long as education is available to help immigrants make that jump. It is not, and there are no plans to make it so.

3. *9/11 shows our present immigration and visa policies put America at risk.* Immigration policy cannot address the problem of homegrown terrorists, but it should be repaired so it no longer allows fanatical subcultures of foreign origin, devoted to America's destruction, to flourish here. Whether it is Timothy McVeigh, an American citizen, or Mohamed Atta, an Egyptian here on a temporary visa, the very presence of such subcultures in this country is an obvious risk.

4. *We need to debate the consequences of a 50% increase in the U.S. population by 2050.* The Census Bureau estimates that the U.S. population will increase to 400 million in 2050, the vast majority of whom will be immigrants and their children. Such an increase will exacerbate many social problems ranging from an overwhelmed welfare system to urban sprawl, school overcrowding, and the destruction of arable farm land. Hospitals, courts, and government agencies will be further stressed. Are we willing to accept these challenges in return for the benefits that high immigration brings? As a nation we are still mostly unconscious of the tradeoffs that we are already accepting in our daily lives. We need to become aware.

5. *We are forming a permanent underclass in America.* It happened with the welfare state, and now it's happening with immigration. Research by groups such as the Center for Immigration Studies, the Urban Institute, and the Rand Corporation show that rates of income, home ownership, and citizenship have all declined steadily among immigrants since 1970, reversing more than 100 years of the opposite trend. The 2000 U.S. Census shows that the median household income by the mid-1990s had risen for a decade among most groups; among Hispanics, the fastest-growing immigrant group in the U.S., it dropped 5.1 percent. In California, where roughly a third of the 34 million people are Hispanic, many immigrants live and die speaking Spanish, never become American citizens, and never assimilate at all. They live in a different culture and a different economy. It's not a matter of whether the U.S. can

afford this economically. It certainly can, and both big business and consumers are benefiting from the low inflation that low wage workers make possible. The question is whether, in the long run, the U.S. can afford it culturally.

6. *The present policy of tacitly accepting illegal immigrants is politically dubious and legally wrong.* Time and again, strong business lobbies championed by U.S. legislators have beaten back the INS when the agency has tried to crack down on illegal immigrant laborers. The mass amnesty for illegal Mexican immigrants that came close to passing before 9/11 was a political lunge for the Hispanic vote that trumped fair policy-making. If the U.S. had passed that law and granted amnesty to four million Mexicans, on what possible legal grounds could it reject a similar plea from the four million illegal aliens of other ethnicities now living in the U.S.? It is not pleasant to contemplate increased enforcement of the existing 1986 law that prohibits the hiring of illegal aliens. Yet failure to do so means that we as a nation are embracing a two-tiered class system of the privileged and their servants. Guestworker programs and tacit acceptance of illegal immigration fundamentally promote such an unequal society. Is that who we are? Is that who we want to become? If so, so be it. And I don't doubt for a minute there are benefits to that path. But we should at least be aware and consciously debate the question first. ◉

Assimilate, then Celebrate

"Celebrating diversity" and "embracing the other," these are the vogue words these days. They both describe ways for the majority population to alter its attitudes and behaviors to absorb immigrants.

But old-fashioned "assimilation," which puts the responsibility on the immigrant to do the hard work of adapting, is definitely out.

Multiculturalism, the idea that we're a nation of many subcultures rather than of one national culture, was the death of the ideal of assimilation. And it's a crying shame.

And now, multiculturalism added to mass immigration is threatening to sink the ship. Many American subcultures —Mexican-Americans, Chinese-Americans, Indian-Americans, and many others—now number in the millions, enough to form an entire country of their own. But these new countries are located inside our borders.

Under multiculturalism these foreign-born populations are encouraged to succeed not through assimilation but rather through ethnic self-determination, to become self-sustaining enclaves of business and religion and culture linked to one another by nothing but a U.S. mail address.

It's time to rethink why we trashed the ideal of assimilation, and to bring it back, at least partially. Can we do this in Rochester?

There are so many strong institutions in our city to help immigrants settle into southeast Minnesota—the Intercultural Mutual Assistance Association, the Migration and Refugee

Services, the Adult Literacy Center, the Rochester Diversity Council, many Rochester schools, and so on.

But are we asking the immigrants themselves to do enough? To take on enough responsibility for their own assimilation? Are we asking them explicitly and insistently not to forget or to renounce their former identities, but rather to subordinate them as they become Americans?

In earlier eras, for all its strong points, we botched assimilation by misunderstanding it and too brutally enforcing it. In schools, we whipped children for speaking a single German, or Chinese, or Indian word; we put Japanese families in internment camps; and we committed other crimes.

Assimilation is not (should not be) about the enforced forgetting of a former culture and identity. That goes against human nature and is thus literally inhuman and bound to fail. And we don't want immigrants to leave every thread of their old selves behind—we benefit far too much from their wisdoms, languages and cultures for that.

Assimilation is (should be) about subordinating the old identity to a new American one. And it's a sacred civic obligation to demand that from immigrants for the sake of security and for the sake of the transcendent ideals of freedom and consensual government that we serve.

Assimilation was enshrined by our nation's founders, including George Washington, who cautioned immigrants to shed the "language, habits, and principles (good and bad) which they bring with them." Instead they should be ready for "intermixture with our people" and thus be "assimilated to our customs, measures, and laws: in a word, soon become one people."

In families you don't adopt a Chinese baby expecting her to speak only Chinese and eat with chopsticks when she's grown. It's the same way in marriage. You take vows to change and to subordinate yourself in certain ways. You sacrifice.

It should be no different with citizenship. Yet for some reason, when it comes to immigrants, we extend to this gigantic number of permanent life partners a free pass. "Celebrate diversity!" "Embrace your roots!"

We keep repeating feel-good multicultural mantras as year by year America becomes less unique and more like the rest of the world, just another kaleidoscope of competing tribes and factions.

Pick your separatist movement—the Basques, the Palestinians, the Kurds, the East Timorese, the Zulus, the Uighurs, the Chechens, the Quebecois, the Zulus, and on and on. The failure of the larger nation to achieve a national cultural unity is the tragic flaw behind all these disasters. The United States was given the gift of unity from the beginning. Now we are squandering it.

On Monday afternoon, I dropped in at Riverside Central Elementary School, where many children are from immigrant families. Riverside is well known for the work its teachers do to help these youngsters overcome language and cultural barriers to get an equal start in life with other kids.

The school's mission statement is posted on the wall. It reads in part: "We encourage students to become good citizens who embrace each other's differences."

How about a new mission statement for students at Riverside and across America that would read as follows: "We encourage students to embrace each other's differences and to become good citizens, above all by learning how to subordinate their individual ethnic differences in the interest of national unity and for the sake of America's highest ideals." ●

Somalis for Dean

An evening that began glumly at the Canadian Honker restaurant—where Bob Rouillard and several friends were "commiserating about the Bush presidency"—ended on a strong upnote thanks to a sudden brainstorm.

Somalis for Howard Dean!

An operating room technician for Mayo Clinic, Rouillard had never been involved in politics. Then, when he recently became a young father, he started thinking about what kind of world he was going to leave his kids.

"We were depressed at the Honker," Rouillard said. "Then we said 'Hey, this isn't a support group. We like Howard Dean. Let's have a fundraiser!'"

On Friday, they hosted one of several outreach sessions they'd brainstormed at the restaurant—a presentation to Somali immigrants they hoped to draw into politics.

The meeting room at the Somali Community Resettlement Services was standing room only with more than 50 Somalis. As usual, the Somali men sat on the left side of the room and the women, dressed in their traditional full-length dresses (called *guntiinos*) and headscarves, sat on the right.

"Thanks for coming to make Minnesota a better place," Rouillard said to the crowd, which erupted into raucous applause. He rattled off a half dozen issues on which he felt Howard Dean was the best candidate for Somalis.

Then he said: "But the most important thing about Howard Dean is that he believes in us. He's turned the power over to us. It's a huge grassroots campaign. And I want all of you to feel that power, too."

A show of hands revealed that only 20 of the Somalis were citizens already registered to vote. A handful more said they'd be registered by Election Day.

One Somali woman raised her hand. "Whether we are citizens or not, and whether we can vote or not, we will help. So sleep well tonight!"

Amina Arte, a Somali-born community worker at the Intercultural Mutual Assistance Association, provided translations for the speakers. At one point she gave a short speech on a distinctly Somali topic.

"It's important to put your old clan memberships aside," she told the group. "It's important to be united in a democracy. So no matter what your clan, try to be united and to think about the good of the whole community."

Abdi Abdinur, of the Somali Community Resettlement Services, said there were members of virtually every Somali clan in the room—about 19 clans.

Nura Abdullah, who has six children with her in Rochester, said after the presentation that when jobs are scarce, old clan conflicts flare up. "When the economy is strong, all that clan stuff goes away," she said.

The sweet smell of sambusa, traditional Somali meat pastries, filled the meeting room when the speakers finished and the pastries were handed out.

One issue stood out above all others for the Somali immigrants: jobs. Many in the crowd had lost jobs in the last two years, especially as assemblers on the IBM and Celestica assembly lines.

"We believe the DFL is the party that helps people with jobs, health care, and education," said Biyod Shakai, a mother of eight who lost an assembly line job in 2001. "We liked it better when Bill Clinton was president."

The value of the dollar, which has strongly depreciated in the past year, was also cited as a major concern. The dollars

233

Somalis remit to relatives still living in Somalia buys about 30 percent less today than it did only a year ago.

A backlog of more than 900,000 visa applications is another major concern of the Somalis who have family members stuck in refugee camps in Africa. Candidate Dean has promised that as president he would speed up processing those applications.

According to the 2000 U.S. Census, 11,164 Somalis live in Minnesota, with 1,131 living in Rochester. Somali groups say the census dramatically undercounted the true number, which they claim is about three times as high.

The Somali immigration began a decade ago when warring clans ousted the Ethiopian president Siad Barre, and the country fell into chaos. A famine in 1992 and 1993 killed a half million Somalis and increased the refugee flow.

After a decade, many Somalis speak good English and, as the Friday night session proved, are ready to rumble in the democratic process.

When the DFL Olmsted County chairperson Lynn Wilson began her speech to the Friday group by saying "Thank you for coming to my community and making it better," the crowd at first stirred uneasily.

Then several Somalis shouted at once: "You should say 'our community' and not 'my community'! This is our country too now!" ●

Importing Dharma

The Buddhist monk Bhante Sathi's journey to Minnesota began with a hunger strike aimed at his parents.

He was 16 years old, living in the Sri Lanka town called Kandy where his father owned a clothing shop, and he desperately wanted to become a monk. He wanted to throw away the modern boy's clothes his father had given him, and put on the ancient maroon robes that monks wear in Sri Lanka.

But Buddhist law says a young man can't become a monk unless his parents give permission—which Bhante Sathi's parents refused to do. So he stopped eating for three whole days. When his parents still didn't give the okay, he ran away to a forest monastery far from his home.

After a few days he telephoned home with an ultimatum.

"I told my parents, 'if you allow me to become a monk, I will come home and be ordained in a monastery close to you. But if you do not allow me, I will not come home.'" Finally seeing their son's total determination to become a monk, the parents relented.

Today, Bhante Sathi (pronounced *Bahn*-tay *Sah*-tee), 31 years old, lives in Chanhassen and teaches Buddhism and meditation at schools, meditation centers, and churches around the state.

Last Saturday, in the wrestling room of the Rochester Community and Technical College, Bhante Sathi sat cross-legged on a thick blue wrestling mat, surrounded by a dozen college students and beginning meditators. For seven hours, he led the group in 20-minute meditations interspersed with storytelling about the Buddha's life, short lectures explaining meditation techniques, and discussions of Buddhist philosophy.

"Buddha didn't discover anything new," he told the group. "He simply realized the workings of living beings and their minds. Buddhism isn't even a religion because it doesn't ask you to believe anything or take anything on faith. It simply invites you to practice and learn for yourself."

A visitor to the class might have been amused to see Bhante Sathi, barefoot in his flowing maroon robes, leading his students in a super-slow-motion walk across the wrestling mat.

This was a "mindful walk" in which the students concentrated on every tiny change and sensation that occurred in their legs as they walked—and got so bogged down in tracking these details they could hardly take a step.

After he became ordained as a teenager in Sri Lanka, Bhante Sathi (the name means "Venerable Sathi") worked as an editor of ancient Buddhist texts written in English. He lived in Kandy until 1999, when he visited a Buddhist temple in Southfield, Michigan, and the short visit turned into five years.

He visited Minneapolis and sensed a strong demand for the *dharma*—the teachings of Buddha—in the state. He moved to Chanhassen in 2004 and since then has been traveling wherever he has been invited, while offering weekly meditation classes at the Heartwood Mindfulness Center in Minneapolis, and at the Unitarian Universalist Church in Mankato.

As a wandering teacher in Minnesota, Bhante Sathi is part of a wave of Buddhism that is fast spreading throughout the United States. In the early 1950's, there were fewer than 100,000 Buddhists in this country, according to most sources. Then, in the 1960's, the Beat culture became infatuated with Zen Buddhism, which uses brain-teasing meditation "koans" such as "What is the sound of snow falling?" to train the mind.

Other types of Buddhism have since landed in America in wave after wave, not only as cultural fads serving Americans eager for exotic spiritual practices, but following millions of new Asian immigrants to the U.S.

Tibetan Buddhism, for example, taught by the Dalai Lama, began surging in America only after tens of thousands of Tibetans were forced into exile by China, which invaded and has occupied Tibet since 1959.

Pure Land Buddhism (from Japan and China), Chan Buddhism (from China), and Theravada Buddhism (from southeast Asia) all now boast tens of thousands of followers in this country. A popular Buddhism guide lists 1,500 meditation centers in the U.S., with possibly more than a million Americans who would say that Buddhism is their religion.

Bhante Sathi's brand is the Theravada school. Scholars believe it is oldest form of Buddhism and the one that is closest to what the Buddha himself taught during his lifetime in northern India around 600 B.C.

Seated on a folding chair after his recent retreat at the Rochester RCTC, Bhante Sathi reached into his robe for a cell phone that buzzed loudly. He flicked it open to listen to yet another invitation to teach the *dharma.*

"People are more and more worried these days, but without reason," he said after the call. "Most of us are always dealing with our ego, which takes a great deal of energy. In meditation we learn to let go of the ego, to live in the moment, and to see things as they really are.

"When you reduce your ego in this way, you feel more released and free."

The Great State of Minnisootaa

When you talk to men and women from the Oromo tribe of Ethiopia who have fled persecution there to live in Minnesota as refugees, the conversation often takes a surprising turn.

Lencho Bati, who lives in Mankato and teaches African geography at Gustavus Adolphus College in St. Peter, says that over the past six years he has periodically returned to live in Ethiopia.

But he won't say where. That's because when he goes back he does it with the utmost secrecy working for the Oromo Liberation Front, the guerilla militia that's fought a bloody civil war with Ethiopia for the past decade.

And when Bula Atomssa, the president of the Oromo Community of Minnesota, sits down to explain why some 15,000 refugees from the Oromo tribe of Ethiopia have settled in the state over the past decade, he doesn't start by explaining what happened in Ethiopia ten years ago.

He starts by describing the Abyssinian conquest of the 1880's. Then he segues to more than a century's worth of guerilla conflicts and civil wars, continuing to this day, in which the Oromo have consistently tried to reestablish their independence from the central Ethiopian power.

It makes Ethiopia sound like Ireland, where heated political arguments in pubs still start with the 1649 Cromwell invasion. Ireland, as the saying has it, is a place where more history is produced than can be consumed locally.

The point being that the spillover produced from the age-old conflict between the Oromo people and the Ethiopian government is now, via the refugee stream it produces, directly affecting the state of Minnesota.

Or Minnisootaa, as it's spelled in Oromo on hand-written signs throughout the Oromo Center, the social service center for Oromo immigrants run by Atomssa in Minneapolis. Its four-person staff runs refugee and employment services, after-school programs, elderly outreach, and HIV/AIDS prevention.

A 34-year-old with a degree in soil and water conservation from Haromaya University in Ethiopia, Atomssa came to the U.S. in 1998 after taking part in an anti-government rally and getting jailed and tortured for his trouble. He won political asylum status here in 2000 after proving that he would likely be executed if he were forced to return to Ethiopia.

"America is my second country," he says. "It saved my life. If there is no America, there would be no me."

Yet he admits that despite now being married in America, and having an infant son, and running all the Oromo Center programs that he does in the Twin Cities, his heart and mind are usually more in Ethiopia than the U.S.

"Irish Americans think about Ireland, and Jewish people think about Israel," he said. "It's the same with Africans. It's hard to forget. You still want to go there, you still want to help there."

Before the Abyssinian conquest, the Oromo, the largest ethnic group in Ethiopia, had evolved a unique political and social system called "Gada." The Gada system included a constitutional government, universal male suffrage, protection of women's rights, and checks and balances including the mandatory replacement of the entire governing body every eight years.

Atomssa's goal is to return to Ethiopia to help the Oromo people revive the Gada system, modernizing the ancient laws so they fit easily into the global network of democratic nations.

Human rights groups including Amnesty International and Human Rights Watch have published reports detailing the rising

239

persecution of the Oromo people by the Ethiopian government. The abuses include press censorship, extrajudicial killings, arbitrary arrests, torture, and the expulsion of thousands of Oromo students from national universities.

Even the U.S. government, which is generally uncritical of Ethiopia because it is considered a close partner in the war on terror, said in a 2003 report that thousands of Oromo are presently being held in jail without charge on the mere suspicion of involvement with the Oromo Liberation Front.

Lencho Bati says that the recent slaughter of Anuak people, a tiny ethnic group of 100,000 in Ethiopia compared to the Oromo's 28 million, at the hands of the Ethiopian military shows that the present Ethiopian regime is losing its grip on power and is resorting to desperate measures.

"It's a clear sign that Ethiopia is heading towards disaster," he said.

In a world where persecuted foreign ethnic groups are closely linked to their politically active and increasingly affluent U.S. immigrant diasporas via cell phones, the Internet, and air travel, it will increasingly be the case that mayhem and trouble in faraway places will result in increased ripples, and at times flood tides, of immigrant political activism in the U.S.

So far, California, where candidates' positions on Mexican issues have swayed elections, has led the nation in this trend. But with our large refugee and immigrant populations, look for the trend to spread here to Minnesota.

Er, Minnisootaa.

"I Thought Things Couldn't Get Worse"

Dessalines Similhomme's mother, Tifam, has lived in her pajamas the past month. So has his sister, Pelita, and his brother, Idely. The reason is that on the evening of September 19, Hurricane Jeanne slammed into Haiti.

The storm came so quickly, Similhomme's family had to flee without pausing to gather any of their possessions. Within minutes their house was destroyed. First, a wall of water from the ocean swept through their home, toppling the furniture and floating the beds. Then a wall of mud surged from the other direction, demolishing the house and burying the rubble.

A Rochester resident since last year, Dessalines spent a full week of frantic days and nights, wondering if his mother and siblings had survived the onslaught that has killed 3,000 Haitians and left more than 300,000—that's about four Rochesters —homeless and without food or fresh water.

Finally, he reached a friend in his hometown of Gonaives, the Haitian city that took the worst punishment from Jeanne, who had a cell phone, and got the news that Tifam, Pelita, and Idely were alive. But their only possessions were their pajamas, and they were living in a two-room apartment with 25 other people. Until today, they have not had a drink of fresh water.

"I feel very bad and it's hard to sleep," said Dessalines, who works at Sam's Club as a stock clerk. "I think about my mother, my brother, and my sister all the time, and also about all of the families who have lost everything."

It's especially ironic that Dessalines should be suffering, as he's spent most of his 43 years trying to help his fellow

Haitians, first as a church pastor in Gonaives and then, after immigrating to the United States in 1994, in yearly trips back to Haiti to distribute food, clothing, bibles, and cash to the poor.

Last July, he bought and delivered enough rice, corn, and beans to feed everyone at the Church of the Prophetic God in Gonaives, for a day, and then to take bags of dried food home. A videotape he took during the trip shows row upon row of young men and women, dressed in their Sunday finest, gulping down platefuls like there was no tomorrow.

Dessaline's own journey to Rochester has been epic. In 1993, in Haiti, he was arrested, beaten, and thrown in jail. His captors readily admitted they'd been paid to arrest him by a consortium of voodoo priests, who were upset that his preaching was taking too big a bite out of their franchise.

The next year, released from jail as arbitrarily as he'd been put in, but afraid to return to Gonaives for fear of assassination, he met a United Nations official who encouraged him to apply for asylum in the U.S. He did so, and a few months later, with his wife and four children, he boarded an airplane for Cedar Rapids, Iowa. He got a job shrink-wrapping cosmetic products on an assembly line within eight days, and stayed in Iowa for nine years.

The on-the-scene reports he gets from his friend with the cell phone are nothing short of hellish. The 3,000 dead are only the bodies that have been recovered. There are still hundreds of human corpses left buried in the mud, which is six feet deep in places, along with dogs and goats and pigs that were also entombed alive in the sludge.

The stink is horrendous. When the UN disburses food, riots break out, and killings and fatal tramplings occur. Human waste lies in standing pools everywhere. The one hospital in Gonaives, named Providence, was flooded, killing all the patients. Now it is running again, and filled with patients suffering from gangrene. The cuts people got during the flood, even small ones, are getting infected and requiring amputations by the dozen.

These accounts are corroborated by the American journalists and international aid workers who have rushed to Haiti. "Alleyways have become filthy canals, turning Gonaives into a putrid version of Venice," wrote Deborah Sontag in The New York Times on Saturday.

The United States has pledged $21.8 million in relief aid to Caribbean countries affected by hurricanes, which means that Haiti, by far the worst hit by the storms, will share that total with Jamaica, the Bahamas, Grenada, and the Dominican Republic. CARE, one of the most active relief groups to work in Haiti in recent decades, is also distributing aid.

When the hurricane hit Haiti last month, Dessalines had just been to Menards to shop for a water pump and generator he planned to take with him on his next summer trip to Gonaives.

"Even before the storm, there was no clean water to drink," he said. "I thought things could never get worse than that. But they did." ●

IV **THE MINNESOTA ANUAK**

A Lost African Tribe of Minnesota

In a tiny apartment in Austin, six men scrunch close on a sofa and two folding chairs. The air is sweet with Ethiopian incense. In the nearby kitchen, African women prepare a meal as the men discuss a crisis being shown on a home video. One of the men, Omot Ochan, explains that the images show the survivors of a July 7, 2002, attack on his native tribe in northern Africa.

According to the United Nations, which runs several refugee camps nearby, 69 men, women and children were killed that day; 39 were seriously wounded, and 8,700 left homeless and starving. Nearly all the dead and wounded are members of the Anuak (pronounced AN-yoo-ak) tribe, an indigenous people of remote western Ethiopia.

The video shows a filthy hospital in Ethiopia packed with sick young men lying listlessly on cots, their bodies broken and thin, their bloody bandages flecked with flies, their eyes despairing.

In some shots, the wounded men wince as they turn over to show bullet holes gaping in their sides. The men in the Austin apartment literally wince as they describe recognizing some of the wounded men in the hosptal as friends and relatives. Like the men in the video, they are members of the Anuak tribe, but they escaped the violence in their land to come to Minnesota in recent years. Today they are meeting frequently to discuss how to help their relatives back home as the Anuak suffer an especially intense bout of tribal killings and ethnic cleansing.

They have formed a group called the Anuak Relief Committee to support and raise money for those left wounded or homeless by the July massacre. The committee, which also acts as an informational clearinghouse for the Anuak community in Minnesota, is based in St. Paul and has members from southeastern Minnesota and the Sioux Falls, South Dakota, area.

I look out the apartment window and see a group of American teenagers tumble out of an SUV and rush into a McDonald's restaurant. We're a long, long way from northern Africa. Yet in this living room in Austin, the fates of Minnesota and Africa intertwine. After all, some of the Anuak men have been here for more than five years and are U.S. citizens. Now they are trying to get the U.S. government to intervene to save their families back home.

Southern Minnesota is home to the world's largest community of Anuak refugees, which numbers about 1,200. Most arrived in the area in the mid-1990s, after the 1991 government change in Ethiopia triggered chaos in the remote western part of the country where the Anuak tribe lives.

"Our people are like the Indians in the United States," Ochan explained. "We want to be independent and to run our own lives. But the Ethiopian government is suspicious of anyone who wants to be independent, and we have suffered from that."

Everyone in the Austin apartment, not far from the Hormel Foods plant where several Anuak work, has a horror story to tell from the early mid-1990s, when they fled Ethiopia.

"There was nothing to eat and nothing to buy," said Obang, who now lives in Rochester and asked that his full name not be used so that he could protect family members who still live in Ethiopia. "You could see many people dying in the street. You didn't know who your enemy was. If you saw a man with a gun, it could be an Ethiopian soldier, a Sudanese rebel, or someone from the former military. If they didn't like you, they could shoot you. So we ran."

According to accounts given by Minnesota Anuak in the two years following the takeover of the new Ethiopian government in 1991, the government sent troops into the Anuak's fertile and oil-rich territory to take control. Random killings, and sometimes massacres of the Anuak ensued. Thousands fled through the Ethiopian jungle, where many died from lion attacks, into refugee camps in northern Kenya.

Obang's journey began when he woke up one morning to the sound of gunfire and screaming. "I saw the soldiers shooting and I ran," he said.

"I was trying to think what to do, but there was nothing in my head. I could feel the bullets going between my arms and legs and around my head. I saw my friends fall down from the gunshots all around me. One was crying in the river where he had been shot. I crawled down to the river and I got into the water and the mud and I held him and I carried him. We stayed in the water for four hours before we could get away. Many people were injured and dying. Since that day, I have never worried about something they call dying. I never worry about what's coming because it's not in my power to change."

After living two years at the Ifo refugee camp in northern Kenya, a tent city of 70,000 where, at its worst, dozens of people a day died of simple infections and diarrhea, Obang was granted refugee status. The International Organization for Migration, an international aid group based in Geneva, relocated him. He worked as a dishwasher at a Chicago Hilton hotel and as a meat cutter at the John Morrell & Co. slaughterhouse in Sioux City, Iowa, before taking a job assembling computer cabinetry at the Crenlo Inc. factory in Rochester.

Obang studies English and is taking graduate-equivalency classes and studying English in Rochester. He hopes to attend college here one day. He became a U.S. citizen last fall.

Most of the Anuak refugees in Minnesota, like Obang, spent two or three years at the Ifo refugee camp before immigrating to the United States. They came to Chicago, St. Paul, Sioux City, and other Midwestern cities before following jobs into smaller cities like Austin, Rochester and Willmar.

"The United States is special," Obang said. "The best thing is that citizens give their opinions to the government, and the government listens to them. That's freedom. So we are asking the U.S. government to help the Anuak."

Through USAID, the U.S. government sent $58.8 million in foreign aid to Ethiopia in 2002, and has requested a budget of $77 million for 2003. Making receipt of this foreign aid contingent on the Ethiopian government's improved actions toward the Anuak is their goal, Obang said.

"The the horrible videotape turns and turns. The tape was made by a Minnesota Anuak who was visiting his family just after the July 7 massacre. It shows the remains of two Anuak villages, Elea and Pinyman, burned to the ground. Once clusters of round straw huts, the villages now are nothing but black circles burned into the ground. Inside the circles are the shattered ceramic urns and gourds that once stored corn flour and oil. A mass grave is shown at one point as the video's narrator explains there was no time to bury victims in individual graves.

In western Ethiopia where the Anuak live, life still balances on a knife's edge. Every nightfall brings the dread of another possible massacre. So every night here in Minnesota, after finishing their jobs at the meatpacking plants or factories, the Minnesota Anuak frantically telephone loved ones in Gambella, the Ethiopian town where many of the homeless have congregated. They collect the latest news. They have done this every day since July, buying fistfuls of telephone cards, with a different person calling home each night and then all the next day sharing the news.

The Anuak Relief Committee has met in emergency session in a different apartment every weekend since July to strategize how to raise money, how to raise awareness of the Anuak's plight outside of Africa, and how to find other ways to help.

Among themselves, the Minnesota Anuak have raised $20,000 to send to friends and family who survived the July attack, Ochan said. The money is wired to a bank in Gambella, where a friend on the telephone can immediately confirm that the money has arrived and been deposited.

The group has also launched letter-writing campaigns aimed at the U.S. government, the Ethiopian government, and Human Rights Watch, Amnesty International and other human rights groups. In these letters, the Anuak call upon the Ethiopian government to conduct a full investigation of the conflicts and to strongly consider relocating the refugee camps, the source of the recent violence, to the fringes of Anuak territory. So far, there has been no substantial reply.

The best source of information about the Anuak tribe is Cultural Survival, a 30-year-old research and activist organization based in Cambridge, Mass. Founded in 1972 by Harvard anthropologist David Maybury-Lewis and funded then by the U.S. Agency for International Development and the Ford Foundation, the group since 1981 has published a half-dozen reports detailing the Anuak's tragic story. The report titles alone tell much of it: "Ethiopia's Policy of Genocide Against the Anuak," "Anuak Displacement and Ethiopian Resettlement," "Oil Development in Ethiopia: A Threat to the Anuak" and "Armed Struggle and Indigenous People."

In 1986, Cultural Survival put the Anuak on its list of "endangered cultures," citing the Ethiopian government's clearance of Anuak land for resettlement as the major threat. Many Anuak were dying, the report said, when farmers tried to fight off Ethiopian soldiers with only their rakes and spears. Estimates of the number of Anuak living today range around 100,000, with perhaps one-tenth of that number having fled the country and now living in exile.

As the indigenous people of western Ethiopia and southeastern Sudan, the Anuak have reaped much greater than its share of the sorrows brought by the civil wars, droughts, and famines that have plagued both countries over the past 30 years. The tribe's rich but remote territory has absorbed wave after wave of refugees from its eastern, western and northern borders. From the north and the east, the Ethiopian government has sent several hundred thousand famine victims to resettle on

Anuak land since the early 1980s. From the west, hundreds of thousands of Sudan civil war refugees have poured in. These waves of settlers and refugees have overrun and destroyed much of the Anuak's traditional farming, hunting and fishing grounds, and brought to a boiling point deep tribal rivalries that had long remained at a simmer.

The current crisis erupted in the refugee camps. Most of the camps' refugees are members of the Nuer tribe of Sudan, with whom the Anuak have had bitter relations for more than a century. The July massacre, according to the telephone reports gathered by the Minnesota-based Anuak, started with a garden-variety Anuak-Nuer shouting match, but turned deadly when a gang of Nuer left and quickly returned to settle things with AK-47 assault rifles.

Tragically, a Thanksgiving weekend massacre, which resulted in 33 deaths, was possibly caused by Anuaks taking revenge for the July slaughter.

"After so many years of being killed, and being killed, and being killed, it may be that an Anuak just burst," Ochan said. "We don't know the full facts yet. But after the July massacre, the Anuak may have thought, 'Unless we do something, they will just kill us again and again.' But now, of course, more violence is all the more likely to happen. It's so tragic."

At the meeting in Austin, the young children of the somber adults run through the cramped living room on their way to a bedroom, where, laughing and giggling, they jump up and down on the bed.

Yet these days, dark images of death are impinging on the paradise the Anuak are trying to create for themselves in Minnesota. Delivered by videotape or by telephone calls back home, these nightmares violently thrust the past into the present, bringing urgent tasks and responsibilities.

"We have finally escaped to America," Ochan said. "But when we see our families back home getting killed we say, 'Maybe we should have stayed and suffered with them. Maybe that is the right way.' It's easy to feel hopeless. But we will keep on. We believe that if we can express and share our suffering with the world, we can make some change." ●

Minnesota Anuak
Fear 400 Dead in Ethiopian Massacre

There will be no last names given in this article. The reason is that if the last names are published, those people or their relatives could be shot and killed.

Let me explain. I am talking about the relatives of some 1,200 Minnesotans.

At 1 p.m. on the afternoon of December 13, more than 200 uniformed soldiers of the Ethiopian army marched into the town of Gambella in remote western Ethiopia, near the border with Sudan.

The soldiers spread out through the town and knocked on the doors of the houses and huts made from corrugated steel and straw matting. Some of the soldiers had pieces of paper with addresses and names. If no one answered their knocks, the soldiers broke down the doors and grabbed all the men and boys inside the house, looking under beds for anyone hiding.

Once the frightened prisoners were in the street, the soldiers beat them with their guns and then told them to run. When they did, the prisoners were shot in their backs. Meanwhile, civilians in town from a different ethnic group than the victims appeared wielding spears and machetes.

"I am going crazy right now," said Romeago, a Minneapolis resident whose sister's home was burned down. "My sister and her kids ran for their lives into the bush. We have no idea if they are safe. We are just praying."

Sometimes the spear-wielding civilians, watched by the passive Ethiopian government soldiers, ran the prisoners through with their spears or simply hacked them down like small trees. They crumpled and died in the street.

Eyewitnesses to the massacre, including one man named Omot who lives in Gambella, and with whom I spoke on the telephone Monday, say that more than 400 bodies have been recovered, many of them from a mass grave.

The United Nations, which runs three refugee camps in the region, has confirmed that violence took place in Gambella and said all of the dead are members of the Anuak tribe, an indigenous people of Western Ethiopia who have been the target of ethnic cleansing for more than a decade. But the UN did not confirm that 400 had died.

About 2,000 Anuak refugees came to the United States in the 1990s, with more than half of them settling in southern Minnesota. About 200 Anuak rallied on Saturday at the state Capitol, marching and making speeches to grab the attention of Minnesota citizens, legislators and the press. It was a freezing cold day, however, and I was the only reporter present.

"The problem is hunger," said Obang, a Minneapolis citizen whose brother is missing and feared dead. "There is nothing to eat. Even if you have money, you have no place to go to get food. You are afraid of being killed."

The Anuak live in a verdant but remote area that has active gold pits and is also known to have oil deposits. Over the past two decades, more than 100,000 refugees from the Sudanese civil war, many of them members of the Nuer tribe, have been settled in the region. Tens of thousands of Ethiopians from poorer parts of the country have also been resettled to the Anuak land.

On Dec. 13, according to the testimony of Anuak survivors, the government and "highlander" Ethiopians collaborated in the massacre.

Omot, the man I interviewed by phone, lost a son in the attack.

"He was a driver and they shot him in his car," Omot said. "I survived by hiding in the bush. I saw a uniformed soldier kill one boy, a student."

Omot also saw a young man who had been shot in the leg

255

and could not walk, and was crying out for help in the street. Omot couldn't help the boy for fear of being shot himself.

The thought of that boy haunts me.

Is he still alive, I wonder? Or was he shot like a crippled dog by the soldiers?

What would it be like to be shot and wounded and left abandoned to die slowly, on the side of a street in the middle of one's own town?

That question kept me awake last night. That and whether Minnesotans will rally to help the suffering relatives of their fellow citizens, the Minnesota Anuak. ●

How News of an African Genocide Broke on a Minnesota Blog

The response to my column three weeks ago, in which I reported on a genocide occurring in Ethiopia, has been so extraordinary I'd like to share it.

I got 55 e-mails and more than a dozen phone calls from places like The Hague, New Dehli, Cape Town, Melbourne, Geneva, and Washington DC, as well as from southern Minnesota, Wisconsin, and South Dakota.

The McGill Report was the first news source anywhere to report on a new genocide that is occurring on the other side of the planet. I wrote the column because more Anuak refugees live in Minnesota than any other state, and they have been thrown into a panic about family and friends back home.

My account of the massacre was based on interviews with two dozen Anuak in St. Paul and Minneapolis who had spoken by telephone with eyewitnesses in Ethiopia on the day of the massacre and in the days immediately after.

"You were the first to report on this and we're very grateful," wrote Greg Stanton, president of Genocide Watch in The Hague, in an e-mail. On January 8, after having done its own research in Ethiopia to corroborate The McGill Report article, Genocide Watch put the Anuak killings on its genocide alert list and published an article filled with damning new evidence.

By breaking local news, the McGill Report broke global news. Anuak refugees all over the world who were desperate for news of friends and relatives from home, sent my column zipping around the Internet.

Samantha Power, the author of the Pulitzer prizewinning book, "A Problem from Hell: America and the Age of Genocide," e-mailed to say she was outraged to learn about the new genocide and was going spread news of it.

Most meaningful of all to me were two dozen e-mails from Anuak refugees around the world who wrote to say—often in these very words—"God bless you and thank you." These letters were filled with a heavy grief but also with a great dignity and a profoundly touching gratitude.

Just that someone had listened to them, had moved many Anuak deeply.

"Sir, I would like to thank you for being a real friend of this small and defenseless tribe," wrote Ujulu Goch, from Washington, DC. "God has always worked through someone to help needy people like the Anuak. But Sir, this is not the end of the tragedy. It's the beginning of the extinction of my tribe from the face of the earth."

Obang Metho, from Saskatchewan, Canada, sent me six attachments in his e-mail – letters he had written to U.S. Secretary of State Powell, U.N. Secretary General Kofi Annan, and other diplomats and aid groups.

He also sent a poem called "Why Do I Rebel?" that captured a note of inspired defiance:

I rebel because honor
And justice are the work of duty and destiny.

I fight because honor and justice
Are the fixed demands of duty and beauty.

I speak up because love of liberty
And the well-being of every human
Are the splendid ornament of the moral life.

Here in Rochester, we can be an early warning system for crimes and atrocities committed all over the world, which would never receive the cleansing light of international attention if not for us. We are free; most of the world is not; therefore it's our opportunity and our responsibility to be such a watch dog.

We can do this simply by being open to what our immigrant neighbors have to say.

Reverend LeRoy Christoffels, the pastor of the Worthington Christian Reformed Church, which has many Anuak refugees as parishioners, said his church was raising money for an Anuak relief effort.

John Frankhauser, of Spokane, e-mailed to say he had brought an Anuak pastor, Reverend Okwier Othello, to his church last summer to meet with Anuak members of the church. "He spoke of the danger he faced when he returned to Gambella," Frankhauser wrote. "We were impressed with his gentle spirit and the way the other Anuaks respect him as their pastor."

Reverend Okwier Othello is the first name on the list of the dead that I have. Frankhauser had received eyewitness accounts of his murder and gave details of his death that are too grisly to recount here.

It was Martin Luther King Day when I wrote this column, so I went to his "Letter from Birmingham Jail" to find some lines that seemed relevant.

There are parallels between the way King encircled Birmingham and Atlanta within a single moral sphere, and the way the ripples of grief and outrage from the Anuak massacre had so quickly spread around the world.

"I cannot sit idly by in Atlanta and not be concerned about what happens in Birmingham," King wrote in his jail cell. "Injustice anywhere is a threat to justice everywhere. We are caught in an inescapable network of mutuality, tied in a single garment of destiny. Whatever effects one directly, affects all indirectly." ●

Stranded in Nairobi

NAIROBI—Two days ago, I arrived here on my way to Pochalla, Sudan, where 10,000 members of the Anuak tribe of Ethiopia are huddled in foodless, shelterless, friendless misery.

They were driven to Pochalla, a refugee camp in the south Sudan desert, by the Ethiopian army, which is presently conducting one of the most vicious yet still almost entirely unknown genocides in the world today, against the Anuak people.

About 2,000 Anuak live in Minnesota, which is why I have come here. The Minnesota Anuak are utterly distraught and anxious to hear news from relatives who have fled for two weeks through the Sudan desert to Pochalla, running from marauding soldiers while totally exposed to the searing desert heat.

Dozens have died from starvation and exposure on the trip.

My forward progress to Pochalla has been blocked by two developments.

The most serious is reports today that Ethiopian troops have crossed the Ethiopia-Sudan border and are advancing toward Pochalla.

It might be just a rumor but it might not, and I need to spend at least another day trying to get better information. Since December uniformed Ethiopian troops have slaughtered up to 1,000 Anuak civilians, including unarmed herders and farmers, and burned several Anuak villages to the ground.

On Dec. 13, more than 400 Anuak were killed in Gambella City, the capital of Gabella Province of Ethiopia, the Anuaks' traditional homeland. That massacre and the subsequent pogroms against Anuak villages started the exodus of refugees seeking safety in the Sudan desert.

The other bother is that my luggage—two travel bags containing my camera, malaria medicine, fresh clothes, documents and gifts from Minnesota Anuaks to their relatives at the Pochalla camp—never arrived in Nairobi. Last night, I spent from 3 a.m. to 4 a.m. on the telephone to the Amsterdam Airport, where it seems my bags are hung up. Today, my fourth day in Kenya, I am dreaming wistfully of fluffy white socks and fresh underwear.

I've been through this in China and Southeast Asia, where I lived for 10 years, so I can settle myself by remembering that everything will work out—only it will be on a Third World timetable, not my own. So, on a Third World timetable, I wait.

This morning I walked from the Christian missionary guest house where I am staying to a nearby coffee shop, where I collected Swahili words from the wall posters and sipped black coffee to the piped-in sounds of Eminem.

I bought a copy of the Daily Nation newspaper and thumbed my way through it. Today's front page news is flooding caused by heavy rain the past several nights, and the burning down of Kenya Seed Company under suspicious circumstances.

The editorial pages, meanwhile, are filled with nervous articles, commentaries and letters on a single topic—a security crisis in this city, for which the phrase "crime spree" doesn't suffice. All of Nairobi is being mugged by highly organized criminal gangs that run extortion rackets and prostitution rings, traffic in drugs and guns (mainly assault rifles) carry out nightly armed robberies of civilian homes and businesses, and even run critical public services, including the city's Matatu, or minivan transport system.

The entire African continent is awash in guns. First the Cold War armed hundreds of national and private militias fighting wars of independence, liberation movements, tribal defense actions and underworld feuds. Since 1989, the free market system under globalization has done the same thing.

Now the guns that flooded Africa under the righteous banners of "liberation and self-defense" are being trafficked by criminal enterprises feeding demand from city-based gangs and underworld entrepreneurs.

The most feared gangs in Nairobi are the Mungiki, the Kamjesh and the Twenty-Threes.

Last night, when I wanted to walk six blocks from my guest house to a restaurant, the staff sternly advised against it. "After 9 p.m. in Nairobi, if you are white, you are a marked man," the doorman, who is black, told me. "Even I would be afraid to take a walk at this time."

Driving back from the restaurant in an unmarked car that belongs to the guest house, my driver and I were stopped by Nairobi police, who asked for my passport and driver's license. Police checkpoints are set up around the city at night to catch stolen vehicles that are one of the local gang's biggest businesses.

Back at the guest house, we passed through a tall iron gate topped with razor wire, into a gorgeous courtyard ringed by an 8-foot-high concrete fence covered with lush, green ivy. The walls surround the entire missionary compound, and it made me sleep easier last night.

Meanwhile, the Anuak refugees in Pochalla, like me, just sit and wait. ◉

A Gunfire Evasion Seminar

LOKICHOGGIO, KENYA—A dozen years ago, this place was a temporary settlement of woven grass huts belonging to the Turkana tribe, desert nomads whose tall men strike naturally elegant poses in their porkpie hats and kilt-like skirts.

Turkana women look like supermodels draped in body-length shawls of brilliant colors and piles of beaded necklaces that cover their necks from shoulder to ear. Their walk is a sashay. Sometimes babies peek out from crescent hammocks slung across the women's backs.

Today, Loki, as it's usually called, is transformed into a frontier boomtown whose growth has been fueled by the 20-year-long Sudan Civil War. In 1992, the United Nations and a dozen other humanitarian agencies opened offices here to serve the millions of refugees the war was generating across the border.

The heart of this desert outpost is a gated compound containing United Nations and other aid agency headquarters. Ringing the compound are a half-dozen safari tent hotels, private airline companies and airplane garages, and the most culture-clashing shopping strip this side of the alien taverns where creatures from a thousand galaxies exchange interplanetary gossip in the Star Wars flicks.

Here in Loki, the Turkana women carry bundles on their heads near a cosmetics shop where U.S. and European women shop for Nivea skin cream. The sleek Turkana men saunter side-by-side with aid workers, U.N. officials, and bush pilots dressed in khaki shorts, sunglasses, T-shirts and clodhopper boots.

This morning, my guide and translator, Barnabas Gilo, and I received a two-hour United Nations security briefing to qualify us to fly tomorrow morning from Loki to Pochalla, Sudan, where some 10,000 refugees of the Anuak tribe of Ethiopia have settled in the past three months.

The Anuak refugees are fleeing an especially vicious outbreak of an ethnic cleansing being conducted by the Ethiopian military against their tribe over the past decade.

The ethnic cleansing has sent about 1,200 Anuak refugees to southern Minnesota, where they work at the Hormel plants in Austin and Willmar, as shelf stockers at Wal-Marts, as security guards and as nursing-home staff. Many now are American citizens and are raising Anuak-American children and families.

The briefing was conducted by Royston Wright, a gruffly good-humored Australian and 20-year United Nations field worker who clicked through a PowerPoint presentation with an African parrot perched on his shoulder.

The briefing mainly covered directions to follow if Barnabas and I come under gunfire attack while in Pochalla. Our instructions in this case are:

> 1. To run from where we are being attacked to a safe place. (It sounds obvious, but Wright pointed out that many people freeze with fear when they come under fire and forget to run from the location that is being targeted.)
>
> 2. Make a long-range radio telephone call to the United Nations at the Loki base. (We are carrying a radio telephone and a satellite phone with us.)
>
> 3. Stay hidden until the U.N. sends a rescue plane out to find us, following a signal from the GPS unit embedded in our radio telephone. God willing.

The walls of the briefing room were hung with color-coded maps of southern Sudan showing levels and types of danger—

land-mine areas, ambush-prone areas, unexploded ordinance areas, areas where military conflict is occurring, etc.

The Pochalla refugee camp is Level 2 out of four security levels ranging from Level 1 (calm and quiet) to Level 4 (all hell is breaking loose.) After passing a short test covering the basics of an evacuation procedure, if one is needed, Barnabas and I are cleared for the visit.

Before heading to the mess hall for dinner, we stop by the office of the Sudan Relief and Rehabilitation Commission. This is the relief arm of the Sudan People's Liberation Army, the rebel-led militia that has fought the Khartoum government to a standoff over 20 years and now controls most of southern Sudan.

At the SRRC, we meet a group of 50 young Anuak men who have just finished a torturous two-day ride in the back of an open truck through the Sudan desert from Pochalla, where famine forced them to try to escape.

Only last month, they had completed a two-week exodus on foot from their home province in western Ethiopia, Gambella, into Pochalla, across the border in Sudan. They were fleeing the killings being carried out by uniformed Ethiopian military units against the Anuak tribe, which to date have claimed more than 1,000 lives.

The refugees' hoped-for destination is the UN-run Kenyan refugee camp of Kakuma, where they could get not only food and shelter but also regular classes in reading and writing and mathematics. In other words, a bit of a life. ●

"Sir, Are You Conducting a Genocide?"

ADDIS ABABA, ETHIOPIA—It is surreal to prepare for an interview in which my first question will be "Minister, are you conducting a genocide?"

I have a meeting scheduled soon with Dr. Barnabas Gebre-Ab, the minister of federal affairs for the Gambella State of Ethiopia.

Gambella is the Ethiopian region from which some 10,000 refugees have recently fled across the border into neighboring Sudan, carrying with them stories of murder, rape, and the torching of entire Anuak villages by the Ethiopian military.

The Ethiopian government was not previously known as partial to genocide, so the Gambella atrocities have raised an unusually high level of alert at the United Nations and among international humanitarian and aid groups.

Ethiopia receives more than $500 million in annual foreign aid, a lifeline for this famine-plagued country that would tragically disappear if donors decide that the government is attempting to wipe out one of its own indigenous tribal groups.

The flow of refugees from Gambella began last Dec. 13, when more than 400 members of the Anuak tribe there were slaughtered by Ethiopian military, aided by members of other ethnic groups wielding machetes and spears. According to eyewitnesses, the Ethiopian troops went house to house in Gambella calling out the Anuak men, telling them to run, and then shooting them in their backs. Those who refused to run were slashed down by Ethiopian "highlanders" with their machetes as the soldiers looked on.

The carnage continued in Gambella town for three days, after which Ethiopian troops are said to have spread throughout Gambella state where they systematically razed entire villages, shot Anuak farmers and herders, and lit fire to the mud-and-straw "tukuls," or huts, often with Anuak women and children still inside of them.

Gang rapes have also been reported. International humanitarian agencies including Genocide Watch, Survival International, and the World Organization Against Torture have all denounced the slaughter and accused the Ethiopian government of conducting campaigns of ethnic cleansing and genocide against the Anuak.

The United Nations High Commission for Refugees in Geneva held a fact-finding session on the December 13 massacre in March. And the U.S. Embassy in Ethiopia has said in a press release that it gives credence to reports that Ethiopian troops have participated in Anuak extermination. Dr. Gebre-Ab is named as one of the three architects responsible for the genocide in several humanitarian group reports on the Dec. 13 massacre and subsequent pogroms across Gambella state.

Naturally I am curious and apprehensive about whom I will find sitting across from me on the appointed day. My friends and family are worried. "Are you nuts?" is their general tone. Specifically they ask: "Aren't you afraid the Ethiopian government will throw you in jail or worse?"

Not really, is my answer.

Ethiopia is a country of 66 million people with significant ties to the west. It exports coffee, its main agricultural product, and has tourism based on its extraordinary natural beauty and wildlife, early human archeological sites, and a Judaic-influenced ancient Christianity is still practiced here.

Addis Ababa, where I arrived yesterday, is in some ways a modern city. It has the largest Sheraton Hotel in Africa. It's got an enormous international airport and the country supports a commercial airline. Telephones, Internet connections, running water, flush toilets, paved roads, fantastic architecture, beautiful cathedrals, superb cuisine, great museums, great wildlife parks—they're all here.

In other words, Ethiopia is enmeshed in an international web of commercial, diplomatic, collegial, and friendship ties upon which the entire country depends. It is a Third World country that's chosen the path of international capitalism (as China, South Korea, and Kenya have) instead of despotic isolation (as North Korea, Laos, and Cuba have).

Having done so, they subject themselves to the pressure of international censure if they are really carrying out a genocide. Aid will be cut off. Trade and finance and friendships will end. Government members will be paraded as monsters before their diplomatic, business, and social acquaintances on CNN, a modern form of shaming in the public square.

Unlike Saddam or Castro or Kim Jong-Il, the Ethiopian government under the leadership of Prime Minister Meles Zenawi long ago made its choice to develop via international trade and commerce, not paranoid dictatorship.

Therefore, I predict Dr. Barnabas Gebre-Ab will be no obvious monster. He will have a well-appointed office in a modern building. He will be sociable and smiling. He will probably speak English and be fluent in the codes and pleasantries of international diplomacy.

He will be more Adolf Eichmann than Adolf Hitler. I could be wrong. I have registered my presence in Ethiopia with the U.S. Embassy here just in case. ●

Ethiopia's Minister of Genocide

ADDIS ABABA, ETHIOPIA—I finally went man-to-man with Ethiopiaa's Minister of Genocide.

He greeted me with a serious nod in his Addis Ababa office and offered me an orange Fanta. He was eager to tell the world his side of the story, he said. He was fed up with the reports coming from the United Nations and from humanitarian groups about widespread ethnic cleansing of the Anuak people of western Ethiopia. He wanted to set the record straight.

After the interview he drove me to my hotel, then invited me for a beer at a local restaurant where we spoke for another hour. His two bodyguards, grim-faced young men carrying AK-47 assault rifles, stood watch nearby as we chatted into the Ethiopian night.

I couldn't stop him from talking.

"If I died tomorrow, I would die with a clear conscience," he said. "I have made mistakes. I am not a perfect man. But I know that I have always done my best in life."

Some Anuak relief groups have named Barnabas Gebre-Ab, Ethiopia's Minister of Federal Affairs for the State of Gambella, in western Ethiopia, as the highest-ranking of three officials responsible for the targeted killing of more than 1,200 Anuak in the past three months in Gambella.

Last December 13, more than 400 Anuak were killed in a single day in the town of Gambella, the capital of the state of Gambella. Eyewitnesses say the Ethiopian army has since conducted scorched-earth raids against many Anuak villages killing men, women, and children.

Some 1,200 Anuak immigrants live in southern Minnesota where they've come over the past decade fleeing earlier episodes of ethnic cleansing. The newest violence in Gambella means that more Anuak refugees will ultimately emigrate from Africa to live in Minnesota.

No group has definitively linked Gebre-Ab to the killings. Yet he is the Ethiopian government official with direct responsibility for day-to-day government and military operations in Gambella state where the killings have occurred. He is the civilian chief of the Ethiopian military force that is posted in Gambella. And at least one source, the former governor of Gambella, says he heard Gebre-Ab give an order to the top Ethiopian military commander to use violent force against the Anuak.

In a column I wrote the day before I met Gebre-Ab, I predicted that he would be more Adolph Eichmann than Adolph Hitler. I expected to meet a bland functionary who saw himself as "just carrying out orders," as opposed to a zealot who justified atrocities by appealing to a greater cause.

Boy, was I wrong. Gebre-Ab is a zealot but not a fascist one. He is a communist one.

"In our revolutionary days we read one model after another —Mao Tse-tung, Sun Yat-sen, Castro, and especially Lenin," he told me over beers.

Like many top Ethiopian government figures, Gebre-Ab fought as a revolutionary for more than a decade to topple the cruel communist regime known as the Dergue. Gebre-Ab was a medic in the revolutionary militia, hiding out for years until the Dergue was finally overthrown in 1991.

After the revolution, Gebre-Ab earned a doctorate degree in England before returning to Ethiopia to accept a government post. His articulate English has a light British accent, plus vocabulary words taken straight from Das Kapital. He spoke frequently of Ethiopia's "lumpens," or criminal class, borrowing the Marxist term made famous in the phrase "lumpen proletariat."

During my trip to Ethiopia, I asked people many times

"Why would the government of this country want to wipe out the Anuak tribe?" There are several possible answers. One is that Gambella state, the Anuak's ancestral homeland, is geographically remote but is agriculturally fertile and contains gold and oil reserves. This makes it attractive for economic development and population resettlement programs by the central government.

The Anuak have consistently pushed for a greater degree of self-rule than Ethiopia wishes to grant, fueling tensions. In addition, the black-skinned Anuak people have historically been persecuted by the lighter-skinned Ethiopians, who in the past have even raided Gambella to abduct slaves.

To these reasons I would add a third, which is that strong ideologies, in particular utopian ones like communism, often breed atrocities.

The vision of an ideal society shines so brightly that any amount of brutality is justified as a means to that glorious end. Such a zealot might thus justify wiping out an entire Anuak village including women and children, just to kill one or two Anuak resistance fighters the village was harboring.

The tragedy of My Lai, and the torture of Iraqi prisoners at Abu Ghraib, shows that Americans have no monopoly on virtue in this area.

As we finished our beers, Gebre-Ab described how he had hungrily read through all the great works of communist revolutionaries for inspiration. It struck me that he and his fellow revolutionaries are now discovering that revolution doesn't work as a principle of governance.

It's been thirteen years since the Dergue was overthrown. Today, rather than fostering democracy, the Ethiopian government is adopting the Dergue's own former methods to keep power and maintain domestic rule.

Its future therefore belongs not as a member of the international family of open, tolerant, liberal democracies, but in an international court of law. ●

Genocide of the Anuak Broadens to Women, Children, and Villages

ADDIS ABABA, ETHIOPIA—A genocide in western Ethiopia that began last December with a massacre of some 400 Anuak tribe members has broadened into widespread attacks by Ethiopian military troops against more than a dozen Anuak villages in the western Ethiopian province of Gambella, according to Anuak refugees and humanitarian aid groups.

Scorched-earth raids carried out from January through April have destroyed a dozen Anuak villages in Gambella, refugees said. The raids have driven more than 10,000 Anuak into refugee camps in neighboring Sudan and Kenya, according to the United Nations High Commissioner for Refugees.

While the December 13 massacre in Gambella town, the capital of Gambella province, was directed only at educated male Anuak, the new phase of the genocide has seen women and children killed, hundreds of Anuak homes and fields burned, and gang rapes of dozens of girls and women, according to Anuak refugees.

Fleeing earlier episodes of ethnic cleansing, more than 1,200 Anuak refugees have immigrated to Minnesota since the early 1990s. The present crisis, however, is by far the bloodiest phase of the continuing genocide of the Anuak in Ethiopia.

More than two dozen Anuak survivors interviewed in mid-April in south Sudan said that on Dec. 13, several hundred uniformed Ethiopian soldiers led the slaughter of more than 425 male leaders of the Anuak tribe in the town of Gambella. The troops used a list of names to identify educated Anuak men whom they dragged from their homes and shot with AK-

47 assault rifles in the streets.

Ethiopian troops also incited hundreds of ethnic Ethiopian "highlanders" living in Gambella to go to their homes to fetch machetes, knives and spears, and to join them in the slaughter, eyewitnesses said. Survivors said the Ethiopian troops burned hundreds of Anuak "tukuls," traditional mud and straw homes, and gang-raped hundreds of Anuak girls.

The Ethiopian military broadened its attacks after Dec. 13 by dispatching troop trucks and, in one case, allegedly a helicopter gunship, against Anuak villages throughout Gambella state. The total casualties from these attacks is said to be more than 1,000.

The eyewitness Anuak accounts have been corroborated by independent investigations made by humanitarian groups including Genocide Watch in Washington, DC., and the World Organization Against Torture, based in Geneva, Switzerland. Amnesty International and the governments of the U.S., the European Union, Canada have all called on the Ethiopian government to immediately investigate the reports.

"The Ethiopian People's Revolutionary Defense Front and highland Ethiopian civilians [have] initiated a campaign of massacres, repression, and mass rape deliberately targeting the indigenous Anuak minority," Genocide Watch wrote in its February 2004 report, following a research team visit to Pochalla. "A severe escalation of violence [has] the potential to provoke a full-scale international military confrontation if not immediately checked."

The Genocide Watch team documented numerous instances of attacks on Anuak as the Highlander attackers sang or chanted slogans like "Let's kill them all!" and "Now is the day for killing Anuak!" Hand grenades thrown into huts was frequently reported, as was looting and, on February 1, the exhumation of a mass grave in the Jabjab region of Gambella by 11 Ethiopian soldiers, apparently to remove evidence of the massacre.

In Addis Ababa on April 22, Barnabas Gebre-Ab, the

Ethiopian Federal Minister with statutory responsibility for Gambella state, insisted that all reports of an Anuak genocide were "fabrications."

Gebre-Ab admitted the region had suffered "tragic" bouts of violence in recent months but said the killers were not the Ethiopian military but, rather, armed revolutionary cells of the Anuak people themselves.

"These are Anuak," Gebre-Ab said. "It's an Anuak group which claims to have formed a liberation front in Gambella, okay? So these are the ones who are killing. They kill engineers. They kill health workers. Teachers. If they are Highlanders, they kill them. Deliberately. And we are hunting them. We have to hunt them down.

"If you want to challenge the political order through violence, we won't let you go. So we are doing our job. Because we are giving them a mortal blow, they are fabricating about this rape, and this and that, it's all fabrication."

According to Gebre-Ab, it was a mob of "vagabonds" and "social scums" including many Highlanders who precipitated the widespread killing of Anuak on December 13. "It's related to animosity. It's hatred, you know," he said. "Why couldn't they control themselves? Why did they go into this emotional outburst and start to kill? Because they are social scums."

"In all societies there are backward elements," Gebre-Ab said. "They are illiterate. They are backward. They are liable to commit crimes."

On December 18, five days after the December 13 massacre, Gebre-Ab released a statement blaming the killings on the Oromo Liberation Front and the Eritrean Peoples' Liberation Front, two resistance forces fighting the Meles regime that are based in areas far remote from Gambella state. A few days later, the Ethiopian defense ministry announced on national radio that inter-tribal conflicts between the Anuak and the Nuer tribes.

Okello Akuai, the governor of Gambella state last December

13, strongly disputes Gebre-Ab's account of the massacre. An Anuak himself, Okello fled for his life on January 8 and today lives in exile in Europe.

"Gebre-Ab gave the order to the local military," Okello said in a telephone interview. "I know that because I was at the military camp when it happened. I was sitting next to the military commander in the region, Tsegaye Beyene, when he got the call from Gebre-Ab on December 13."

"From there they started killing people in the town," Okello said. On the second day of the killing, Okello said he pleaded with Tsegaye to stop the killing. "I quarreled with him, I told him to stop the killings," Okello said. "He said to me, 'All Anuak are the same, they are butchers.'"

On the early morning of December 13, before the killings began in Gambella, an unidentified group attacked a vehicle carrying eight Highlander government officials, killing them all. According to Okello and other Anuak eyewitnesses, the Ethiopian army displayed their corpses in downtown Gambella and incited local Highlanders to their murderous fury by saying that Anuak had killed the eight, and that the murders needed to be avenged by killing all grown Anuak men living in Gambella.

On December 14, the second day of the massacre, Okello said he called Gebre-Ab in Addis Ababa to report on the killings and to plead that they stop. Gebre-Ab's telephone line to his military commander was not working at the time, so Gebre-Ab told Okello to relay a message to Tsegaye.

"I told Gebre-Ab that the military was killing people," Okello said. "And Gebre-Ab told me, 'Tell Tsegaye to increase the military force.'"

Okello also said Gambella municipal employees had earlier reported to him that a list of educated Anuak men marked for execution had been drawn up. Okello said that eyewitness reports to the massacre written by Anuak women who had lost husbands and brothers had been destroyed.

In an interview last week with the Reuters news agency, the Ethiopian Prime Minister, Meles Zenawi, called reports of the Anuak genocide a "fiction." He said the Ethiopian military had intervened to stop killing by armed Anuak insurgents and that "without the intervention of the army, the killings would have continued." No more than 200 people have died, he said.

The statement to Reuters was Meles' first public mention of the violence in Gambella since it started on December 13. Neither Meles nor Gebre-Ab explained why a radical Anuak militia—even if it conducted armed attacks on the Ethiopian military—would also kill large numbers of Anuak farmers and herders, loot Anuak homes, and rape Anuak women.

The Anuak King, Adongo Agada Akway, whose permanent home is in the village of Otallo, southern Sudan, is presently living in Nairobi where he is meeting with foreign diplomats, journalists, United Nations officials, and other humanitarian workers to try to bring international pressure on the Ethiopian government to stop the genocide of the Anuak people.

"What is happening in the Anuak Kingdom is exactly what happened in Rwanda, and what happened in Darfur, western Sudan," King Adongo said. "Innocent people are killed in all these cases. They don't know why they are being killed. And in every case it is designed by the regimes in those countries. The Ethiopian government is the one that gave the orders."

The King estimates that the ethnic cleansing of his tribe by the Ethiopian government has decreased the tribe's population by 10 percent since 1991, when the present government took power. There are about 100,000 Anuak living both in a small portion of eastern Sudan and, primarily, the Gambella state of Ethiopia.

Historically, the lighter-skinned Ethiopian tribes have shunned the darker-skinned African tribes, and sometimes raided the tribes to acquire slaves.

The Anuak are one such dark-skinned African people indigenous to regions of the lower Nile, others including the

Nuer, Dinka, and Shilluk. All these tribes are racially distinct from the olive-skinned Ethiopian tribes such as the Tigray, the Oromo, and the Amhara.

The Anuak's ancestral homeland of Gambella is not only geographically remote from the capital of Addis Ababa—it is also agriculturally fertile, relatively sparsely populated, and blessed with gold and oil reserves. This has made their land much coveted by the central government for economic development and population resettlement.

"Gambella is potentially a very rich area," said Gebre-Ab. "It could be the breadbasket of Ethiopia."

Throughout the 20th century, the Anuak Kingdom has been studied by many Western anthropologists who have lived among the Anuak for long periods, including the famous British social anthropologist E.E. Evans-Pritchard.

The Anuak have been admired in particular by anthropologists for their system of dispute resolution, in which all major arguments throughout the Kingdom are resolved by open discussion between all the disputants in front of the King and his cabinet which holds session every day in Otallo, Sudan.

King Adongo is now struggling to apply his culture's ancient system to one of the greatest crises the Anuak Kingdom has faced in its history.

"Before taking up arms we want to find a democratic way," he said. "A way of reconciliation. We don't want to aggress anybody. We want to have peace talks with somebody who aggresses us. We want to have a meeting with the Ethiopian government with the intervention of the world community. There is no alternative unless people sit down." ●

The Refugees of Pochalla

POCHALLA, SUDAN—A group of women huddle together, talking quietly. In their hands they hold small yellow berries called olemo that are the shape and color of the 25-cent gumballs sold in machines at the mall. Occasionally, one of them takes a small bite from a berry and makes a pucker face. The women are debating whether to feed the berries, one of the few sources of food and moisture available in the drought-stricken refugee camp, to their starving children. The berry causes diarrhea, so the choice they debate is a sickening one—risk their children's health in hopes of gaining a little nutrition or risk their death from starvation.

The recently formed Pochalla refugee camp is in Sudan, but it is not in Darfur, in the country's west, where humanitarian officials say the worst genocide since Rwanda is presently underway. Rather, Pochalla, in southeastern Sudan, is filled with refugees of the Anuak tribe of Ethiopia, who claim to have fled attacks on their villages led by the Ethiopian army.

According to the United Nations, some 8,500 Anuak refugees descended upon this traditional Anuak village, just across the border from Ethiopia, in the early months of this year, more than doubling its population and straining its resources beyond the breaking point. A nearby riverbed has run dry, people are drinking from road ruts and eating leaves, and they whisper in the muted register of oppressive hunger.

Amnesty International, Human Rights Watch, and the State Department have all made it clear in their recent annual reports that Ethiopia's human rights record is poor. Ethiopian forces have rounded up student protestors belonging to separatist groups, journalists have been jailed, and political dissidents have been detained for long periods. The State Department last year estimated that up to 1,500 unlawful killings were committed in Ethiopia in 2002, some by government security forces.

But somehow, news about Ethiopia's seemingly interminable famine, and the good-faith attempts of many Western aid groups to address it, always trumps Ethiopia's human rights infractions in the headlines. In addition, the Ethiopian government, which receives roughly $300 million in annual foreign aid, has drawn much positive attention for its "modernization" and "democratization" efforts. The economic development policies of Prime Minister Meles Zenawi have been held up as exemplary by economists and development experts in the West, including Jeffrey Sachs, the director of the Earth Institute at Columbia University (who has advocated increasing aid to Ethiopia under the United Nations Millennium Project, which he heads), and the Nobel Prize-winning economist Joseph Stiglitz, also at Columbia.

In 2001, Stiglitz wrote an article for The Atlantic Monthly in which he lauded Meles for his integrity. He was "quick to investigate any accusations of corruption in his government." And he was "committed to decentralization—to ensuring that the center did not lose touch with the various regions," Stiglitz wrote.

Now, the Anuak refugees are telling a different story about the Meles government—a tale of human rights abuse more ominous than any previously reported. The persecution of the Anuak reveals the dark side of Ethiopia's vaunted federalism, and their fate will say much about the future of this fractious African nation. While not on the scale of the Darfur tragedy (which has killed 30,000 and displaced 1.2 million) or the Ethiopian famine (7.2 million Ethiopians in danger of starvation) the violence described by the Anuak refugees compels attention precisely because of the tribe's small size.

279

There are just 100,000 Anuak. Almost 10,000 of them are now refugees in Sudan and Kenya. Anuak leaders and several human rights groups—Genocide Watch, Survivors International, and the World Organization Against Torture—say more than 1,200 Anuak have been killed in an explicit campaign by the Meles regime, or a rogue element within it, to wipe out the tribe altogether. They aren't slow to use the word genocide.

Evidence of a campaign of slaughter and rape by Ethiopian troops comes from several sources. There are eyewitness accounts of Anuak mass graves and the testimony of a former governor of the Anuak region, who says an Ethiopian army commander told him on December 13 about plans to eliminate the Anuak.

But mostly, there are the Anuak refugees, all of whom recount the same basic story: Several hundred Ethiopian soldiers came to the town of Gambella, the capital of Gambella state in remote western Ethiopia, on the morning of December 13. There they incited the members of several local tribes that have long-standing tensions with the Anuak, collectively known as highlanders, to assault the Anuak with machetes and spears. The soldiers, according to the refugees, went door to door calling Anuak men into the street, where they were shot to death by the soldiers or hacked down by highlanders. They then torched the Anuak's mud-and-straw huts, which are called tukuls. Survivors have compiled a list of 424 killed in the attack, noting the manner of their death, either by "bullet" or "machete," gleaned by examining the corpses.

Through April, the refugees say, Ethiopian troops carried out scorched-earth raids on a dozen Anuak villages, where tukuls were burned along with seed stock, farmers and herders were shot, and women were raped and taken as sex slaves. It's difficult to verify these accounts, coming as they do from isolated villages without telephones, electricity, or running water. The fact that roughly two-thirds of the Pochalla refugees are not from Gambella, but rather from small villages in the state, however, suggests that something bad—bad enough to make people walk days through the bush to reach this camp—did happen.

Those lucky enough to get here face a precarious existence. The Pochalla refugee camp is rust-red and table-flat, a dusty desertscape strewn with lean-to shelters and shattered human beings. There are no old people here—they either died on the weeklong trek through the bush or remained in Ethiopia to face an uncertain fate. Young children, caked in grime and dressed in rags—if they are dressed at all—scamper around, pulling little bent-metal toys on strings and making tiny forts from straw. But their voices, like those of their parents, are mere whispers, and they cough.

A medical worker at the camp estimates that 60 percent of the refugees suffer from diarrhea or low-grade infections, with the threat of malaria, yellow fever, and other ever-present illnesses. By late April, a dozen people had died at the camp from disease or hunger, the refugees say. The World Food Program, from a base camp across the border in Kenya, airdrops lentils, salt, and oil into Pochalla once every six weeks, but the food disappears quickly.

So far, the Meles government has denied there is any organized campaign against the Anuak. Meles told Reuters on April 29 that reports by Western NGOs that 1,137 people had been killed between December 13 and March 31 in the Gambella region were "a fiction." Barnabas Gebre-Ab, the Ethiopian minister for federal affairs for Gambella and the civilian chief of the armed forces in the state, tells me that some "tragic" deaths had occurred in Gambella on December 13 and that a mob of "social scums"—highlanders who supposedly had whipped themselves into a fury of ancient race hate against Anuak—was responsible. The only role the Ethiopian army played was to stop the killing before it spread, he says.

Why Ethiopia would try to eliminate a small tribe of mostly illiterate herders and farmers remains something of a mystery.

In recent years, tensions between the Anuak and the central government have reached a boiling point over several issues, including rights to oil discovered in Gambella, Anuak representation in the Gambella state government, and, especially, the placement in Gambella of Sudanese refugees of the Nuer tribe, who, for centuries, have competed with the Anuak for land, grazing, and fishing rights.

Since December, an armed Anuak resistance group called the Gambella People's Liberation Force has formed. On January 24, according to both the Ethiopian government and Genocide Watch, armed Anuak in the town of Dimma killed more than 150 Ethiopian soldiers in an ambush.

But perhaps the real reason the Anuak have been singled out is that the Meles government has decided to use them as a way to send a warning to other, more powerful separatist forces in Ethiopia. Formed by idealistic Marxist revolutionaries, including Meles himself, the government came to power after a grueling 17-year war waged against one of the cruelest regimes in African history.

In the early years, a ruling coalition of the country's many ethnic groups was formed, a democratic constitution was written, and a grand strategy of "ethnic federalism" was announced. The dream was peaceful co-existence, but today, virtually all of the human rights abuses tallied each year stem from the Meles regime's suppression of one or another separatist movement. There is a liberation front for almost every one of the "ethnic federalist" states in the country—the Oromo Liberation Front, the Eritrean People's Liberation Front (still battling Ethiopia over disputed boundaries), the Ogaden National Liberation Front, the Sidama Liberation Front, and, now, the Gambella People's Liberation Front begun by the Anuak.

A 36-page article written under the pen name "Mathza," a pseudonym widely believed in Ethiopia to be used by Meles, and posted on the Web on April 6, seethes with rage against the "power mania" of "separatists, parties, organizations, groups, private press and individuals" who "condemned the government for not handing over the administration to them on a silver platter." "Fantasizing to dismantle the ethnic-based federal system is tantamount to conspiring to create chaos," Mathza writes.

Most ominously, Mathza reminds his readers that "the bogus statements that Ethiopians were always united, that they enjoyed harmonious co-existence, that they were happy under the previous governments, etc., are all lies. The truth is the country was held together by force, not voluntarily, a situation that was likely to explode any time with dire consequence." The author says Switzerland and the United Kingdom are models for Ethiopia's ethnic state system, but the real model evoked is Yugoslavia, with Meles himself in the role of Tito, holding the country together with an iron fist. Mathza cites the recent violence in Gambella as the kind of local incident "instigat[ed] and fuel[ed]" by separatists who then "cry foul and human rights violations" when the Ethiopian army intervenes. All of which offers a clue as to why the Anuak, so tiny a tribe, would be so worrying to the regime. Mathza paints Ethiopia as fragile, filled with explosive tension points, a tower of matchsticks.

In such a country, even a little olemo berry could trigger a dangerous chain reaction. ●

Another Darfur Victim: The Anuak of Ethiopia

The genocide in the Darfur region of Sudan that has killed tens of thousands of Africans and displaced more than a million has claimed another unlikely victim—the Anuak tribe of western Ethiopia.

On December 13, 2003, the Anuak tribe suffered a bloody chapter in a genocide of its own when uniformed Ethiopian troops attacked the Anuak capital city of Gambella, killing more than 425 Anuak and driving 10,000 of its tribe into exile in Sudan and Kenya. Numbering only 100,000 together, the Anuak tribe is now teetering on the verge of extinction as the killings continue to this day.

But with the world's attention fixed on Darfur, the Anuak genocide has been entirely overlooked by the international media as well as by the United Nations, humanitarian aid groups, and the international public at large.

Darfur has sucked every last drop of the world's attention and, it seems, patience for African genocide, leaving not even a glance for the Anuak. Since December 13, 2003, the Anuak have not received even a minute of coverage on any of America's major TV networks or major cable channel news shows.

The oversight is doubly ironic as the two genocides are so similar. In both cases a sovereign power—one based in the capital of Khartoum, Sudan and the other in Addis Ababa, Ethiopia—has attempted to wipe out a black African minority living in a remote yet coveted Western province.

In addition, roughly a third of the Anuak live in eastern Sudan only a few hundred miles southeast of Darfur. The fortunes of the Anuak tribe for the past two decades have been vastly influenced by the Sudan civil war of which the Darfur massacre is but the latest chapter.

More than 100,000 Sudan war refugees, for example, were relocated to the middle of Anuak territory in Ethiopia in the 1990s, quickly igniting bloody clashes between the unarmed Anuak and the well-armed refugees, most of whom belong to tribes with longstanding tensions with the Anuak.

Once again, tragedy in Sudan is shadowing the Anuak.

"Darfur and Gambella are the same place to me, just the names are spelled differently," said Obang Metho, an Anuak who fled Ethiopia to live in Saskatchewan, Canada. "It's the same thing, the same problem."

In the single bloodiest attack against the Anuak in more than a decade of targeted massacres carried out against the tribe, several hundred uniformed members of the Ethiopian army drove in troop trucks into the western Ethiopian city of Gambella on December 13, 2003.

According to dozens of eyewitnesses, the Ethiopian soldiers went from door to door in Gambella, calling out the names of Anuak men and boys. When they came into the street they were told to run and then shot in the back, or hacked to death with machetes by light-skinned Ethiopian citizens who carried out the military's orders to kill Anuak.

Similar massacres occurred in more than a dozen Anuak villages in the province of Gambella in late 2003 and early 2004, driving thousands of Anuak into squalid refugee camps in Pochalla, Sudan, and a Nairobi slum called Ruiru, where they still live today.

Men, women, and children who lived normal lives going to work and school in Gambella have been living starved and sick in camps for nearly two years.

While little-known internationally, the Anuak genocide has become big news in Anuak diaspora communities around the world, and also in Ethiopia, where the government's attacks against the Anuak minority tribe became an issue in the 2005 national elections.

News of the Anuak genocide in western Ethiopia first broke in Minnesota, where some 1,500 Anuak refugees live after fleeing earlier periods of ethnic cleansing against their tribe that were carried out by the Ethiopian army.

Almost immediately after the December 13 massacre began, Anuak refugees in Minnesota started receiving telephone calls from their relatives and friends in Gambella. The Minnesota Anuak could hear gunshots and screams in the background of the phone calls and sometimes heard Ethiopian soldiers yell "Put down the phone!" before the line went dead.

The Anuak and Darfur genocides share many similarities, besides their both being directed by sovereign governments against defenseless minorities.

Determined to wipe away the entire culture of their victims, the killers in both Darfur and Gambella not only massacred humans but also torched houses, crops, food in storage, seed stocks, and agricultural equipment and infrastructure. Entire villages in both cases have been flattened by fire.

A key weapon in both genocides has been rape. More than a dozen Anuak women interviewed in the Nairobi and Pochalla refugee camps described to this reporter being gang raped and seeing many other women being gang raped by Ethiopian soldiers.

The humanitarian agency Genocide Watch sent a research team to Gambella in January, 2004 and recorded similar accounts, including that Ethiopian soldiers often told the women as they raped them that "We are going to kill your men, so the next generation of Anuak will be produced by us."

Anuak women in refugee camps have begun to have babies fathered by Ethiopian soldier rapists, recent visitors to the refugee camps say.

More than 1,200 Anuak refugees live in southern Minnesota, having arrived here in the middle 1990s after fleeing an earlier ethnic cleansing that took as many—if not more—lives as the 2003 and 2004 killings.

Some 7,000 Anuak refugees live scattered around the world in a diaspora that today is grieving the death in Ethiopia of their mothers, fathers, brothers, sisters, and friends at the hands of Ethiopian soldiers.

The Anuak, like the tribes of Darfur, are black-skinned people of African descent. In Sudan and Ethiopia, the black-skinned tribes are shunned and oppressed by lighter-skinned tribes whose leaders hold national power. As in the case of the American Indian, in Darfur and Gambella the dark-skinned natives are sitting on oil fields that the light-skinned leaders want.

"The government wants the land but not the people" in both Darfur and Gambella, Metho said. "So in both places, people are being killed by their own governments." With only 100,000 Anuak still living, compared to 1.7 million members of the Fur and other African tribes of Darfur, the proportional damage to the Anuak culture is even greater than in Darfur.

Some Anuak leaders fear that the genocide of their tribe may already be functionally accomplished. With Anuak deaths from the recent government-led massacres totaling more than 1,200 since 2003, and 10,000 Anuak in exile as refugees, the birth rate may now have permanently dipped below the death rate, the threshold at which genocide becomes effectively a fact.

With the Sudan peace agreement reached last December, and a fragile-but-holding ceasefire holding in Darfur, the Sudan-Ethiopia border at Gambella is sure to gain in strategic importance.

The reason is that by virtue of oil in the region, as well as the fact that a half-dozen rivers make it both fertile and a potential transportation hub, the region is key to economic development for both countries.

In Ethiopia, government officials refer to Gambella as "potentially the nation's bread basket," and they court foreign investors interested in exploring and developing the oil fields there.

In Darfur as well, the discovery of oil in recent years has attracted the interest of international oil companies and investors whom the Sudan government desperately wants to attract.

There is, of course, only one problem in Sudan and Ethiopia. That is the Anuak who live in Ethiopia, and the Fur and other dark-skinned tribes of Darfur. Neither tribe poses anything close to a military threat against the central government, or are pushing for full autonomy, but both have asked for a share in the bounty once oil exploration money pours in.

That's been enough to bring the wrath of their governments upon them.

With local enmities so ancient and deep, the only hope for peace in both cases is for the international community to shake off its lethargy and bring pressure to bear on each of the governments to stop the killings. Yet that will only happen if the world knows what is happening in the first place—to the Anuak of Gambella, as well as the victims of Darfur. ◉

"We Were in Over Our Head, But We Loved Them"

The ethnic cleansing of the Anuak tribe by the Ethiopian army has taken a long time to grab the world's attention.

Not so the churches of Minnesota, however.

In the months following the massacre of 424 Anuak in remote western Ethiopia on December 13, 2003, more than a dozen churches opened their doors to panicked and grieving Anuak immigrants who live in Minnesota.

Some 1,200 Anuak refugees live in the state, having arrived here as refugees in the mid-1990s after fleeing targeted violence against their minority tribe in Ethiopia, by the Ethiopian military and by other ethnic groups.

Because most Anuak are Christian, as the result of more than a century of missionary work among black Africans in Ethiopia, many Anuak in Minnesota joined Christian churches when they first arrived in the state.

That membership became a lifeline for many Minnesota Anuak in 2004.

That's because every Anuak in Minnesota has relatives or close friends who died or became refugees in the past year. But because they can't return to Ethiopia for either financial or political reasons, they face a serious psychological burden dealing with their losses at such a distance.

"When people hear that their relatives have died but they can't go back, that's psychologically so hard," said Pastor LeRoy Christoffels, pastor of the Christian Reformed Church in Worthington, Minnesota. "That grief is a serious thing and we try to help them with that by offering spiritual care."

About 30 Anuak belong to the church, Christoffels said. Besides grief counseling, the church has also raised and sent money to help some 10,000 Anuak refugees still living in a camp in south Sudan.

The Calvary Baptist Church in Roseville has been the most active, raising more than $30,000 to send a human rights team to Ethiopia to interview witnesses and document the massacre in January, 2003.

Other church leaders have traveled as well to the United Nations in New York and Geneva; to the European Union headquarters in Brussels; and to Washington to lobby U.S. political leaders to put pressure on Ethiopia to stop the targeted killing of Anuak.

The Calvary Church also sent food and relief supplies to Anuak refugees and survivors in Ethiopia, and worked with the human rights groups Genocide Watch and the World Organization Against Torture to write reports.

Paul Lindberg, a missionary who works with the Calvary Baptist Church and the Eagle Brook Baptist Church in White Bear Lake, has made several trips to Ethiopia, most recently last month where he organized reconciliation meetings between Anuak and ethnic Ethiopians living in Gambella.

The Christ Lutheran Church in Eagan has raised $24,000 to drill up to ten well holes at the refugee camp in Pochalla, Sudan, according to Omot Ochan, an Anuak leader and member of the church.

At the Austin Vineyard evangelical church in Austin, pastors Richard and JoAnn Chinander sponsored two Anuak Days last year. More than 250 Anuak came to the first one, last April 4, while still in shock.

"Our Anuak families came to us crying and saying 'Our families have been killed and we don't know what to do,'" Mr. Chinander said. "We told them we are a small church, and that we were in way over our head, but we loved them and we wanted to help them, and that we would." ●

Diapers and Death

"We thank our husbands for staying home today to change our children's diapers," a Minnesota woman belonging to the Anuak tribe of Ethiopia said the other day.

At a crowded Minneapolis meeting hall last weekend, some 50 Anuak women gathered to anxiously discuss, to sometimes weep, and above all to intently compare notes with each other on the best ways to raise their children born in America, so far from their African homeland.

The call for diaper duty gratitude to husbands earned polite applause.

But when Akuthi Okoth, an Anuak woman who'd flown in from Indianapolis for the day, rose to speak she struck a deeper chord that stirred a thoughtful silence followed by appreciative cheers.

"Sisters, listen!" she thundered. "You put your husbands through school here in the U.S., while taking care of your children all by yourself. Yet when your husbands finish school, they don't help you go to school yourself. Sisters, you must insist! It is your right to get an education!"

"If the men are going to sit around that's fine," Okoth pleaded, "but we aren't going to wait for them. We'll get up and get things going and see what we can do."

It was women's rally, and complaints were voiced by frustrated women against wayward men.

Yet Mommy Track issues were the least of the problems discussed, and the Minnesota Anuak women's dilemma is greater even than the culture shock, loneliness, and exhaustion that all immigrant mothers face.

They are trying to keep themselves and their children healthy and sane while their very culture—parents, grandparents, brothers, sisters, friends, and the entire African society that first gave them grounding in the world—is being driven towards extinction by genocide.

The 1,200 Anuak immigrants in Minnesota—more than anywhere in the world outside of western Ethiopia—are here because the Ethiopian government has been ethnically cleansing their tribe for more than a decade.

On December 13, 2003, the bloodiest day in Anuak history horrifically unfolded when uniformed Ethiopian soldiers flooded the Anuak capital town of Gambella and went door to door, dragging Anuak men and boys from their homes and shooting them dead in the streets.

More than 420 Anuak men died that day in Gambella, and several hundred others were killed as Ethiopian troops fanned throughout Anuak territory where they burned entire villages to the ground, raped women, and looted and burned field crops and stored grains. The marauding continues today.

Virtually every Anuak woman at the Minneapolis meeting had lost fathers, brothers, and close friends in the massacre.

"It makes you very sad and bitter," said Akuthi Okoth. "Anuak women still in Ethiopia live without their husbands or sons, and they are still being raped, and their children destroyed. Those Anuak women have no voice, but we Anuak women in the United States can be their voice."

Because more than 10,000 Anuak were driven to flee their homes after the December 13 massacre, all of the Anuak women at the Minneapolis meeting had relatives and friends now living in refugee camps, one of them located in the parched Sudan desert, and the other in a putrid Nairobi slum.

Hundreds of Anuak men and boys are also being held without charge in federal prisons in Gambella and in the Ethiopian capital, Addis Ababa, where stories of torture and extrajudicial killings are rampant.

The December 13, 2003 massacre was first reported in The McGill Report on December 22, 2003, after dozens of Anuak living in Minnesota received frantic cell phone calls from their relatives in Ethiopia while the massacre was still underway.

This March, Human Rights Watch, the world's largest human rights organization, released a report stating that the Ethiopian army "has committed widespread murder, rape, and torture" against the Anuak tribe.

"The widespread attacks directed against the Anuak civilian population," the report said, "bear the hallmark of crimes against humanity under international law. In many areas, abuses are ongoing and frequent."

The Anuak community of Minnesota has worked closely over the past two years with local churches and student groups to hold educational meetings and fundraisers to buy food and clothing for Anuak refugees, and to pay for trips by Anuak leaders to the U.S. State Department and the United Nations.

More than $50,000 in relief funds has been raised, and the Human Rights Watch report is testimony to the Anuak's success at raising world awareness of the Anuak genocide.

Yet all has not gone smoothly with the Minnesota Anuak's efforts to absorb the tragedy in their homeland, and to help their endangered culture.

The problem, the Anuak women stressed over and over, is the discord and fragmentation the Ethiopian violence has sown right here in Minnesota, at both a political and family level.

At the political level, instead of promoting unity among the Minnesota Anuak, the December 13 massacre has had the opposite effect.

Faced with the possible genocide of their tiny tribe, which numbers only 100,000 remaining members, some Anuak in Minnesota have said that raising money to buy guns to fight the Ethiopian army is the best response.

Others have dismissed that option as suicidal, and focused

on raising relief money instead. Yet another group has argued that lobbying elected officials in the U.S., which is by far the largest source of aid funds to Ethiopia, is the Anuak's best hope for ending Ethiopia's ethnic cleansing of their tribe.

Since December 13, four Anuak men in Minnesota have emerged as leaders of four separate relief groups. Each has his own constituency, works with his own group of American friends and sponsors, and favors one or another relief strategy. Two of these leaders don't speak with each other; a third is exceptionally fluent in English but is considered aloof by most Anuak; and a fourth is widely respected but for personal reasons keeps a low profile.

"Anuak tend to be from specific regions, such as villages by one river or another in Ethiopia," explained Okony Cham, an Ethiopian Anuak who graduated this spring from Mankato State University. He had been invited to the women's meeting as the videographer. "Even in the U.S., Anuak who come from one region in Ethiopia don't follow the leaders from other regions."

In Anuak history, threats from tribal enemies either in Sudan or Ethiopia have mobilized Anuak in different villages to unite. This is happening now under the Ethiopian army's assault.

But this time, a unified Anuak response in Ethiopia is especially hard to muster because so many of the tribe's leaders fled the country in the 1990s, especially to Minnesota, which is home to the world's largest Anuak refugee population.

The rapings and killings of Anuak that began on December 13 and continue to this day, has also deeply divided many Anuak families in Minnesota and elsewhere throughout the U.S., the Anuak women said last weekend.

They swapped tearful stories of coping with divorce, debts, alcoholism, and children in trouble at school and with police—all of which increased sharply after December 13, 2003.

One woman said her husband took to gambling at a Shakopee casino and wrecked their family. Another woman described making endless three-hour car rides to and from a courthouse in another county, to act as a translator for a troubled Anuak boy who was constantly in trouble with the law.

Rising from their folding chairs to address the group, the Anuak women spoke in long emotional gulps, again and again tracing their families' problems to feelings of rage at the Ethiopian government and army.

Yet having no means to directly express their rage at the actual perpetrators in Ethiopia, the rage is aimed instead at those nearest them, their families.

"It's like kicking the dog when in reality you are mad at your boss," said Ariet Oman, who had flown to the Minneapolis meeting from Spokane.

"We need to support each other as a sisterhood," she said. "Not just donating money, but doing whatever we can. Just go knock on your sister's door. We can be there emotionally. Give your shoulder to cry on."

Akuthi Okoth stressed the importance of remembering that the name Anuak means "sharing" and that hospitality was a cornerstone of Anuak culture. "Let's not just have an Anuak sisterhood, but let's have American sisters, African sisters, all sisters. And let's remember there are a lot of people suffering, not just the Anuak people. So let's try to help them too. Let's expand our kindness to them too. Let's try to support them too."

Several Anuak men had been invited to the meeting and made speeches.

Lero Odala, who recently moved to Mankato with his family from Boston, said that Anuak men in the U.S. are looking to Anuak women for a good example.

"Women can make men more attentive to their responsibilities," he said. "We men, who are afraid and incapable of uniting, are asking you to lead us to victory."

Akway Cham, another male guest, advised Anuak women "to be independent of men because you have your own gifts from God. Women know love better than men."

Warajo Ojulu, a tall Anuak man wearing a gold robe with an embroidered map of Ethiopia on the front, read a poem of appreciation to the women.

"Mom is the one who carries us for nine months, and then cares for us for many years," his poem read. "Mom is not someone we can compare to anyone else, because she is the root of everything. Mothers have to unite for the future of their children, and for their children's lives after they pass away. Children can see a bright future from what their mothers started."

Ariet Oman's eyes were glistening when she heard these words, and Akuthi Okoth stood up and said: "To hear a poem written by a man that endorses the mother's love, that means so much to us. Let's take that from here." ●

An Easter Message to the Minnesota Press

"For Christians, it is called Holy Week, the one we're passing through," a somber editorial in the Minneapolis Star-Tribune begins today. "It's supposed to be about death and this year, especially, it is."

The editorial asks how we can use death itself to seek a larger purpose in life, and thus to avoid for our loved ones, our fellow citizens, and for ourselves the disconsolate and tragic end to life that is so common in this world.

In the spirit of this editorial, I would like to add one more dimension to this search we Minnesotans undertake this Easter. I address these thoughts specifically to my friends and colleagues in the Minnesota press.

Yesterday, Human Rights Watch, the world's largest human rights organization, released a report accusing the government of Ethiopia of "widespread murder, rape, and torture" against the country's minority Anuak tribe.

The report says that the Ethiopian government's "targeted" campaign of violence against the Anuak "bears the hallmark of crimes against humanity under international law," and that murder, rape, and torture is "ongoing and frequent."

The world is full of misery and mass murder. Why should the Minnesotan press pay special attention to this one?

Because for the past decade, the ethnic cleansing of the Anuak from Ethiopia has resulted in more than 1,000 Anuak refugees fleeing for safety to our state, which is now home to the largest diaspora settlement of this tribe in the world.

With only 100,000 remaining members, the entire Anuak

tribe with its unique culture and language is under immediate threat of extinction by ethnic cleansing, according to the Cambridge, Massachusetts-based rights group, Cultural Survival.

What role might we in the Minnesota press play in trying to stop the violence against the Anuak tribe by genocide?

If we clearly see that we are able to play such a role by exercising the freedoms that we enjoy but that the Ethiopian press does not, would we then not only have an opportunity but also a responsibility to help end the genocide of the Anuak?

There is not only a free press argument, and a humanitarian argument, but also a self-interest argument for extending a hand of help to the Minnesota Anuak. The Minnesota Anuak live in the Twin Cities primarily but also in Mankato, Austin, Worthington, Rochester, and other towns where they work in food processing plants, at megastores as shelvers, and are taking higher education degrees.

For the past year, life has been hell for the Anuak of Minnesota who all have lost family members and close friends to gruesome murders. Parents, children, and siblings have been murdered; mothers, wives, and sisters have been raped. In many cases loved ones have dropped out of sight with no word about their fate.

Since December 13, 2003, when approximately 425 Anuak were massacred on a single day by the Ethiopian army, more than 50,000 Anuak in Ethiopia have been made homeless as they fled the carnage into the malaria-infested bush and to a refugee camp in southern Sudan.

Many Anuak in Minnesota have quit their schooling and risked losing their jobs to spend their life savings to fly to Africa, to discover the fate of their loved ones.

Some Anuak have flown back to Africa only to find their parents, brothers and sisters all killed. In other cases there is simply no trace of them. In the luckiest cases, the Minnesota Anuak find their loved ones living in rags and tatters in refugee camps in the Sudan desert or in Nairobi slums.

The impact on Minnesota of the Anuak genocide can thus be measured in many ways—economic, social, cultural, spiritual. Educations ended and jobs lost is an obvious economic loss. Time and money spent searching for loved ones in Africa also translates into more domestic crises in Minnesota as rents go unpaid, marriages fray, children get in trouble, and dependence on social services is extended.

Many Anuak in Minnesota, feeling utterly helpless, are suffering depression in silence or need grief counseling to survive every day. Thanks to the Human Rights Watch Report, the Anuak genocide is now virtually undisputed. Though the numbers of dead and missing are smaller, the genocide of the Anuak tribe is now a fact as solid as the genocides of Rwanda or Darfur.

As potential first-responders, the Minnesota press has the opportunity to demonstrate how the free press in a democracy can safeguard and extend precious freedoms across national and geographic borders, throughout the world.

Our meditation on death this Easter would be fruitful, I believe, if we in the Minnesota press decided to extend the powers and blessings we enjoy to the Anuak. ●

V **A GLOBAL CITIZEN THINKS ABOUT WAR**

A Global Citizen Thinks About War

I

I would wish this war to be fought for the liberation of the people of Iraq.

I would wish that America had the will to fight and win this war to free ourselves and others in the world from the threat of weapons of mass destruction and to spread the gifts of liberty and equality and democracy.

I would wish we had the strength to embrace the global empire that we have become and to rise with wisdom and courage to the challenges of leadership as the world's standard-bearer and guarantor of those shining ideals.

I would wish we had the will to accept the costs of that leadership.

Yet reality is not made from my wishes, and the reality is that we are pursuing the war on Iraq to maintain the economic status quo in America, while mouthing ideals to mollify our conscience and to preserve the fiction that we can live forever like kings of the earth yet never pay the price.

II

It's a damned difficult thing to think about war. One reason is that in war by definition the usual rules don't apply. Death, not life, is the goal of war. Destruction and not progress is its goal. Thank God we don't have much experience making decisions in such a state. And yet our lack of familiarity with war leaves us unprepared to think through the situation well when the time comes to make such a decision. And such a time is now.

III

There isn't a tougher moment for a global citizen than the one where you must sit down and decide on war—whether to go to war personally or through the support you give as a citizen to the government's war effort.

In normal life, a global citizen cultivates the ability to see connections between her daily life and the lives of others who live across the oceans and around the world. Even subtle clues speak of a grand interconnection to a global citizen, and these clues pull her towards uncovering what possibilities and responsibilities these connections may imply. The simple stitching in a pair of shoes made in Malaysia, or the tang in tea leaves picked in Sri Lanka, or the lilt of an Irish accent overheard at the grocery store checkout line, all of these speak to a global citizen of the interconnectedness of today's world.

War offers a sudden stark illumination of the usually hidden global connections that underpin our daily lives. In fact, war or its imminent possibility offers so violent an exposure of these underlying realities that many people, understandably, choose to shield their eyes and turn away.

The contemplation of such human connections—of the responsibilities they imply and of the possibility that they might suddenly be destroyed—may be so painful that the task is deferred or denied. In the present case, despite the heightened awareness of our nation's dependence on Middle Eastern oil, it would be amazing if more than a small fraction of the country's 16 million owners of gas-guzzling SUVs took the lesson seriously enough to cut back on their driving, much less sell their cars. An even harder task is to imagine, in sufficient detail that it changes behavior, how innocent people will die when U.S. bombs accidentally, yet inevitably, stray into residential areas in Baghdad, or when close fighting erupts in the cities.

IV

There are four basic perspectives on this possible war. Two of them are held by supporters of the U.S. president's efforts to forcibly oust Saddam, and two are held by those who are opposed to his plans.

The war's supporters define the goal of the war as:

A. To liberate the Iraqi people from tyrannical rule in order to establish a beachhead of liberal democracy in the Middle East;

B. To ensure the long-term stability of the global economy in order to protect the long-term prospects of the U.S. economy;

The war's detractors meanwhile define its purpose as:

C. Foreign adventurism in the affairs of a brutal regime which nevertheless controls only a small portion of the world's oil and poses no immediate threat to U.S. national interests;

D. An imperial land grab orchestrated by a handful of scheming oligarchs and fat cats whose goal is to preserve their grip on power, boost their oil company stocks, and protect their lavish lifestyles.

The (A) crowd—the liberal hawks—is the most interesting group because it counts among its members many who forged their politics in opposition to the Vietnam War. Now these former draft card burners are cheering Bush's plan to blast Saddam out of existence. They see the possible bombardment of Iraq as the latest in a series of wars and revolutions that have expanded liberal democracy around the world. The former Democratic Senator Bob Kerry, Dissent magazine editor Mitchell Cohen, and American Prospect editor Richard Just are liberals who favor forcibly removing Saddam.

Those in the (B) camp, meanwhile, see the war's main purpose as maintaining global stability by eradicating Saddam as an agent of global terror. The bible to this group is "The Threatening Storm" by Kenneth Pollack, a former CIA analyst in the George H.W. Bush administration, who offers extensive documentation of Saddam's long efforts to acquire nuclear and other weapons of mass destruction. If Saddam had the bomb, Pollack argues, he would almost certainly use it to seize Saudi Arabian and Kuwaiti oil fields, or to destroy them while trying. The only real disagreement in this camp is over how much time the U.S. should spend to develop domestic and international support for the war and to work with Iraqi opposition groups before sending in the troops.

Two camps favor answer (C)—libertarians, always wary of foreign entanglements, and geopolitical thinkers who see Saddam as a brutal yet eminently rational and self-protective man who is, therefore, deterrable. To these folks, the likelihood of Saddam using weapons of mass destruction will actually increase if the U.S. strikes now, perhaps by activating sleeper terrorist cells in the United States, or by launching chemical or biological weapons against Israel once a war starts. Those who chose answer (C) also chide the administration for justifying its war plans with principles it would be impossible to follow consistently, such as neutralizing every possible nuclear power and deposing every nasty dictator in the world.

The partisans of answer (D) are a passionate assemblage of unreconstructed leftists, progressives, idealists, and politicized artists and writers who paint the perpetrators of the possible war in cartoonish grotesques. America is the new global empire and a bloody capitalist crusader; George W. Bush is a reckless cowboy, a malleable dunce, the pet of a Texas oil cabal; Rumsfeld is the devil incarnate; Powell is a noble man sadly corrupted; and etc. These are caricatures, yes, but they are not for that reason necessarily wrong.

V

Who can doubt that George W. Bush, who slurs his words to sound like a swaggering Texas Ranger, in some part of his soul is itching to avenge the man who tried to kill his pa? "Saddam's misfortune is to sit on the second biggest oilfield in the world, and Bush wants it," writes the British spy novelist turned global citizen, John le Carre. "If Saddam didn't have the oil, he could torture his citizens to his heart's content. Other leaders do it every day—think Saudi Arabia, think Pakistan, think Turkey, think Syria, think Egypt." More nuanced liberal critiques, such as Michael Walzer's, actually favor a forcible ejection of Saddam, but one that is mounted by the UN to enforce its inspections, as opposed to a police action to further the American ruling elite's "aggrandizement of their wealth and power." Says Walzer: "There can't be any disengagement from the war against privilege and corruption, both of which are embodied in our current government."

VI

Where does the U.S. administration fall among these choices? By my lights it is pursuing the war to maintain global economic stability (B), while publicly justifying the aggression in terms of traditional American ideals (A). The most frequently implied of those ideals is that of the U.S. as the righteous redeemer of an evil world. Of course, rhetoric aside, no one believes that Gulf War II won't be just as much about preserving U.S. access to oil supplies as Gulf War I was. In that earlier desert excursion, you'll recall that the U.S. government's first explanation of the war's rousing purpose—"to save democracy in Kuwait" —was quickly dropped when the U.S. public realized no such thing existed.

VII

Between his candidacy and his presidency, George Bush changed his vision of America's role in the world completely. As a can-

307

didate he was isolationist, while as President he is aggressively internationalist under the banner of the war on terror. This complete reversal of position undermines the credibility of U.S. international actions, because it draws into question whether we have the will to follow up military action with long-term support that builds friendships and creates new democracies.

Also, there is something in Bush's manner, and I am not the only one, that makes me doubt the sincerity of his podium rhetoric. His dropped g's, his fondness for cowboy metaphors, and his sly schoolboy demeanor, as if he were always about to towel-snap somebody, puts me off. He doesn't possess the personal gravitas to speak convincingly of great political ideals. To me the isolationism of candidate Bush sounded more authentic, more ardent, more convincing. Especially when compared to his upbringing, during which he showed not the slightest interest in foreign travel or in the world, his newfound passion for "liberating" other countries others rings hollow in the ear.

VIII

I believe that unless we generously share the gifts of freedom and equality with others, we will lose them ourselves.

My dilemma is not that ousting Saddam by force is a bad idea. It's possibly the right idea. But it's being carried out by the wrong person.

It's wrong because Bush's actions don't reflect his words. Wrong because he's a Yale graduate with a fake Texas accent.

Wrong because he lacks the humility that's a necessary adjunct to strength. Wrong because when it comes to a guiding vision of the world, he promised us one thing and now he is delivering another. How can you trust such a man?

IX

A chance encounter with an old friend helped me to formulate where I stand on the U.S. military effort to oust Saddam. My friend is a retired physician who spends his summers in Minnesota and winters in sunny Scottsdale, Arizona. He's got a beautiful big house in each place; he dresses in spiffy tailored suits and silk ties; and he drives a nice car that is close to brand new. We met at a swanky Indian restaurant next to the Phoenix Arts Center where, after we had downed our three-course meal of chicken tikka, shrimp biryani, vegetable dishes and imported beer, we attended a concert of the Emerson Quartet. In other words, we enjoyed an evening the likes of which 99 percent of the earth's inhabitants could never dream of enjoying.

My friend is resolutely against the war to oust Saddam. "Bush just wants to kill the guy who tried to kill his father!" he said. "And for this petty reason he wants to drag the entire country into an incredibly dangerous and costly war that no other nation in the world will support!"

My answer to my friend was this: "You're right. But don't you also realize that you and I are living in the newest global empire, and all that's happening now is that one cost of citizenship in the empire is coming due?"

X

From the flight deck of the U.S. Abraham Lincoln, which is heading now from the Pacific Ocean to the Gulf region, a U.S. Air Force pilot told a TV journalist recently: "Our job is power projection. We have guys flying hundreds of miles off this ship to do the nation's business." The pilot's voice was untinged by the reticent or embarrassed tones that characterized U.S. military pronouncements for three decades after the Vietnam War. It was the pure, unconflicted, pitch-perfect voice of the world's newest global empire.

America maintains five global military commands posted on four continents; its economy pumps life-giving capital into scores of developing countries; its consumer goods and movies and music are universally admired and accepted; its language is the international language; its currency is a safe haven; and for all the resentment our global presence engenders, just ask

309

the people where it really counts—e.g., South Korea, Israel, Bosnia, or Kosovo—whether they approve of America's global prowess and military might.

Our cushy lives so rich in material pleasures, educational possibility, health care, and leisure, are all supported by commercial tendrils of empire that efficiently suck low-priced goods from developing countries, while also inexorably attracting the smartest and most ambitious natives of other countries to our shores. Compared to our next-door-neighbors here in the U.S., we may feel we don't own enough or make enough money and thus we may want more. But compared to the rest of the world, we already have everything. We are all fat cats. We have everything because a global empire—a commercial, cultural, and military global power—supports us.

We are a *military* global power, and if we were not we would not enjoy the commercial and cultural advantages that we do.

XI

The key questions that citizens of America's global empire must therefore ask themselves are: Do I believe in the motivating ideals of this empire? Am I willing to accept the costs – in taxes and other forms of treasure—that it takes to maintain the empire and the lavish life that I am able to live because I am a citizen of the empire? Do we have the stomach to face the reality that we have much of what we have because of our brute military power, and not because we are smarter or better than everyone else?

Will we be able as a society to develop into the first global empire that is also liberal, democratic, humble, and wise? Will we able to develop the needed leadership skills to engender in the rest of the world an attitude of respect and fondness and gratitude towards us, instead of the anger and bitterness and resentment of our arrogance that is now so common? In other words, will we learn what we need to become the first global empire in world history that actually survives to a ripe old age?

XII

The early signs are discouraging. The U.S. military blew into Afghanistan, did its urgent business and vowed eternal support of the long-oppressed Afghan people, but now has basically flown the coop. Why should we believe that our government will do any more to support a stable democratic government in a post-Saddam Iraq? Where are the Bush government's efforts right now to build a national consensus around the need to rebuild postwar Iraq into a democracy, just as we helped Germany and Japan to become democracies after World War II?

Why aren't we working right now to develop the good will of Iraqi people prior to our bombing the daylights out of them? Vastly more democratic radio broadcasts, U.S. propaganda leaflet drops, and covert operations with opposition groups inside Iraq would help reverse the mistrust of ordinary Iraqis for the U.S., built up from more than a decade of disastrous economic sanctions.

Where is the U.S. government's leadership in helping to educate Americans about Arab culture and society? We may soon send an occupying force into the Middle East, there to stay for many years. The occupation will not succeed unless the occupying force shows the Iraqi people some respect, some knowledge of their culture, and even over time perhaps some affection.

XIII

The first rule of international travel—for soldiers, diplomats, journalists, businessmen, and tourists—is that a nationon's government is not its people. Despite the despots who too often lead them, the ordinary people of the world across all cultures are usually hospitable, generous, and kind. No military occupation leading to democracy will work in Iraq without making a real connection with its people at this basic human level.

Learning how to speak their language, recite their poems, read their books, play with their children, and sing their songs would help. When we march into Baghdad, we'll need to make friends with the people we almost killed.

XIV

Fevered worries on the dawn of a new war rise up now like shrieking demons. We remember the hurt and the pain of the Vietnam War, not just the hell of the war itself with the 58,178 dead but also the lingering wounds of war that scarred the decades that followed—the returning veterans who were shamed for killing for their country; and all the young men with PTSD, of whom some now still cry uncontrollably at a pin drop and suffer flashbacks and night sweats; and then all the broken marriages, the flip-outs, the drug addictions; and the tragic stories like that of Lewis B. Puller, the decorated Marine who survived multiple amputations and depression and alcoholism, only to succumb, finally, to suicide.

Are we ready again for another war so soon? Will the cost be equally as terrible? Will it be worse? Can we survive such wounds? Are we doing the right thing?

On what grounds are we willing to risk our lives and our souls once again in a military venture that is sure to kill many innocents?

XV

Could we in the United States ever imagine the lives of foreign people with such detail and empathy that we would be compelled to act as morally towards them as we do towards our own friends, families, and next-door-neighbors?

Could we ever find a way to believe that the innocent citizens of Iraq are truly our neighbors and thus are deserving of every respect, including the courtesy that we not blow them up?

As G.K. Chesterton said, "We make our friends. We make our enemies. God makes our neighbors." Can we find a way to really love our global neighbors?

Moral philosophers offer possible answers to such questions, which lie at the heart of global citizenship. The Greek philosopher Diogenes declared himself to be not a patriot who owed allegiance to any particular city-state, but rather to be "a citizen of the world." The Roman Stoics said that all human beings should enjoy the privileges of citizenship because they shared the unifying trait of rationality. In an Enlightenment treatise that's rising rapidly in popularity, *Perpetual Peace*, Immanuel Kant echoed the Stoic line with a twist, i.e., that governments should respect the human rights not only of citizens but of foreigners, an idea later enshrined in the U.S. Constitution.

XVI

So are we making progress after all? Without a doubt. The United States is itself the greatest example, because here all people are owed government protection of their basic human rights regardless of race, religion, color, sex, age, caste, or station of birth. Persecuted refugees from the world over have flocked to the United States for decades because of this.

But a global war of which Iraq may only become the third (after 9/11 and Afghanistan) major battlefield threatens to reverse this progress. The erosion of human rights of both U.S. citizens and immigrants, which is already underway in this country, is one sign of that. So are the possible deaths—i.e., the loss of the right to life—of innocents in Iraq. I am not saying that any amount of backsliding on human rights is indefensible; if the threat to global society is big enough, surely some amount of loss is acceptable. But if those rights are being eroded any-where, as they are now, it should be very carefully observed and monitored, like a persistent low grade fever.

To extend the metaphor, such a fever should only be tolerated for a certain period of time, after which the patient recovers and goes on to gain new heights of health. When will the present period of global rights retraction be over? Have we set time limits and goals? If not, why not?

313

XVII

If the war happens it will be tragic and God-damned, because innocents will surely die. But if it happens, its explicit goal should be not simply the eradication of Saddam as a potential nuclear threat, which is spurious because we all understand that Saddam is deterrable, as he has been for thirty years. Rather, it should be done for the express purpose of the liberation of the people of Iraq; and it should be done without gloating or breast-beating; and only after longer deliberation and with a genuine commitment to long-term support of liberal democracy in the Middle East.

XVIII

If the war does happen, as seems certain, once the bombs start to fall there will be only one question, which is, what can we do now?

What can a global citizen do?

We might take a leave of absence from our jobs and fly to Iraq to help with humanitarian aid. We could send money for that aid too, of course.

We could also make an effort to find the Iraqi citizens who live in our area, and reach out to them to talk and share ideas. There are about 90,000 Iraqis living in the United States, according to the 2,000 U.S. Census. Find them by asking around at work, at church, or networking through friends. I did this recently and in southeastern Minnesota I found a couple of Iraqi-Americans in Rochester, and another couple of them at a restaurant in Minneapolis. At the restaurant, I chatted with the owner, and he introduced me to an Iraqi friend visiting from London, who had a brother who was executed by Saddam. This man had every reason to hate Saddam, and he does. But he's also opposed to Bush's plan to oust him with bombs.

The reason? "This is something for Iraqis to do for themselves, because they don't trust the United States, and it will be a disaster." He quoted an old Arab saying to me: "Me and my brother against my cousin; me and my cousin against the for-eigner." "In Iraq, the U.S. is the foreigner," the man told me.

"They simply are not welcome by the Iraqis, but the U.S. doesn't understand this." If you ask around, you'll surely find Iraqi-Americans with strongly different opinions, but that's just part of the process of learning about the messy, conflicted reality we face as we enter Iraq.

Whatever your profession, you could probably also find some Iraq angle to research and pursue. If a teacher, what is education like in Iraq? If a doctor, what humanitarian medical efforts are underway to relieve the disastrous health effects of the economic embargo of the past decade? As a journalist, you could find local Iraqis to interview for the local newspaper. And so on.

XIX

The point would be to listen, mainly. Which is just what we haven't done much of, either as a government or as a people, before we launched ourselves into this likely war with Iraq.

We haven't listened because we've been too busy enjoy-ing life, eating at fancy Indian restaurants, and drinking fine imported beers, and paying $1.50 a gallon for gasoline and calling it an outrage, and living like absolute kings.

It's been fun, but it's a risky way to live. Just consult your history books on Rome's Julius Caesar, France's Louis XIV, and England's George III. The moral: empires that don't listen always pay the price in the end. ●

At a War Rally, Echoes of Earlier Wars

You didn't see doubt at a "Support Our Troops" rally here in Rochester yesterday, but I don't know why—there were lots of Vietnam veterans in the crowd. Hundreds of people waved American flags and cars were parked a half-mile in every direction. "Liberate Iraq" was the favorite placard and card tables were stacked with inspirational articles, poems, and letters from the Internet.

A biker club showed up—I counted 75 Harley Davidsons parked—and there were plenty of leather chaps, vests, and biker boots in the crowd. Lots of folks sat in folding chairs on the grass and it felt a bit like a tailgate party. An Uncle Sam on stilts was walking around.

A country music song was playing on the PA system when I arrived:

> *Some people say we don't need this war,*
> *I say there are some things worth fighting for.*
> *Some say this country is asking for a fight,*
> *I say after 9/11, that's right.*
> *They say you shouldn't worry about Bin Laden.*
> *Have you forgotten?*

The song recalled for me the high-minded rationales for the Vietnam War and how the patriotism in the early part of that war turned ultimately, for so many veterans, into bitterness and betrayal. Are we applying the right lessons from that experience to this war?

A Fox radio broadcaster was the event's emcee. A singer from Plainview, Donna Chapel, sang the national anthem, and then all the kids in the audience came to front to lead the audience in reciting the Pledge of Allegiance. A Mayo Clinic ambulance helicopter flew overhead, in lieu of an F-15.

A woman from an eagle aviary in Wabasha, Minnesota, on the Mississippi River, showed a beautiful eagle to the crowd, pumping her arm so the eagle spread its wings to an impressive four feet across or so. A few anti-war protestors stood off to the side, maybe 20 of them, holding up signs abjuring all war and violence, and a half-dozen city police stood nervously between them and the pro-war crowd. U.S. Representative Gil Gutknecht told the audience in his speech that "periodically the tree of liberty needs to be nourished with the blood of patriots."

The best speech was by a local county sheriff, Terese Amazi. She said: "Many people ask me, 'What can we do to make our neighborhoods safer?' And my answer is, know your neighbors. Somewhere along the line we've gotten away from knowing our neighbors, and we've got to get back there."

How far might the idea of "neighbors" expand? Could it reach to Iraq? ●

Baghdad in the BWCA

On the shores of Emerald Lake in the Boundary Waters Canoe Area, 60 miles north of Grand Marais along the Gunflint Trail, I sat around a campfire recently with my two best Rochester buddies of four decades, eating batter-fried walleye and sipping grape Gatorade.

We talked about the war in Iraq.

It was strange to be imagining that hot, dusty, wounded Arab land still so shrouded in violence and grieving, while we sat in the quiet mystic depths of pristine Minnesota nature.

The call of loons filled the air with mournful echoes.

Had the war in Iraq been a good idea or bad idea? We all agreed that things aren't going especially well in post-war Iraq, but on balance did we think it a good thing or a bad thing that the U.S. had ousted Saddam from power?

My friend Chris, a neurologist at the University of Minnesota, said that Americans don't have enough information about what's going on in Iraq to make a good decision whether to leave or stay. The media just isn't giving us enough information, he said, and the reports they do offer often aren't the truth, only sensationalism packaged to sell like entertainment.

Still, Chris said, it was clear enough that we had got ourselves into a quagmire in Iraq, so pulling out was by far the most sensible thing.

The sun slowly fell and the sky burned a deep, glowing pink at the horizon. A black crow flapped and cawed. Mosquitoes buzzed.

My friend Rick, a Rochester lawyer, fired back.

"Chris, you are expecting the media to give you all the

information you need to make a decision. But we'll never have all the information we want. We need to make decisions before that. I find myself looking inward and asking 'How would I feel if I were an average Iraqi person? In that case, how would I feel? What would I want?'"

The bottom line for Rick was that Iraqis now have a freedom to make their own future that they didn't have before. They no longer fear execution of their entire families on the basis of mere rumors that they didn't like Saddam. "If I were an Iraqi I'd be overjoyed that Saddam was gone," Rick said. "I'd feel that as bad as things might be now, I had new opportunities."

A fish jumped in the lake, making a loud "plop!" and leaving only ripples by the time we looked. The sweet scent of fried walleye mixed with sharp piney smells in the air.

As for myself, I believed in Rick's simple formula, to "look within." We can't learn every language in the world and each one of us, realistically, can't travel to many places to search out the truth, either. Surely the Boundary Waters wilderness teaches the wisdom of Rick's path.

Loons and bald eagles, not Fox and CNN, are the authorities in our wilderness. Our imaginations must do the distant travel.

The three of us joked throughout the trip about "being in the now."

"Chris, are you paddling in the present?"

"Rick, are you eating your oatmeal mindfully?"

For six days our eyes saw calm wilderness lakes and rugged rocks and perfect nature, while inside we saw Baghdad. We heard and saw the fireworks of shock and awe. We saw children lying in hospital beds.

What I want to ask is what lessons the treasure of our northern wilderness might hold for the peace of the entire world?

What responsibility do we have to share those lessons?

"Harmony of knowledge, will, and feeling toward the earth is wisdom, for it has to do with living at peace with other forms of life," wrote the Minnesota conservationist and writer, Sigurd F. Olson, after one wilderness trip. "Since the beginning of civilization, harmony with nature has been almost disregarded, though it has been recognized by a few great minds as the only solution to the problem of finding peace and contentment."

On the first day of our trip, a giant snapping turtle floating like an astronaut in two feet of crystalline water poked his nose above the waterline to peer a few moments at the three of us.

A wise old soul, we decided.

The persistence of our violent inner visions shocked us.

All through the trip, loons cried their strange whoops and sighs, their calls that pierce the heart so hauntingly, their laughing shrieks and mournful cries of perfect nature. ●

Alden Pyle at Abu Ghraib

For a New Year's gift this year some old friends of our family, Europeans who immigrated to the U.S. after World War II and then became American citizens, sent my parents a book: "The Quiet American" by Graham Greene.

My Mom and Dad expressed puzzlement at this choice of gift, but by chance I had had coffee with our friends only a few days earlier and we had discussed the war in Iraq. So I knew immediately the message they were sending, which was that America was entangling itself in a new Vietnam.

More than that, they were saying that once again, in Iraq as in Vietnam, America's seemingly congenital innocence in the ways of the world was leading this country into another conflagration likely to not only wound us as Americans, but the whole region of the world we'd invaded.

The eponymous "quiet American" of Graham Greene's novel was Alden Pyle, an idealistic foreign officer sent to Vietnam to funnel U.S. tax dollars to a mysterious "third force" that would spread democracy in southeast Asia. Instead, the money was used to murder innocents and Pyle ended up assassinated in a muddy ditch.

"He was impregnably armored by his good intentions and his innocence," Greene wrote of Pyle. "You can't blame the innocent. They are always guiltless. Innocence is a kind of insanity."

Pyle's insanity came to mind last week as I saw those horrific photographs from the Abu Ghraib prison. There was Pyle grinning over a pile of naked Iraqis. There he was again, holding a hooded Iraqi prisoner bound by a dog leash around his neck. And again, Pyle laughing insanely as another Iraqi prisoner was forced to strip and fondle himself.

What bothers me the most about those photographs is that I still don't accept my European immigrant friends' argument that Iraq and Vietnam are equivalent, and that in George W. Bush we have Alden Pyle as President.

But there is no doubt that those photographs make it a thousand times more difficult to prove my point.

That's because up to a point, the photographs prove that my friends are 100% correct. This tragic episode has revealed once again—as did the internment of Japanese Americans in World War II, the My Lai massacre, the Waco massacre, and many other examples—that America has no monopoly on applying perfect justice or righteous moral conduct in war.

Our global idealism, which we nurture despite having little direct experience of foreign cultures and world history, often leaves us Americans caught tragically unaware when history rudely breaks in, as it did on 9/11. The photographs from Abu Ghraib have fallen onto our heads with the same explosive force as did the falling twin towers.

There is the same sad sense of shock: can this really be *us?* Followed by a rush of confused emotions, failed attempts to forget and deny, and nagging questions about the long-term meaning and consequences of these horrors.

The MP's who subjected the Iraqi prisoners to these tortures are said, at best, to have been poorly trained as prison wardens, and at worst to have been following orders that flowed from President Bush himself.

But how trained are we as Americans in the conduct of good citizenship during war? Does it even feel like we are at war? Have we ever been asked to sacrifice, really? Have we ever been asked to serve? Even to volunteer?

Are those who are asked to serve asked equally throughout society? How many Harvard and Yale men are fighting today in Iraq? How trained are we for that matter at asking critical questions of our own government as it takes away civil liberties in the name of fighting a war on terror?

These questions are answered mostly in the negative thanks to the dangerous innocence of the American character as exemplified by Alden Pyle.

The world is much better off without Saddam. But thanks to those photographs, America has lost a lot of ground in that argument along with, once again, our innocence. But if we have lost it, for goodness sake let us now leave it good and lost.

Let us through patient but relentless self-questioning replace our dangerous American innocence with real knowledge of the world and thus of our rightful role as a prosperous and free nation within it. ●

VI **NINE PATHS OF GLOBAL CITIZENSHIP**

Global citizenship, one might say, is a kind of super-citizenship—the familiar idea of rights and duties of membership in a civic group, only taken to a higher power, which is the power of the entire planet.

The central idea is that global citizens spend time each day thinking about their responsibility to maintain not only the health of their particular city, state, and country—but also about the civic and moral duties they owe the planet and its people.

Global citizenship has its own heroes and a history that runs parallel to, and usually just below the visible surface of the more prominent social and political practices and theories of every age. Today, thanks to 9/11 and global warming and other striking contemporary proofs of our interconnected and endangered world, the idea may finally be coming into its own.

There are roughly nine major paths towards global citizenship. Any person who on a daily basis tries to reconcile the pressing needs of his or her family, career, and community with the inner urge to act each day somehow for global betterment, will find spiritual ancestors and some practical advice in one or more of these paths:

1. The Path of Reason
2. The Path of Faith
3. The Democratic Path
4. The Humanitarian Path
5. The Ecological Path
6. The Free Trade Path
7. The Feminist Path
8. The Corporate Path
9. The Perennial Path

Citizenship is membership, but it is also remembering, with the first and most essential memory being that of dependence for our lives as individuals upon the good health and the goodwill of the global community of human beings. And, upon the environmental health of the planet.

This is not always an easy thing to remember even within the cozy confines of family, city, or nation. It's all the more difficult when our fellow citizens—those with whom we need to vividly remember our connection—live in foreign countries far away and out of sight of our daily lives.

Adam Smith remarked once that if a European man lost his little finger in an accident, he would be thrown into a torment. Yet that same man, "provided he never saw them, would snore with the most profound security over the ruin of a hundred millions of his brethren" in China.

Today, thanks to CNN and a hundred other news sources, we would most certainly see in graphic visual detail the ruin of millions of Chinese, if God forbid that calamity came to pass. Yet we also know, for reasons Smith could not have foreseen, that our sleep usually remains quite undisturbed by the suffering of peoples half a world away.

Millions of human souls in recent years died violently in North Korea, Sudan, the Congo and a half dozen other hell spots on Earth in the 1990s, for instance, without disturbing American sleep much. Responding only to what their audience ratings meters tell them they should do, our TV news media follows reports on the war in Iraq with bulletins on Michael Jackson's pedophile case, and on and on it goes, distracting us hour after hour and year after year.

Then a killer flu virus suddenly arrives on our shores from China, or acid rain floats in from Canada, or a terrorist-piloted jumbo jet explodes on our own shores. Only then do we pay attention.

To a large degree, those catastrophes are the direct result of not regularly remembering and acting upon the vital life connection we know exists between ourselves and the other inhabitants of our planet, especially those who live very different lives in a land far away, until it is too late.

Until recent years, pondering cosmopolitanism was mainly a pastime of the elite for whom it was either necessary business or diverting pastime, such as wealthy international traders, diplomats, or philosophers. The elites who ran the great European colonial empires all had a cosmopolitan view; as did the early explorers of Portugal and Spain; and the globe-trotting Jesuits who were as greedy for global souls as merchants were for gold and spices. Renaissance philosophers like Hugo Grotius spun theories of international law straight from their vision and genius, without having much practical daily application.

Similarly, the Greek stoics, the first forefathers of anyone who tries to forge a cosmopolitan outlook today, philosophized on the equality of all mankind while owning household slaves.

Yet the inconsistencies and incomplete theories of these global-thinking pioneers make them no less useful to us today. No doubt we will have to update, modify, and ultimately transcend their example as mankind goes on, if it is lucky, to successfully complete the next step in its ever-expanding consciousness. We had better soon become global thinkers or all die as local ones.

But one thing is sure, which is that whatever new global consciousness arises, it will grow out of the ideas passed down from those who have put them, such as they are today, already in our minds. The new theory will have to save what is useful to today from the global thinking pioneers, and kick away what is useless or false. The first step is to become consciously aware of the ideas that already move us and limit us from our own living past.

1. The Path of Reason

Patron Saint: Socrates
Main Idea: Reason and virtue are universal
values of mankind
Followers: The Stoic philosophers (Zeno,
Seneca, Marcus Aurelius), the Cynic philosphers
(Antisthenes, Diogenes, Crates), Hugo Grotius,
Immanuel Kant, Martha Nussbaum

"I am neither an Athenian nor a Greek, I am a citizen of the
world," said the sage of Athens (quoted by Plutarch). As such he
was perfectly democratic in his application of the standards of
reason across all borders and with all comers. Applying reason
to belief, individually and personally, citizen by citizen, was
Socrates' way. For him good ideas could come from anywhere
in the world. Spreading these ideas to the young men of Athens
got Socrates killed; yet in submitting to the will of Athens that
he be executed, instead of choosing exile, Socrates showed
the limits of his cosmopolitanism. The Stoic schools took the
cosmopolitical aspect of his thinking to its greatest extreme,
arguing that the entire world was entirely material and endowed
with reason and soul, and it was thus every individual's role,
wherever they may live on the earth, to live according to the
dictates of rational nature. The Renaissance philosopher Hugo
Grotius built the first system of international law out of the
notion that all humans are rational and social, and thus are
bound in a moral world that transcends national boundaries.
When Immanuel Kant wrote "perpetual peace is guaranteed
by no less an authority than the great artist Nature herself," he
picked up where the Stoics left off. His essay "Perpetual Peace,"
arguing for universal peace based on universal laws, is the mani-
festo of modern cosmopolitans. Martha Nussbaum extends the
theme arguing that the global spread of liberal arts education
would support freedom, democracy, and human rights.

2. The Path of Faith

Patron Saint: Albert Schweitzer
Main Idea: Service to God by revering and
supporting all life
Followers: Augustine of Hippo, St. Francis,
St. Paul, G.K. Chesterton, Reinhold Neibuhr,
Mother Theresa, Habitat for Humanity

"As long ago as my student days, it struck me as incomprehensible that I should be allowed to live such a happy life while I saw so many people around me wrestling with care and suffering," Schweitzer scrawled on a notepad only a week before his death in Gabon, Africa. "There gradually grew up within me an understanding of the saying of Jesus that we must not treat our lives as being for ourselves alone." As a result, Schweitzer sacrificed a promising career as a concert organist in Europe to go to medical school and then move permanently to Africa as a medical missionary. By giving up his cushy life to follow Jesus' call to live for others, Schweitzer both followed, and established his credentials, as a modern avatar of the path of the missionary—usually but not always in modern history, a Christian. Faith not reason is the motivational spring of these cosmopolitans. God's plan, not man-in-progress, is the engine of human history. Humanist critics point to the many crimes of Christian missionaries and of the evangelical urge; yet the fact remains that missionaries more than any others, until the multinational corporation was invented, have overcome the gravity of local life in order to travel the world, to endure loneliness, to learn foreign languages, to befriend foreign people, and even to die in foreign lands having religiously converted others but been entirely culturally converted themselves. Religious humanitarian groups such as Catholic Relief Services and Lutheran World Relief are among the largest and most active NGO's serving refugees and the world's poor today.

3. The Path of Democracy

Patron Saint: Woodrow Wilson
Main Idea: Global political, legal, and trade
cooperation
Followers: Jonathan Schell, Vaclav Havel,
the League of Nations, the United Nations,
the International Court of Justice,
the World Trade Organization

These global citizens see global health primarily as the absence of war, with world peace arising primarily by individual action taken in the political sphere. The government's role is to work with other nations towards global cooperation in all matters of common interest including health, humanitarian relief, education, the environment, and armed police actions. Citizenship to them implies individual action through voting, vocal political dissent, and other means of pressuring governments toward these ends. A few Wilsonians see the world ideally evolving towards a single global federalism; most favor continued national sovereigns working ever more closely through international treaties, protocols, laws, and practices that are backed by public opinion. To them, Woodrow Wilson's idea for the League of Nations—especially his principles of democracy, freedom, self-determination, and the rule of law—was not proved fatally flawed by the League's failure; rather it was a noble idea ahead of its time. The most prominent Wilsonian today is Jonathan Schell who argues in The Unconquerable World that the string of strikingly non-violent democratic revolutions that occurred in the late 20th century in the Soviet Union, Poland, Czechoslovakia, South Africa, South Korea, Indonesia, Spain, and other countries is evidence that America's present military dominance goes against the grain of history and shows the enduring might of people power.

4. The Humanitarian Path

Patron Saint: Henri Dunant
Main Idea: Humanitarian action based on
universal human rights
Followers: Aryeh Neier, Paul Farmer,
International Red Cross, Doctors Without Borders,
Human Rights Watch, Amnesty International

In 1862, Henri Dunant, a French businessman in northern Italy, witnessed one of the bloodiest battles of the 19th century—Napoleon's armies driving the Austrians out of Italy at the town of Solferino. Young Dunant, 34 at the time, walked through the battlefield afterwards and saw soldiers shot through, their guts opened, missing arms and legs, but still alive and with no medical or nursing help at all. Writing up the experience in a small book called "A Memory of Solferino," Dunant immediately poured all his time and funds into travels around Europe to get governments to send representatives to a conference to address the problem of wounded soldiers and prisoners of war. The 1864 conference drew up the Geneva Convention which codified rules for the treatment of wounded and prisoners, and formed the Red Cross. The phrase "human rights" would not become current for another 90 years, but the Red Cross became the first transnational humanitarian organization based on the idea of human rights. The group's fundamental principles then as now were humanity, impartiality, neutrality, independence, voluntary service, unity, and universality. After World War II, especially after the United Nations General Assembly passed the Universal Declaration of Human Rights in 1948, human rights groups have proliferated by the thousands, creating a global civil society composed of "non-governmental organizations" working transnationally through aid efforts and conferences. In addition, the language and law of human rights has become a pillar of U.S. foreign policy, used in the justification and adjudication of numerous foreign military and humanitarian projects. Human rights activists in the United States have given the movement special impetus by transferring to the global human rights movement many of the political, organizational, and ideological practices and beliefs of the U.S. civil rights movement of the 1960s.

5. The Ecological Path

Patron Saint: Rachel Carson
Main idea: Living in harmony with nature is a key to peace
Followers: Aldo Leopold, Sigurd Olson, Arne Naess, Edward Abbey, Wendell Berry, Bill McKibben, World Wildlife Fund, World Conservation Union, Greenpeace

Ecological consciousness is the Copernican revolution updated to modern times: it puts mankind not at the center of the universe but rather in one small corner in the great web of life. Backed by the authority of modern science, the ecological view holds that the health of the whole earth depends on the health of all the parts, with a flaw or cancer in any part possibly leading to the death of all. Theoretically, this insight could lead to a humble politics, one that takes into account the possible consequences of every action not only locally but throughout that web of life, including the citizens of faraway lands. Aldo Leopold, the author of the ecological classic "A Sand County Almanac," connected ecology and civics when he wrote of man being "a plain member and citizen of the biotic community." Leopold's friend and colleague, the naturalist Sigurd Olson, hiked in the wilderness of northern Minnesota and believed it offered lessons of global import: "Harmony of knowledge, will, and feeling toward the earth is wisdom, for it has to do with living at peace with other forms of life. Since the beginning of civilization, harmony with nature has been almost disregarded, though it has been recognized by a few great minds as the only solution to the problem of finding peace and contentment." Sooner or later every environmental writer comes to roughly the same conclusion. Putting the earth first—biocentrism trumping anthropocentrism—inevitably makes all men citizens in stewardship of their common home, the glistening blue sphere of Earth.

6. The Free Trade Path

Patron Saint: Adam Smith
Main Idea: Unregulated global capitalism improves everyone's life
Followers: Milton Friedman, F.A. Hayek, Ronald Reagan, Margaret Thatcher, libertarians, multinational corporations (except when protectionism suits them better)

The British liberal economist and moral philosopher Adam Smith theorized in 1776 that every man, "intending only his own gain" in making and selling goods, was actually working for the benefit of all men, whether he was conscious of this or not. In so doing, Smith invented a notion—the invisible hand of the free market—which remains one of the most power-ful globe-encircling ideas to this day. The key notion is the price system, which magically finds a specific trading point at which parties on both sides of the transaction are satisfied. In other words, economics isn't always brutish competition with a winner and a loser. In a free market, everyone can win. This idea became the foundation of "neoliberal" economics that, under the leadership of Ronald Reagan and Margaret Thatcher, fueled the phenomenal growth of globalization in the post-war period. With Milton Freedman's "Capitalism and Freedom" as their bible, neoliberal policymakers in the 1980s and 1990s drove vast global programs of government-led privatization. Global financiers used the philosophy to rationalize moving vast amounts of investment funds in and out of foreign banks in search of the highest returns. By the middle 1990s, the downsides of these policies, such as the destructive impact of investment funds suddenly withdrawn from an entire national economy, or the crushing financial terms imposed on foreign countries by the International Monetary Fund, had drawn thousands of protesters to annual conferences where global economic bodies, such as the World Trade Organization, met. The Nobel prizewinning economist Joseph Stiglitz and the journalist William Greider have offered penetrating critiques of the free trade or "neoliberal" path, while also acknowledging the good that economic globalization sometimes has done. The enduring allure of the free trade path to the global citizen is captured by its modern prophet Milton Friedman: "When you buy your pencil or your daily bread, you don't know whether the pencil was made or the wheat was grown by a white man or a black man, by a Chinese or an Indian. The price system enables people to cooperate peacefully in one phase of their life while each one goes about his own business in respect of everything else."

7. The Feminist Path

Patron Saints: The women of the
Chipko movement in Mandal village,
Uttar Pradesh, India
Main idea: Feminine values are universal, practi-
cal, civic, and green
Followers: Carolyn Merchant, Carol Adams,
Carol Gilligan, Elizabeth Spelman,
Women's Environment and Development
Organization, the Gorilla Foundation,
Feminists for Animal Rights

The name "Chipko" comes from the Hindi word for "hugging," which is what the village women of Mandal in northern India did to the trees in a nearby forest in 1973, when logging companies threatened to clear-cut them. The protest was spontaneous and the women refused to budge even as the bulldozers charged, as if they were protecting their own children. It was Ghandi's principle of non-violent resistance or satyagraha, put at the service of a forest. The fact that women often are on the front lines of environmental battles around the world, and that they often find common cause despite language and cultural barriers, suggests the feminist view has much to offer aspiring global citizens of either gender. In particular, feminist group action not only on global environmental issues but also on social and economic justice issues is often marked by intense collaboration, open and free discussion, listening, and compromise. Further, feminist writers like Carol Gilligan and Elizabeth Spelman have argued that women tend to develop mastery of relationship maintenance skills to a higher degree than men. Gilligan's idea that women tend to follow an "ethic of care" as opposed to men's "ethic of justice" seems especially apt in a global citizenship perspective. The ethic of justice looks to abstract moral principles as guides to action, while the ethic of care stresses attention to the particular case and person, being open to different outcomes and stressing the maintenance of personal relations in each case to the degree possible. Virtues often exercised more naturally by women than men—hospitality, modesty, restraint, kindness, and the impulse to repair—these feminists argue, are the indispensable virtues to any global civic life.

8. The Corporate Path

Patron Saint: Rev. Leon Sullivan
Main idea: Doing business globally with a
social conscience
Followers: Business in the Community,
Business for Social Responsibility, Robert Haas,
David Grayson, Simon Zadek, Levi Strauss & Co.

As economic globalization progressed in the 1990s, a back-lash formed among critics who saw it as a form of empire, enslaving a new generation of underpaid workers in Third World countries to wealthy First-World masters. Riots in Seattle in 1999, where the World Trade Organization had its annual meeting, showed the depth of the anti-corporate sentiment. That confrontation and others led to the rise of the latest trend in doing business with a social conscience, known as CSR for "corporate social responsibility." Cynics say CSR is a branch of corporate public relations. It is true that some companies, such as Levi Strauss and The Body Shop, have put significant resources into social programs. But no companies have scored notable successes in the social and profit categories simultaneously. The patron saint of this path, the Rev. Leon Sullivan, built a worldwide network of self-help worker training centers and in 1971 joined the board of General Motors, becoming the first African-American to hold a board seat on a major corporation. In 1977 he authored the "Sullivan Principles," a human rights code of conduct for U.S. and other multinationals operating in South Africa, while apartheid was still the law there. By getting American companies in South Africa to commit to equal opportunity employment for black as well as white employees, the Sullivan Principles turned multinational corporations into agents for social change. This example, at least, shows that multinational corporations can and sometimes do play a critical role as global citizens by expanding human rights and democracy worldwide. Environmental and labor cases involving major multinationals like Nike, Union Carbide, and others tend to grab headlines. Yet the overseas staffs of U.S. multinationals, which number about two million U.S. citizens, create a de facto overseas diplomatic corps that shows a human face of America to the world—a great act of global citizenship. Also for every factory worker scandal, U.S. multinationals also offer employment and social and educational opportunities to foreign workers that they could never otherwise afford. History also shows that multinational firms are sensitive to pressure from consumer protests and NGOs, which have driven companies towards increasing social accountability over the years. Working as an expatriate employee of a multinational corporation remains the most practical path available to most Americans to experience global citizenship firsthand.

9. The Perennial Path

Patron Saints: Mahatma Ghandi, the Dalai Lama
Main idea: Spiritual oneness through shared suffering and renouncing ego empowers individuals and secures the world
Followers: Aldous Huxley, Joseph Campell, Michael Lerner, Ken Wilber, Jacob Needleman, Joseph Goldstein, Huston Smith

What did the Buddha say to the hot dog vendor? "Make me one with everything." The "unitive knowledge of the divine Ground of being" is how Aldous Huxley put it in The Perennial Philosophy, summarizing the universal truth that is taught at the oft-shrouded heart of the world's great religions: "All is one." Each of us is in essence but a tiny shard of a single Godhead. It's an obvious insight to many, yet hard to translate into meaningful civic action. Today's followers of the Perennial Path are trying to find just such practical paths by which individuals can turn their spiritual search into effective global citizenship. Jacob Needleman, the historian and philosopher, speaks of the need for America to overcome its intensely selfish worldview by building a "community of conscience," one citizen at a time. America's founding fathers provide ideal mythic models from which each citizen can be reassured that the possibility for true greatness can be tapped by seeking the light of divinity within. That act puts man, Needleman says, "in accordance with his structure and nature as an image of God" and allows him to fulfill his highest purpose: "To care for the inner divinity and through that to care for our neighbor." The New Age philosopher Ken Wilber suggests that a widespread breakthrough in consciousness to a "worldcentric" view, which previously has been the domain of social elites, may be the next step in human evolution that began with egocentrism (self-focus), and then successfully progressed then to sociocentrism (partially subjugating the needs of self to the needs of the group). "In this transformation," Wilber writes, "from the sociocentric to the worldcentric, the self de-centers once again: my group is not the only group in the universe, my tribe is not the only tribe, my god is not the only god, my ideology is not the only ideology." Some Perennial Path leaders, such as the Buddhist teacher Joseph Goldstein, say that working spiritually to eradicate the sources of conflict within oneself, such as through meditation, is the highest form of peace work that a human being can do. ●

POSTSCRIPT: A NEW STORY FOR A NEW WORLD

There are lots of problems with cosmopolitanism, the ancient idea that people should consider themselves as citizens of the world.

There is the practical problem that a person who is deeply rooted in a local culture doesn't necessarily have the skills to understand global cultures. There is the moral problem of declaring that one's responsibilities to strangers equal those owed to fellow citizens and family members. And there is the semantic problem that "global citizenship" can mean very little outside the context of an actual sovereign state.

Can you see people getting overcome with emotion, singing loud and proud, writing a stirring poem, yelling themselves hoarse, or going off to fight a war to defend their identity as cosmopolitans?

"Cosmopolis the beautiful?" "I'm proud to be a cosmopolitan?" I don't think so.

And yet we know there's a grain of important truth in the idea of global citizenship. If our hearts don't thrill to the idea, our minds at least respectfully salute.

We know that nine out of ten articles of clothing we wear these days are made outside the U.S.; and that nine out of ten toys used by our children are made in China; and that our cars wouldn't run if we removed all the parts made in Mexico.

Salsa, Tabasco, lemongrass, curry and a hundred other flavors are already more familiar—more *American*—than many indigenous American foods. A nuclear suitcase bomb made in Pakistan is a threat to any place in the United States. Our lives are already thoroughly interpenetrated by the world beyond American borders. We know this.

Yet there is a gap between the reality of life in America, which is cosmopolitan, and the official narrative of life in America, which remains national and regional.

Now here is the funny thing. When the stories that human beings use to explain reality no longer match reality, people don't respond as you'd expect. They don't usually change the story to fit the new reality. Rather, they continue to explain the new reality with the old story.

Throughout the 1990s, America was still telling itself outdated Cold War spy stories and jailing Chinese "spies" on concocted charges. Meanwhile, a new set of enemies was designing new weapons of mass destruction aimed at American cities and citizens. There were plenty of early warning signals that this was going on. But few of us paid attention because it was much easier to continue seeing the world through the old story than it was to see the world anew and to write a new story to fit.

We need a new story in America. The new story needs to fit the new reality, which is cosmopolitan. The new cosmopolitan reality is defined not only by where our clothes, toys, food, and cars are made but also by the Internet's global reach, the globalization of finance, the porosity of borders to viruses, and the fact that 28 million people born in foreign countries now live in the United States—more than ever in our history.

How can we tell our new story in a way that we'd feel our pulses race for justice, goodness, and identity defined in a cosmopolitan way? We've seen the consequence of failing to renew our vision of ourselves in this way. We've seen the price of failing to renew our great story.

So how should we tell our new story? It will need to be set not just in our homes, our cities, our states, or our nation —as great as all those are. It needs to be set on that pale blue lonely planet called earth.

It will be a story of cosmopolitanism, and in order to compete with our present-day fight songs and rallying cries and our national anthems it will need to be dramatically raw, universally human, and heartfelt.

In a media world shaped by consumerism and fantasy, our new story must be rooted in the world's present-day reality and essential human need.

It can't be boring! It will have to show how common men and women can achieve world-changing shifts in perspective and epiphanies like the one described by Paul Simon in his song called *You Can Call Me Al*:

> *A man walks down the street,*
> *It's a street in a strange world,*
> *Maybe it's the Third World,*
> *Maybe it's his first time around;*
> *He doesn't speak the language,*
> *He holds no currency,*
> *He is a foreign man,*
> *He is surrounded by the sound,*
> *The sound,*
> *Cattle in the marketplace,*
> *Scatterlings and orphanages;*
> *He looks around, around,*
> *He sees angels in the architecture,*
> *Spinning in infinity,*
> *He says* Amen! *and* Hallelujah!

Our new global story will need its sexy Cleopatra, its blood-drenched Achilles, its ridiculous clowns and buffoons. It will need its Mother Earth and its angels of kindness. It will need to be as now as war, as here as cornfields, as forever hot as a trend. It will need to be spicy and full of flavors, because only delicious stories spread far and wide.

Yet this story that embraces the full poetry and craziness of mankind will also carry an utterly practical message of sanity. All the ogres and saints of the story will illuminate a path to peace. Because death in the end satisfies no one, not even the monsters and the death-mongers.

All beings ultimately want to go on. They want to live and they want their personal stories finally to merge with the great river of endless worlds upon worlds. They want that eternal journey to be spent not in suffering but in joy.

The great new global story will show many paths to that joy. It will re-tell the ancient message of all sages: that evil leads to evil and good leads to good. So, be good. Be kind. Be kind to your neighbor and kind to yourself.

Right here, be kind. •

artpacks

Publishing, fine art printing, and studio workshops for *the art of your life and the life of your art* ™. Contact us to learn more about our work or order additional copies of *here: A Global Citizen's Journey*.

artpacks
535 22nd Street NE
Rochester, MN 55906

telephone 507-273-2529
virginiawoodruff@charter.net

here: A Global Citizen's Journey

Soft cover books are $18.95
Limited edition hardcover books are $65.00
In Minnesota, add sales tax @ 7%,
$1.33+$18.95=20.28 soft cover and $4.55+$65=$69.55 hardcover
Shipping is $3.50 for the first book, and $1 for each additional copy
Checks, Mastercard, and Visa accepted

quantity
_____

tax
_____

shipping
_____

total
_____

art of your life, life of art ™

December 8, 2008